FED POWER

FED POWER

How Finance Wins

Lawrence R. Jacobs
and Desmond King

OXFORD
UNIVERSITY PRESS

OXFORD
UNIVERSITY PRESS

Oxford University Press is a department of the University of Oxford.
It furthers the University's objective of excellence in research, scholarship,
and education by publishing worldwide. Oxford is a registered trade mark of
Oxford University Press in the UK and in certain other countries.

Published in the United States of America by Oxford University Press
198 Madison Avenue, New York, NY 10016, United States of America

Library of Congress Cataloging-in-Publication Data

Names: Jacobs, Lawrence R. | King, Desmond S.
Title: Fed power : how finance wins
    / Lawrence R. Jacobs, Desmond King.
Description: New York, NY : Oxford University Press, 2016.
Identifiers: LCCN 2015040588 (print) | LCCN 2015050008 (ebook) |
    ISBN 9780199388967 (hardback) | ISBN 9780199388974 (E-book) |
    ISBN 9780199388981 (E-book)
Subjects: LCSH: Federal Reserve banks—History. | Banks and banking,
    Central—United States—History. | Monetary policy—United
    States—History. | Government accountability—United States—History. |
    Equality—United States—History. | Democracy—United States—History. |
    BISAC: POLITICAL SCIENCE / Public Policy / Economic Policy. | POLITICAL
    SCIENCE / General.
Classification: LCC HG2563 .J33 2016 (print) | LCC HG2563 (ebook) | DDC
    332.1/10973—dc23
LC record available at http://lccn.loc.gov/2015040588

9 8 7 6 5 4 3 2 1
Printed in the United States of America
on acid-free paper
Typeset in Century Schoolbook
Printed by Sheridan, USA

Contents

Acknowledgments

This book grows out of our investigations of American political economy during the last decade at a series of conferences convened at Nuffield College and the Rothermere American Institute in Oxford University. For financial support we are grateful to Nuffield College, the Nuffield College Mellon Trust Fund, and the Rothermere American Institute, as well as the Hubert H. Humphrey School of Public Affairs and the Walter F. and Joan Mondale Chair for Political Studies at the University of Minnesota. We are grateful to paper givers and participants at two conferences we convened on the politics of governing the Federal Reserve. None bear responsibility for errors of fact or interpretations.

We would also like to acknowledge the research assistance of Patrick Carter, Peter Polga-Hecimovich, and Jonathan Spiegler in the Humphrey School of Public Affairs, as well as Marissa Theys in the Department of Political Science at the University of Minnesota.

At Oxford University Press, Dave McBride has been an outstanding editor whose support, guidance, and meticulous line-by-line editing has been invaluable. We thank also Kathleen Weaver and Gwen Colvin for their excellent guidance through the production process.

We dedicate this book to our families and their good cheer in joining us on this journey. Fully alert to the hard truths of life, we offer them these words from Seamus Heaney—"Believe in miracle, And cures and healing wells."

LRJ
DK

FED POWER

1

Why Fed Power Matters

IMAGINE THIS SPLIT screen in early 2009 shortly after the inauguration of President Barack Obama. One screen: fiery debate in Congress and in the media over passing a stimulus package. It passes, but only after three Senate Republicans cross the aisle and imperil their political futures—one changes political parties.

The other screen: a hush-hush confidential meeting of the Federal Reserve Bank's top decision-makers to review a joint plan with the Treasury Department to buy up as much as $1 trillion of the $2 trillion in toxic assets that private banks recklessly purchased in the pursuit of profits.[1] How will the Fed and Treasury pull off a rescue of imprudent banks while turning a cold shoulder to millions of Americans who are losing their jobs and homes? The Fed's chair, Ben Bernanke, confides that the "political strategy is to provide an overall structure with ... not a great deal of detail, with the idea ... [of] creat[ing] some buy-in on the political side. It's like selling a car: Only when the customer is sold on the leather seats do you actually reveal the price."[2]

Two massive government commitments and entirely different styles of governance. One is the familiar public process of open debate and democratically elected officials deciding; the other is secretive and controlled by mostly unknown figures with careers in private finance who are looking to car salesmen as models. One features the jousting of contending values and perspectives; the other is insular and rests on the proposition that Fed officials and their circle of economists know the unquestioned truth. One disperses benefits and tax credits to much of the country; the other targets America's largest banks for exclusive deals.

The Federal Reserve Bank is a mutant institution of government. It has enjoyed anonymity from Americans for most of its history even though it wields unparalleled power on domestic policy that is largely free of the traditional system of checks and balances, which routinely grind down presidential and congressional proposals. The exceptionalism of Fed power stands out among the three branches of government within the United States and among democratic, capitalist countries.

Free pass. That's how America's circle of key policymakers, business and civic leaders, and media honchos have reacted to the Fed's extraordinary power. Presidents and congressional leaders squint into the blinding Klieg Lights; the Fed routinely devises new policies in its quiet sanctums and announces them—how and when it chooses.

The deference to the Fed's exceptionalism flows from a pervasive view among America's ruling clique of elites: the central bank is a national steward. The Fed dispassionately adjusts the supply of money and credit to avoid the horrors of inflation and sharp economic downturns; and it rescues the country when financial crisis strikes. Elites accept the Fed's unrivaled power as a practical necessity. They believe the system of accountability enshrined in the US Constitution by James Madison and his colleagues cannot be trusted to protect the country from sliding into financial and economic ruin. Congress and the president can deadlock over taxes or budgets to pay for the country's defense and education, but any such stalemate or political negotiation over monetary policy threatens a Dantian hell. Put simply, the Fed protects America against its representatives—it is a guardian shielded from political interference.

The exceptionalism of Fed power and autonomy is the product of its battle for institutional position in the context of chaotic global financial markets and the extravagant dysfunction of Congress.

Its exercise of power consistently favors banks and investment firms not only in response to lobbying or the seduction of revolving doors, but also because thriving finance helps the Fed itself by generating revenue and pleasing its allies.

The result? Not surprising, but often overlooked: the Fed is an inequality generator. Its normal operations reward the wealthy. The crisis of 2008–2009 accelerated the Fed's grab for power and its advantaging of the advantaged.

At this point, you may be expecting us to unload a screed about the need to "end the Fed," as Ron Paul's book put it. Wrong. Historical and practical experience along with the examples of such other countries as Canada leads us in a more complicated and new direction—designing an American central bank that is simultaneously effective in financial management *and* democratically accountable. America must have a central bank to calibrate the money supply and stand ready as a last resort to avoid the excruciating consequences on everyday people of recessions and financial implosions—wiped out savings, rampant unemployment, and foreclosures that toss families onto the skids of life. Reconciling effectiveness and accountability, however, runs into the Fed's supportive alliance whose members (falsely) insist that the choice is between the Fed or no functioning central bank; and into Ron Paul acolytes who contrive spurious scenarios in which financial crisis confirms the Fed's culpability in producing it—ignoring the cases in which the Fed and other central banks head off or diminish economic convulsions.

America does face a dire future. The threat is not angry populists and unruly mobs stopping responsible monetary policy—as the Fed and its pals insinuate. That is not a reasonable fear on which to waste time. The threat is also not solely the arrival of the next financial crisis, though it is building because of the recurrence of speculative bubbles, economic malaise, mushrooming debt, and wild-west banking in the shadows of the financial system.

The calamitous future stalking the United States is that it lacks an effective financial manager. The Fed's actions undermined its future capacity by sapping its legitimacy—favoritism of select financial firms and neglect of everyday homeowners

combine with its lack of accountability to America's elected of-
ficeholders. Public and congressional distrust of the Fed after the
financial implosion of 2008–2009 prompted lawmakers to side-
track efforts to build an effective and democratically accountable
financial manager.

Now is the time for thoughtful elites and concerned citizens to
prepare to chart a constructive new direction for central banking
in America—one that works and fits with democratic values. This
book traces the Fed's historic trajectory from the nineteenth-
century cauldron of populist rage to the twenty-first-century giant
it has become, its extraordinary and biased actions during the
2008–2009 crisis, and the resulting legitimacy deficit it ran up.
Congressional reforms after the 2008–2009 crisis deepened the
Fed's predicament: they ratcheted up expectations that the central
bank would prevent the next systemic implosion while denying it
the authority to deliver because of fear it would use new powers
as in the past: to favor the already prosperous and widen economic
inequality. It is time to introduce to the United States a new way
of approaching financial management—one that is rooted in its
founding values and the proven track record of other countries.

DON'T BUY THE FED HYPE

Irony is one of history's most delicious gifts. America paraded
out of World War I into extraordinary prosperity. But it also
inched toward the devastation of the Great Depression and World
War II. Four generations later, the collapse of the Soviet Union
persuaded American elites that it was time to strike a pose of
global domination. The Pentagon talked of "discourag[ing] the
industrialized countries from questioning the American leadership" or claiming "a bigger regional or international role."[3]
Meanwhile, a new era of disorder and competition blossomed.

Grandiosity seguing to wreckage is a familiar theme in history.

Today, even thoughtful people cheer on the Fed for its apparent
success in saving America from an epic depression. Why, they

may wonder, would we scrutinize an institution that stopped the run on financial institutions and revived them? These are understandable questions, given the paucity of clear and compelling analysis of Fed actions.

The Catechism of the Fed

But appearances are deceiving, and the Fed and its allies have constructed a seductive but misleading Kabuki theater. The Fed is ringed by an impressive-sounding catechism developed by the central bank and its fraternity of economists.

- The Fed, we are lectured, serves the "public good" as a well-intentioned, "benevolent social planner" selflessly committed to serving equally everyone in society.[4] "The principal reason for the founding of the Federal Reserve," Lawrence Broz insists, "was to assure stable and smoothly functioning financial markets" that benefited "society at large."[5]
- The Fed's "independence," we are informed, insulates its decisions from corrupting outside interests and its distance from elected officials erects a shield against what economists mysteriously refer to as the "time-inconsistency principle."[6] This is jargon for "Trust us. Don't trust politicians." Put more politely, today's government secures loans from private markets to cover spending and debt by promising low inflation to maintain the value of the loan, but bankers suspect that politicians will later change their minds to please lobbyists and voters by printing money to artificially boost employment, which in turn diminishes the real value of the loan.

The powerful fashion and disseminate ideas not simply for the magnanimous pursuit of truth, but to induce our indifference and acceptance of their privileges. The Fed's catechism discourages or undermines legitimate questions and challenges about how private banks, investors, and the Fed organize and allocate money and wealth.

Reality Test

Stripped-down reality: the Fed's laxity invites financial break-down; its operations widen inequality and repudiate democratic responsiveness. Here's an overview of coming themes.

Fed Inaction

The Fed is feted as saving America, and yet its inaction in taming the financial Wild West led to the 2008–2009 crisis in the first place. The Bank of Canada both prevented the full-blown crisis that the Fed invited and tamed the American flames that jumped the border without massive direct taxpayer bailouts.

Generating Inequality

The Fed strikes a pose as a servant of the broad public good—the "permanent and aggregate interests of the community"—as opposed to the self-interest of the few, in the elegant words of the makers of the US Constitution.[7] After the Fed's establishment in 1913, America's economy and supply of jobs did grow because the US monetary system was rescued from perennial banking runs and the dollar was established as a trusted international currency with Wall Street as a prosperous financial center.

The flaw in the public good account is its false equivalency between the gains for finance and for the general public. When the country is spared financial disaster, everyone gains. But let's not ignore—as is usually the case—the lopsided and often concealed benefits for a specific industry and particular firms. A fair accounting would report the unequal rates of return.

The operation of the Fed contributes to widening inequality by facilitating the abnormal swelling of the financial sector as well as by its specific policies. The Fed is handmaiden to the surge of finance to 9 percent of the economy (an all-time high). Finance made up 10 to 15 percent of profits in the 1950s and 1960s; by 2001, the proportion was close to 40 percent and probably substantially larger, after accounting for executive compensation in the financial sector and changes in corporate accounting.[8] With the Fed's babysitting, the drive to earn outsized profits in finance is also crowding out more productive sectors: exchanging capital to generate interest, dividends, or capital gains pays more than the familiar production and trading of goods and services. And economic growth and job creation suffer.[9] Imagine the choice of a scientist or a brilliant college graduate: Should they invest years of their lives in curing cancer or building new forms of sustainable energy, or should they take a job in finance that pays more, and more quickly? Banks and investors are knocked off course by similar tradeoffs: Would you lend to an uncertain project that requires expensive research and development, or a property development that leverages securities for high returns? That loud sucking sound you hear is Wall Street inhaling talent and capital: it costs our economy 2 percent of growth each year or $320 billion—more than three times what the federal government spent on education in 2014.[10]

The normal operation of the Fed is legally bound to pursue a "dual mandate" of "stable prices" and "maximum employment," but it primarily focuses on policing against inflation followed by tweaking the economy during sharp downturns (when inflation is reliably tame).[11] Full employment is lost in the shuffle.

Here's the key part: the Fed tackles threats of inflation and swooning economies by manipulating financial markets to change the money supply. The Fed sets the rates that its 19 designated banks and brokers charge each other for overnight loans, provides overnight loans to commercial banks at discount rates to allow them to meet obligations, and regulates the reserves and liabilities of commercial banks.

The Fed's reliance on capital markets produces winners and losers. It "worsens inequality," in the words of Ben Bernanke, after he stepped down as Fed chair.[12] The owners of stocks and other assets typically enjoy sharper gains and greater protection against lasting deep losses while everyday workers gain less and suffer bigger and more lasting harm, including job loss and stagnating wages.

That's not all. The Fed also fuels inequality through its normal operations. The Fed's main policy tool is buying and selling US Treasury bonds to adjust interest rates. It lowers rates during sour economic times by selling bonds. This expands the money supply to encourage businesses to invest and consumers to spend. When inflation kicks in, it raises rates in order to reduce the supply of money.

Quick Cut-In on Fed Speak. While the media often talks about the Fed "setting" interest rates, the process is indirect and inexact. Banks in the Federal Reserve System are required to keep a certain amount of money on deposit; it can lend its excess reserves to banks that need additional reserves. The "interest rate" that gets so much attention is how much banks charge each other, which ends up influencing how much we get charged for mortgages, credit card debt, and other loans.[13]

Here's why the Fed's interest rate policy matters in terms of who gets what. The Fed's decisions to change interest rates shift economic resources between debtors and creditors. Fed policy to expand the money supply to spur the economy is usually good news for workers, while reducing it to cut off inflation often comes at the cost of employment.

The crisis of 2008–2009 jacked up the upwardly redistributive impact of Fed policy. With interest rates already cut to zero, the Fed went on a buying spree of US Treasury bonds and radioactive securities that few wanted (many were backed by risky mortgages). Expanding credit was the purpose of "quantitative easing" (impenetrable jargon, right?) and its scope was massive—amounting to $3.5 trillion by 2014.[14] Public debate? Congressional hearings? Nope. Its design and launch was (true to form) the Fed's alone, and done in private. More on that in a moment.

A steeper recession was avoided, and that was good news for everyone. But the biggest winners have been the "superrich"— the richest 1 percent of households who control 64.4 percent of all stocks, bonds, and other forms of assets and the top 10 percent who own over 80 percent.[15] The Fed's quantitative easing pumped up stocks and delivered enormous gains to the rich. Its interest rate cuts reduced the lending costs for banks, which in turn allowed them to score profits.[16] Americans in the top 1 percent of real income fell by 36.3 percent between 2007 and 2009 and then mostly bounced back (it regained 31.4 percent in 2009–2012 and more since 2012). It is a similar story with regard to wealth: the Great Recession produced a retreat and then a recovery at the top as the equity markets regained lost ground and reached new highs.[17]

As financiers prospered, economic disparities widened. Since 2008, everyday people lost life savings, jobs, and housing and watched their household wealth and income plummet. While the real income of the superrich recovered from the Great Recession, the rest of America suffered an 11.6 percent hit to their incomes and largely missed out on a "recovery" (0.4 percent).[18] By the middle of 2013, median household income was still 6 percent lower than it was before 2008. The wealth of everyday people—often sunk into their homes—took a punishing blow. Ten million lost their homes or clung to them by a financial thread even four years after the recession was declared over—in 2013, 2.3 million were trying to fend off foreclosure.[19] The impact on wealth among people of color was especially devastating: the already large tenfold advantage of white households over black households in 2007 swelled to a bulging thirteen-fold gap by 2013.[20]

A *Washington Post* business reporter cut through the reams of data to highlight the impact on everyday Americans: "Over a span of three years, Americans watched progress that took almost a generation to accumulate evaporate. The promise of retirement built on the inevitable rise of the stock market proved illusory for most. Homeownership, once heralded as a pathway to wealth, became an albatross."[21]

Rising economic inequality has a number of potential sources: misdirected tax and spending policies, the nosedive of unions, the advantage of skilled workers as technology accelerates, changing international markets, and more.[22] The Fed stands out as an institutional enabler—sustaining finance and its growing distortion of the US economy. The Fed's reliance on capital markets privileges one set of policy tools that favors those with a disproportionate hold on wealth and income. Extraordinary measures to lift the values of assets—like quantitative easing—are even more "heavily skewed" to the already well-off who own most stocks and other investments, as the normally staid Bank of England put it.[23]

Expert Rule and the Anti-Democrats

The Fed's know-it-all swagger quietly rests on a fundamental premise: that its decisions should be dictated by its technocratic experts who know best. The twin foundations of the US Constitution—rigorous accountability and democratic responsiveness to citizens—are jettisoned because they are presumed to invite inflation, runs on the dollar, and fickle politicians.

A former vice chair of the Fed's Board of Governors, Alan Blinder, helpfully gave voice to the central bank's inclination—in his words—to place power "in the hands of unelected technocrats."[24] Blinder instructs us that they make "monetary policy on the merits" in a "technical field where trained specialists can probably outperform amateurs." Fed technocrats are further distinguished by the Olympian vision to break from the short-sightedness of politicians and steer the country toward its long-term interests. What justifies this radical departure from the Constitution's trust in "we the people" and its elected representatives? "It works." Indeed, Blinder is so impressed with the central bank's track record in the "realm of technocracy" that he recommends turning over taxation and other areas of policymaking to "an independent technical body like the Federal Reserve."

Blinder's case for muffling democracy and deferring to experts is refreshingly candid (thank you) and expresses a prevailing—if publicly muffled—sentiment among many of those at the apex of America's ruling institutions. Scholars and public commentators have often embraced technocracy instead of democracy since the ancient philosopher Plato and the eighteenth-century British writer and politician Edmund Burke, who famously proclaimed that each elected representative "owes you...his judgment," which he "betrays...if he sacrifices it to your opinion."[25] The twentieth-century philosopher Joseph Schumpeter tartly dismissed responsive democracy for depending on everyday people who are—in his view—inclined to "drop down to a lower level of mental performance" on matters of public affairs. Schumpeter forcefully pressed for a technocracy that treated elections as a "method" for voters to choose the deciders who, in turn, are free to exercise their superior knowledge, experience, and judgment.[26]

The allure of expert rule swells during turmoil, when the delay and negotiation that accompanies the legislative process are portrayed as an unaffordable luxury. True to form, the Fed's reactions to the 2008–2009 implosion required, Fed fans insist, unilateral action by those who knew best.

Contracting out hard policy choices to experts who reach the best solutions is enticing. And, in truth, specialized knowledge is a component of monetary policy and justifies some degree of (conditional) independence for central banks.

But let's put our thinking caps on. *The technocratic solution is a mirage*—actually three.[27]

Mirage #1. It is absurd to assume that Fed officials—alone among government administrators—are immune from advancing the narrow perspectives and interests of their agency and from listening to the pressure groups that hound it for special treatment. Here is the reality: the absence of regular and meaningful procedures to hold Fed officials publicly accountable opens the door to favoritism. Doubts that "men were angels" convinced James Madison and his fellow designers of the US Constitution to agree that "ambition must be made to counteract ambition" by inviting separate branches of government to obstruct, delay, and block each other. How the Fed slipped Madison's net of accountability is a central theme of this book.

Defenders of the Fed retort with a soothing dose of common sense: Why complain? The Fed's response to the 2008 crisis helped revive the US economy, and it turned a "profit"? What would the world look like without expert rule and favoritism?

It's a fair question, but there are several flaws.

First, equating the avoidance of disaster with the Fed's secret technocracy gives it too much credit. The Fed did stop a Great Depression, but Canada's more transparent and accountable central bank protected its economy from even facing economic Armageddon and made due without the massive rescues familiar in the United States.

Overselling is a theme. Officials in the Bush and Obama administrations insist that the Fed produced a profit.[28] Nice try. "Profitability" conveys a commonsense notion of "earning" and getting back more than was put in; in reality, the Fed relies on a rather peculiar calculation that leaves out the cost of the funds that were offered. It also slides over—again—the winners and losers. How many doomed owners of homes and businesses would have clasped like drowning swimmers onto free credit, and been saved to regain their financial footing and resume "profitability"— paying mortgages, taxes, and payroll?

Second, the claim to expertise masks competing values. Progressives—like Paul Krugman—welcomed the Fed's quantitative easing to circumvent conservative congressional deadlock of government spending. With legislative fiscal policy cut off, quantitative easing became the most significant government stimulus and is credited by independent analysts for dulling the Great Recession. The short-term benefit came, however, at significant cost to democratic norms and constitutional procedures. In an earlier period, President Ronald Reagan and Republicans lauded the Fed's unilateral move in the early 1980s to jack up interest rates to crush inflation. Democrats and progressives fiercely criticized the Fed in the 1980s for consigning millions to unemployment while Republicans and conservatives now lambast the Fed as an "unaccountable power within American government" with "no opposing force to rein it in."[29]

The evocation of expertise reaches for pristine claims to truth, but is cover for situational partisanship. The result is a perverse cycle: Reagan supporters cheered autocratic Fed decisions that slashed inflation at the cost of jobs, which set precedents for Obama progressives to welcome back-door stimulus. The institutional victor is the Fed: the precedent of going it alone sits on the table like a loaded gun for the next set of partisans.[30]

Third, scrutiny of who gets what reveals that the Fed's solutions are hardly neutral, but performed best for a few. The Fed's arsenal of technocratic jargon and pretentions rule out of order or altogether ignore questions about fairness and equity. But let's be clear: In the context of an open democracy, it is entirely appropriate to ask—as one of the pioneers of political science did— "Who Gets What, When, and How?" The Fed contributes to rising economic inequality through its concealed advantages for finance, and its reliance on the policy tools of capital market interventions that favor those who are sophisticated investors and already wealthy.

Mirage #2. For all the talk about how well the Fed "works," its performance contributed to the 2008–2009 crisis. For years, the Fed's tight embrace of a "deregulatory ideology"—as the authoritative congressional investigation of the financial crisis put it— set the stage for near Armageddon by insisting that experts had engineered a new, safer system. Here's the sad litany of mistakes by the Fed and other agencies that the investigators documented: opened up "gaps in the oversight of critical areas with trillions of dollars at risk," ignored "warning signs" of a looming financial crisis, and failed to "stem the flow of toxic mortgages, which it could have done."[31]

The Fed's cluelessness vividly comes to life in transcripts of meetings of its senior policymakers—the Federal Open Market Committee—as disaster looms. (Break time: you are rewatching Alfred Hitchcock's *Psycho* as the Vivian Leigh character steps into the running shower just before Norman Bates's mother repeatedly stabs her—you cringe and want to shout out a warning. That's what it is like reading the Fed transcripts.) Staring over the shoulder of the Fed's brainiacs, we watch them slide in and out of failing banks and investment firms in 2007 and 2008 with supreme optimism of happy days soon to come even as all-out collapse approaches, as subprime mortgages implode, financial institutions teeter without adequate cushions to withstand credit crunches, and newfangled securities and shadow banking prove much less secure than they assumed.[32] "Public stewards of our financial system," the authoritative congressional investigation concluded, "ignored warnings and failed to question, understand, and manage evolving risks."[33]

How often do you see a genuine and fulsome apology from a senior government official? And yet Fed experts so miserably failed that its former head, Alan Greenspan, came clean—declared his "shocked disbelief" at the Fed's failures as financial markets melted down in October 2008.[34] For years, he had confidently preached the usefulness of "greater reliance on private market regulation" and denigrated the false "perception of the history of American banking as plagued by repeated market failures that ended only with the enactment of comprehensive federal regulation." Greenspan was not alone. The boss of a lead financial regulator—the Securities and Exchange Commission's Christopher Cox—proclaimed a "good deal of comfort about the capital cushions" shortly before Bear Stearns and other firms collapsed due to overleveraging. He too would later profess regret.[35]

Of course, the problems were deeper than individual oversight. The nonpartisan Financial Crisis Inquiry Commission on the 2008 crisis singled out the Fed as one of the "sentries...not at their posts," sharing blame for the "widespread failures in financial regulation and supervision [that] proved devastating to the stability of the nation's financial markets."[36]

The failure of Greenspan and the Fed are not a surprising or unexpected outcome. Sheila Bair (chair of the Federal Deposit Insurance Corporation for Bush and Obama) spent years trying to plug the holes in the tattered regulatory structure and prevent the Fed giveaways. She fought (and often lost) a series of running battles with Bernanke and Bush Treasury secretary Hank Paulson and Obama Treasury secretary Tim Geithner to police finance much more sternly, and to cut back on what she saw as overly generous government help to banks and investment firms.[37]

The mistakes by Greenspan and others fit into a general pattern: experts regularly get it wrong because rule by specialists invites shortsightedness, inattention to risks, and narrow definitions of the "public good."[38] Autopsies of contemporary US disasters—from the explosion of the Challenger space shuttle to the breakdowns that led to the 9/11 attacks—illustrate that compartmentalized organizational routines and deference to specialized experts can produce decisions that are rational with regard to discrete issues but damaging to the larger system.[39] The 9/11 Commission revealed, for instance, that the United States possessed sophisticated intelligence capabilities that detected parts of the terrorist plot, but that the process lacked integration by generalists within and across agencies.

The problem leading up to the 2008 financial crisis was the Fed's insularity and narrowness. Intervention to head off the crisis was blocked by its rigid faith (as Greenspan conceded) in the "self-interest of market participants" to generate "private market regulation."[40] Groupthink dismissed prescient warnings about the failure of its assumptions, and narrow professional values and experiences failed to detect links between the discrete financial worlds of subprime mortgages and international markets for credit and risk sharing.

The mistakes by the Fed are not limited to the 2008 crisis. Fed officials and their cadre of analysts proselytize expertise, but their claims that granting them a free hand tames inflation lacks convincing evidence. Careful study finds, as one recent summary put it, "no causal relationship" between central bank independence and inflation.[41]

And of course, the future may bring to light more miscalculations. Here's a big issue that may showcase the consequences of the Fed's decision—a balance sheet that flips into negative territory. Some of the Fed's most audacious policies during 2008–2009 purchased the bad securities and assets that banks did not want (think toxic mortgages tied up with subprime loans and other undesirable investments). The banks smiled as they counted their cash and safely stowed it away as a deposit at the Fed. This little square dance worked fine as long as banks were ditching the bad stuff and afraid of making loans that turn out to be risks. The improving economy begins to change things. People and business are now strutting into banks with stronger prospects and a willingness to pay good money for credit, and banks are keen to pull their deposits out of the Fed to make profits. What does the Fed do? One strategy is to persuade banks to keep their deposits with the Fed by raising the rate it pays. Makes sense, except the boost in deposit rates costs the Fed money—it must literally make payments to the banks that put their money in the Fed. This scenario or others may put the Fed in the red, and, with it, bring renewed scrutiny of the wisdom of the Fed's policies.[42]

Mirage #3. Let's stop pretending that the Fed operates in a cloistered enclave when its policies and operations occur in a community defined by shared values and beliefs. Handing the reins of monetary policy to "unelected technocrats," as Blinder puts it,

offends our deep suspicions of concentrated power and expectations of democratic government. Opposition to the ratification of
the Constitution in the late eighteenth century is long forgotten,
but the resistance was strong and expressed a fear that endures—
rulers "erect an interest separate from the ruled" that advantage
"the respectable men."[43] Over the course of American history, banking
and Wall Street have often triggered political backlashes. William
Jennings Bryan ignited the 1896 Democratic National Convention
with his fiery defiance of big banks who insisted on a gold standard. In the next decade, Teddy Roosevelt railed against corporate
"trusts" and the "malefactors of great wealth."

How does democratic accountability work? For openers, it is
not one thing; it requires an arsenal to foster informed public
debate and check the institutional and individual ambition to act
alone. Meaningful transparency and public deliberation is necessary; much of the Fed's power comes from calculated strategies
to depress public talk and the healthy challenges it invites. Public
deliberation is oxygen for informed press coverage, the engagement of everyday citizens, and public interest watchdogs. But that
is not enough, given the specialized knowledge of monetary policy
and financial regulation and the need for the rigorous tracking of
central banks. The expertise of elected representatives and congressional committees are needed to supply regular and direct
legislative oversight. Finally, institutional architecture matters
enormously. The design of central banks to narrow their responsibilities to monetary policy and to position independent regulators is indispensable. The mesh of accountability created by public
deliberation, legislative oversight, and constrained central bank
design are subject to strain.[44] In combination, however, they do
offer a vital counterbalance to America's central bank that reflects both the framework Madison developed in the US Constitution
and the practical experience of other countries (notably Canada)
that stand out for effective financial management.[45]

Fed power sits on the fault line in American public life—its
march over time to secure increasing autonomy and power is an
affront to American culture and Madison's tradition of accountability. The sobering irony is that the Fed itself has set a dangerous

snare: it promises elusive expert answers, but its go-it-alone arrogance has reignited America's deep-seated distrust of concentrated and unaccountable power. Its moment of apparent triumph has triggered, as we discuss below, revolt against its autocratic powers.

FINANCIAL PATHOLOGY: FINDING THE FED'S BIAS

The pathology department in hospitals is among their most important divisions—it pinpoints why patients die and, when appropriate, assigns blame. Fingering the culprits in the 2008–2009 financial cave-in is revealing.

Why was the Fed so slow to recognize the impending collapse of the financial system? Let's turn the question around: Why would we expect the Fed to vigorously police banks and investment firms?

Favoritism 1, 2, and 3

The well-being and accommodation of finance and the affluent align with the personal interests and professional orientation of Fed officials as well as the Bank's institutional interests. The Fed could no more crack down on finance and the wealthy as it could savage itself.

Operational Favoritism
The Fed's public pronouncements promise broadly shared gains; in reality, the Fed favors finance in several forms. The first is baked into its everyday operations—the operational inequality produced by its reliance on capital markets.

Selecting Winners
A second form of favoritism burst onto the scene with the 2008–2009 crisis—the targeting of benefits and relief from the risk of steep losses or bankruptcy. The Fed took a series of unilateral steps—from opening its services to nonbanks to watering down collateral

requirements—that delivered substantial advantages to one industry and a few privileged firms. Leading the list of takers was Goldman Sachs with an initial haul of $14 billion (the government bailout known as the Troubled Asset Relief Program, or TARP, added an additional $4 billion).[46] In exchange, the Fed asked for little. It refrained from demanding—as nearly all other central banks did—concessions from banks and investment firms (delicately known as "haircuts"). Nor did it demand that firms use the extraordinary assistance to relieve the freeze in credit instead of hoarding the money for their own gain (as they did).[47] Bush's Treasury secretary Hank Paulson conceded to the congressional inquiry that "no specific requirements [were made] for those banks to make loans to businesses and households," even though its purpose was to give them "the capital...that would lead to lending." Even Paulson accepted that this may have been overly deferential.[48]

"Without the federal assistance," the Financial Crisis Inquiry Commission noted, firms like Goldman Sachs would have had to "find the $14 billion some other way"—on much less favorable terms.[49] With credit markets frozen in 2008–2009, the US government's credit to Goldman and the other anointed firms was, according to a prominent economist, an "enormous favor" that was indispensable and unavailable for nearly all—including Lehman Brothers and everyday Americans frantic to keep their homes and other businesses.[50]

The Fed also targeted favors by absorbing the risk that private businesses took on when they gambled. The Fed threw a lifeline to these firms—and not other American businesses or citizens—by purchasing their bets on toxic securities tied to subprime mortgages and by lending to them without its long-standing requirements for safe collateral to protect taxpayers against the failure to pay back the credit.[51]

The Fed "socialized" the risks and losses of finance. "The private debt of highly leveraged financial institutions," Mark Blyth explains, "became the public debt." The rub is that the "banks promised growth, delivered losses, passed the costs onto the state,...which of course must be paid for by [taxpayers and] expenditure cuts."[52]

During the 2012 presidential election, Mitt Romney was privately videotaped warning donors that taxpayers were paying for the 47 percent of "takers" who receive government benefits—from senior citizens on Social Security and Medicare to veterans. Let's turn this question on the Fed's largesse: Who talks about its takers among a fraction of 1 percent?

Missing in Action: Middle-Class Rescue

Rarely do everyday people show up in the Fed's operations. They are either an unrecognized abstraction referred to as "the American People," or absent. Chairwoman Janet Yellen recognized the omission and started to orchestrate press events with staged meetings with "the people."

As Middle America cratered, the Fed and its institutional allies in the US Treasury publicly offered a miniscule response and then, in effect, forgot about it. The nonpartisan Government Accounting Office catalogued the hundreds of billions authorized and spent on banks and investment firms after the 2008 crisis.[53] Its reports on what was done for everyday Americans are quietly stunning. Compared to the luxuriant treatment of the affluent, far smaller amounts were targeted to helping Americans at risk of foreclosure in the aftermath of the 2008 tsunami—$45.6 billion. But that is not all. Of that minor effort, only $2.5 billion was paid out—about 5 percent of the authorized amount. The Treasury's Home Affordable Modification Program promised to help 4 million borrowers. It delivered for just a quarter of that.[54]

The Fed is a political institution that redistributes wealth and power. The bias of government policy was to act aggressively to aid finance and to choose inaction for Middle America. Winners in the marketplace are further advantaged by the Fed.

Motivated Favoritism

Why would the Fed favor the few in finance when its much-lauded mission is to serve the common good? Let us count the ways— three in particular.

Revolving Doors

About a year after Ben Bernanke stepped down from the pinnacle of power as Fed chair, he was hired by Pimco and Citadel—two of the largest financial firms in the world. Pimco's CEO, Douglas Hodge, beamed at benefitting from Bernanke's "extraordinary knowledge and expertise."[55] Translation: ka-ching. In return, Bernanke became fabulously wealthy. (Context: Citadel CEO Ken Griffin's haul in 2014 was $1.3 billion—about half of the entire economy of the country of Belize.[56] Bernanke's yellow brick road from the heights of government power to finance stands out, but is hardly unique.)

"Revolving door" is the shorthand for the rewarding journey from agency to industry positions and back.

The revolving door is prevalent in the wider circle of financial regulators who are serenaded by stupendous paydays. Some regulators searched for their ticket to the gravy train as they designed legislation.[57] A *New York Times* investigation reported that 148 people cashed in their jobs with agencies trusted with regulating finance for well-paid positions as lobbyists as the mega-rescues were crafted in 2009 and 2010.[58]

The payoff for Wall Street of hiring Fed and other financial regulators is straightforward—advice on how to anticipate and game the rules. Hiring Fed officials not only delivers payoffs for gaming in the future (Pimco's rationale for signing up Bernanke); they may also infiltrate the thinking of regulators and influence them from within government.[59] After all, we tailor our workplace behavior today in anticipation of where we want to be tomorrow. Research documents the influence on central bankers of "shadow principals" outside government who control later hiring.[60]

Put yourself in the position of a Fed staffer worried about paying the big college bills for several children in high school and thinking about taking a better paying position in finance. Would you seek out a reputation for compelling firms to pull back from profitable business?[61] In the real world, this is not imaginary: reports of threats and punishments meted out to zealous financial regulators frequently turn up in the press and memoirs.[62]

What about senior Fed officials who had previously worked on Wall Street? Two members of the five-person Board of Governors had worked in finance in a private equity firm (Jerome Powell was a partner at the Carlyle Group) and a global mega-bank

(Stanley Fischer was vice chairman of Citigroup). The top honcho of the important Fed Bank in New York—William Dudley—came from Goldman Sachs and continued to hold a cache of AIG and GE stocks.[63]

The risk here is that Fed officials continue to embrace the mindset of finance. During the 2008–2009 crisis, the Fed was routinely printing conflict of interest waivers to sign off on its officials cutting deals for their former employers. Dudley is a poster boy for the dueling loyalties—he received waivers to keep AIG and GE stocks while bailing them out.[64] Is it too much to expect waivers to short-circuit past loyalties and to guarantee detached scrutiny?

Capture

The allure of revolving doors is complemented by an army of well-heeled lobbyists whose persistent, dominating influence on Fed officials can amount to a kind of "capture."[65] The Fed and, at times, other agencies decided—deep breath—to allow banks to create a newfangled business based on shaky mortgages; declined to enforce existing consumer protection laws against offshoots of banks; relaxed requirements that banks keep enough cash and credit on hand to cover their bets; and more.[66] Do you see the pattern? Again and again, the Fed's decisions adopted "policies generally...favoring the financial sector" and giving it license for "increased profits in the short run" while "making the financial system more fragile and imposing widespread losses on society."[67]

Capture is like a virus that changes forms. It may amount to a literal invasion of government agencies by lobbyists who wield persistent and dominating influence (such as the energy industry writing policy).[68] It also can entail "cultural capture," in which the Fed and finance come to see the world as the rich and finance does. They may agree on who has status (big firms and financial wizards rank highest); share similar networks of colleagues and mentors; and jointly assume that markets work best when left alone (unless crisis requires a rescue).[69] Common mindsets, Nobel Prize–winning economist Joseph Stiglitz suggests, induced officials in the

Fed and other agencies to "think that what's good for Wall Street is good for America."[70] Rather than contentious battles, "government negotiators [come] to the table largely in agreement with the bankers' view of the world."[71]

Example: traditional banking originated loans and mortgages and held them, living off of the interest rate. In the decade before the Great Recession a shadowy world of international banking sprang up to supply short-term borrowing and lending between businesses. This breakaway from traditional banking hit the jackpot: it met the needs of business to make payroll, and it generated income for firms that swapped and quickly repurchased assets and packaged home mortgages as a security. It replaced the traditional "originate and hold" model of lending with "originate and distribute"—a shift that was heralded by economists and bankers as promoting greater security against financial risk. What started out, however, as a concrete service to businesses and a path to risk management flipped into an opaque and complex scheme for speculators to generate outsized profits on "credit swaps" and "mortgage-backed securities." Canada was sufficiently alarmed that it put up limits, but not the Fed or other US regulators. Where were they? Good question. The Fed was not powerless to get involved, but it viewed this financial whirlwind through the eyes of finance; Greenspan fiercely resisted regulation as damaging innovation and deemed it unnecessary given the "self-interests of organizations" and the "unrivaled" success of "free, competitive markets." Bernanke praised the new shadow system as run by "very sophisticated" traders in congressional testimony in 2005. Looking back, Greenspan would concede the "flaw" in his thinking and the congressional inquiry would conclude that "the Federal Reserve neglected its mission" by deferring to financial markets.[72]

Where were the American people and citizen groups committed to fending off special interests and lax regulators when the storms of financial turmoil gathered? Americans, after all, are legendary joiners.[73] They were an occasional force, but in general they were outmatched—amateurs against all-star lobbyists who descended on Washington like "birds of prey" (in John

McCain's lacerating phrase).[74] The immediate, direct, and intense consequences of Fed and Treasury decisions for finance
(spelled: profits, bonuses, and jobs) puts the fear of God into Wall
Street and other parts of the industry to invest overwhelming
resources into lobbying and coordinating their incursions; the
general public has enormous stakes too, but lacks the resources
and all-consuming attention to concealed but weighty decisions
about whether or how to regulate finance and rescue it during
crisis.[75]

Let's go to the videotape for an illustration. The time is 2009–
2010, when the US financial system was wobbling and Congress
was talking about reining in high-risk finance in what became
known as the Dodd-Frank Act. Wall Street and its friends mobilized an army of lobbyists, but still suffered a number of setbacks
thanks in part to a pugnacious opponent—a coalition of hundreds of public interest groups that fought under the flag of
Americans for Financial Reform. The thrusting of interest groups
displayed in passing Dodd-Frank all but disappeared, however,
when the hugely important process of implementing the law
started. Absent the high-octane attention generated by presidential promotion and the media spotlight, fundraising and the mobilization of public interest groups and Americans for Financial
Reform faded. Of course, industry kept funding well-connected
lobbyists to bombard obscure agencies and was rewarded with
outright concessions or the next best thing—delays and stalemate
that prevented action.[76]

Fed Interests
The siren songs of lucrative job prospects and silver-tongued lobbyists that influence Fed officials matter, but there is a still more
perverse factor—the Fed's drive to help itself.[77]

Journalists and researchers have a habit of treating the Fed
either as a well-intentioned steward of the public good or, more
critically, as a passive cash register tallying the demands of finance. Missing in action: the Fed as an institution with interests
and aims of its own.[78] Some view the Internal Revenue Service
as nearly a satanic force driven to enrich itself. And we have no

problem assuming—correctly—that the Defense Department protects their turf and advances their agendas.

The Fed (like other government institutions) maneuvers to advance its agenda, but it enjoys nearly unparalleled advantages. It
boasts extremely well-trained staff in equity markets, economics, and law. It enjoys clear lines of authority that has spared it
for years from the infighting and external interference that saps
other agencies. And, its officials and separate outposts share a
well-developed sense of mission.

The Fed helps itself when it protects and stabilizes finance.
This symbiotic relationship was baked into its inception. To build
active support for the Federal Reserve Act of 1913, the lead lawmakers struck a deal with big banks: they would aggressively
push for the enactment of the new central bank and, in exchange,
the Fed would convert the floundering US dollar into a precious
global currency and transform New York into a world financial
hub at great profit for the banks.[79] Over time, the Fed's development was premised on advancing its interests as an institution
and safeguarding its stake in finance; these became organizing
principles that stitched together its seemingly discrete agencies
and actions.

The Fed's most basic interest is to sustain its flow of resources
to function and to reward the private banks in its system. The
Fed generates enormous sums of money from operating on Wall
Street by collecting interest on its investments and the revenue
from buying and selling them.[80] This stream of cash covers the
Fed's expenses (over $1 billion in 2014) and those of the 12 re-
gional banks ($3.6 billion) as well as a 6 percent dividend paid to
the over 2,900 private banks that are members of the Fed's 12
regional banks. This princely payout is legally guaranteed, often
tax-free, and three times larger than the average dividend on the
stock market's main index in 2014—it totaled over $1.6 billion in
2012.[81] After the Fed has feasted, it turns over the ample left-
overs to the Treasury, which amounted to $98.7 billion in 2014
and about $500 billion from 2008 to 2014.[82]

As the Fed's reliance on finance for revenue tethers their interests
together, it also underwrites the Fed's political independence.

Unlike most other government agencies, the Fed's own sources of revenue releases it from competing annually in Congress for a budget allocation. Fiscal independence also frees it from the scrutiny and political meddling that often accompanies the annual appropriations process. It sails above the normal congressional budget process and the scrutiny of agencies that often accompanies appropriations.

The Fed's institutional dependence on finance is also anchored in its need for information. The Fed and other regulators strike bargains with banks to obtain data.[83] The banks let them collect information on their operations, balance sheets, and internal management in exchange for confidentiality. Without that agreement, information would be delayed or withheld.[84] But the terms of the trade handcuff what the Fed knows and how the Fed can use the data to police finance. Fed chair Bernanke identified the need to collect and process information as one of the "significant challenges" to preventing future shocks to the financial system.[85]

The financial implosion of 2008–2009 created a new set of motivations. The crisis impugned the Fed's reputation and interrupted its operations. But the Fed's rescues served finance as well as itself by sustaining its stream of revenue and attempting to resuscitate its reputation.

As the financial tsunami wiped out jobs and forced businesses to retrench starting in late 2008, the Fed faced another dire threat: even if the financial system did not collapse, a steep and prolonged recession could leave it stuck with losses on the extraordinary commitments it was making to banks and other businesses. Maintaining its rescues and ginning up the massive investments in quantitative easing to stimulate the economy and prevent losses protected the Fed's investments and forestalled a far more intense public and congressional backlash.

Here's another motivation for the Fed's catering to finance: organized warfare in Washington. The Fed's long history of surviving threats to its budgets and turf has instilled a thirst for reliable allies who can mobilize armies of lobbyists (as finance does) when the central bank is threatened by Congress or the White House. When early Dodd-Frank proposals in 2009 took aim at clawing back its authority, finance provided the shock troops to fight them off.

Appreciating the Fed as an institution motivated by its own interests resolves a puzzle: the Fed both aids finance and exercises exceptional independence to stand above the fray of government and industry meddling. How can the Fed be both partial to finance and apart from it? The Fed's organizational interests are to sustain and help finance overall. This may mean aiding certain sectors and firms more than others as well as refraining from intervening at certain junctures—Lehman Brothers comes to mind, among others.

What We Are Not Claiming

Let's pause here to slew goblins and peddlers of false extremes.

Goblin #1. Does the Fed's favoritism of finance make its staff evil ogres or craven tools of the rich? Not as a rule. Many of the people who work at the Fed may be genuinely committed to public service and sincerely believe that deferring to finance serves the public at large.[86] The issue, however, is not morality but rather the plain-vanilla institutional interests and personal motives that propel the Fed's favoritism regardless of who works for the Fed.

Goblin #2. Far-fetched conspiracies of bankers and diabolical schemes to bring down America can be thrilling, but the reality is more mundane—the mutual interests of finance, the Fed, and its ostensible overseers in Congress. The Fed has formed a durable alliance with the well-funded lobbyists of finance and loyal enclaves within the government—from Treasury to particular congressional committees.

Mutually reinforcing rewards bond together the triple politics of monetary policy: the Fed seeks allies to protect and expand its independence and capacity; finance welcomes Fed policies that give it leeway for profit-seeking and rescues when its speculation threatens massive losses; and members of Congress earn campaign donations while government officials gobble up well-appointed positions in banks or investment firms. Triple politics translates into extraordinary leeway for America's central bank: the Fed is attuned to Congress on discrete policies (notably interest rates) that tweak the operation of monetary policy while legislators tolerate Fed initiatives to define the architecture of modern finance.[87] Back-patting helps to explain why Congress largely looked the other way—until after the fact—when the Fed refrained from enforcing regulations before the 2008–2009 crisis and when it supplied massive, permissive credits and guarantees to business.

Goblin #3. You might be wondering what matters more: ambition to land a minted job in finance, the pressure of lobbyists, or the Fed's own drive to protect its turf? It's difficult to pinpoint, but it is fair grounds for debate. (Argue among yourselves.)

Goblin #4. The Fed is not all-powerful. The pioneer of sociology Max Weber observed that institutions and groups with power and ambition rely on their public reputations and credibility to insulate and amplify their sway: they "wish to see their positions transferred from purely factual power relations into a cosmos of acquired rights...that are...sanctified."[88] Put more bluntly, power is not always projected by the gun of soldiers enforcing a dictator's orders—Weber's "factual power." Influence may be most potent when the actions of the powerful are accepted as legitimate and the mass public acquiesces.

The Fed exercised power that may be without precedent in US domestic affairs outside of wartime, and yet this surge undercut its legitimacy and harmed its long-term prospects. Emerging from the shadows to commit massive loans and guarantees publicized its deviant structure outside Madison's system of accountability and precipitated public and congressional questions and resistance.

The Fed's development, then, is characterized by a double action rather than a seamless progression. Reforms, responses to new financial snafus, and struggles for institutional position produced sharp expansions in the administrative might and independence since 1913. The Fed's exercise of its enhanced powers, however, precipitated reactions that threatened its legitimacy and might. This pattern of action and reaction helps to explain its current uncertain position, as we discuss in later chapters.

FINDING THE FED STATE

Studies of political development in the United States lament America's "hapless giant"—the large conglomeration of government agencies and lawmaking bodies that are stymied in domestic affairs by conflicting lines of authority among government divisions and underdeveloped administrative capacity. Library shelves groan from the weight of impressive tomes such as Alexis de Tocqueville's chronicling of early nineteenth-century America, which concludes that "the federal government of the United States is tending to get daily weaker." Distilling generations of similar observations, J. P. Nettl pointed in the late 1960s to the "relative statelessness of the United States" and the prevailing ideology of self-reliant individualism and distrust of government. Contemporary observers continue to proclaim American government large, intrusive, and, true to form, unable consistently to pursue coherent courses of action.[89] Headlines that track the saga of big but ineffective government from the savings and loan debacle of the 1980s to the financial implosion two decades later affirm a long-running story. These recurrent episodes also reinforce the weakness: catastrophic oversights and ineffectiveness feed the low confidence in government among elites and the public, which in turn lead to the next round of (predictable) debacles of ineffective government oversight and inflamed distrust.[90]

Fed Exceptionalism

In a sea of weakness, America's central bank stands out in domestic policymaking for its administrative might and two features in particular. The first is its operational capacity to identify coherent objectives, consistently pursue organizational responsibilities, and act decisively. It enjoys extraordinary resources, clear hierarchical lines of authority, and hundreds of trained personnel with doctorates. No single unit of government wields the capacity in domestic policy to commit trillions of dollars on its own. No part of government boasts the talent that runs the Fed: it attracts PhDs from the most prestigious universities and accomplished talent from business. If the Fed entered a contest populated by "Big Bang Theory" nerds, few would bet against it.

The Fed's powers on the domestic front rival the vast resources and independence of the national security state. Democratic and Republican presidents have taken advantage of constitutional ambiguity, roadblocks to congressional action, and gaps in public knowledge to ratchet up presidential prerogatives and the use of surveillance and covert military operations despite efforts at reform.[91]

For all of the power that the Fed has accrued, it is not immune from intervention. Under rare circumstances, it may face significant sustained public scrutiny and disruption by Congress.[92]

The Fed's second exceptional feature is its autonomy.[93] It enjoys the power to reach decisions and take actions without the delaying and checking by other branches of government and the interference by outside interests that is familiar in domestic policymaking.[94]

Central banks in Europe and other capitalist countries have long argued for some degree of institutional independence as necessary to prioritize low inflation and to fend off demands from well-appointed lobbyists and voters as elections approach. During the Glorious Revolution in seventeenth-century England, the monarchy struggled to secure credit because banks feared it would default on loans, and it was compelled to delegate decisions over borrowing to Parliament and a central bank.[95] Leaders of the American Revolution appreciated that attracting credit required credibility against worries that "surprise inflation" would undercut the real value of debt. Article 1 (Sec. 10) of the US Constitution enumerates the government's commitment to protect contracts and debt obligations, and James Madison's Federalist Paper #44 underscores its importance.

The Fed's degree of independence stands out. Under normal circumstances, the central bank's debates over policy and its decisions are reached behind closed doors. But that does not begin to describe its insulation, or distinguish it from its counterparts. The Fed commits public funds but its governance lies, in important respects, in private hands (regional banks and an appointed board). The wild card, however, is Section 13(3). It was added to its legislative authorization in 1932 and provides the legal equivalent of a blank check to take actions that it deems appropriate "in unusual and exigent circumstances." The Fed used 13(3) to act *alone* to reinvent its role and powers during 2008–2009.

Let's pause for a moment of reflection. "Alone" is a word that is hard to apply to the US form of government. Congress passes a bill; the president can block it with his veto. Presidents nominate senior government officials; the Senate decides whether to confirm them. Congress and the president agree to create a new law; the judiciary can review it to test its constitutional mettle. One branch watching and checking the other is the common thread. Alone? Not so much.

Back to the Fed and what made its 2008–2009 actions exceptional: it unilaterally committed trillions of dollars on favorable terms to a new class of private businesses. While America's constitutional process grinds nearly all significant domestic policy through the ringer of multiple and competing branches of government, the Fed asserted its prerogatives in Section 13(3) to extend massive amounts of credit. Yes, there was a process, but "cake walk" aptly describes it—private approval of at least five members of its own board. The normally reserved former Fed chair, Paul Volcker, declared that the formerly staid central bank was tightrope-walking at "the very edge of its lawful and implied powers."[96]

America's central bank is an exceptional type of governance. We call this the "Fed State."[97]

The Takeoff

Since its inception in 1913, the Fed developed through a series of breakthroughs. The 2008 crisis triggered a takeoff in three respects.

Takeoff #1. Before 1980, presidents expected a compliant Fed. They forced out its chairs who were unresponsive (as was the case under Harry Truman) or ineffective in tackling economic troubles (as did Jimmy Carter). After 2007, it was inconceivable that presidents Bush or Obama would try—let alone succeed—in forcing out the Fed chair or standing in the way of its novel and unprecedented interventions into private markets. Even with a roiled Congress considering incursions into the Fed's authority, the most threatening legislative challenges were steered aside as risks to market confidence and economic recovery. The Fed emerged with more responsibilities.

As the Fed entered its second century, it was mostly free of the normal institutional shackles that impede US government and wielded a skilled and sophisticated staff to guide the private sector and to reshape the fiscal commitments of the public sector.

Takeoff #2. Even by the Fed's lofty standards of institutional capacity, the Fed's interventions in 2008–2009 stood out for their size, scope, and departure from past precedents. Its response began in 2008 with the usual toolkit—it cut the discount rate at which banks borrowed from the Fed—but escalated to launching a blitzkrieg of institution-building by creating an alphabet of emergency lending programs and establishing currency swap agreements with 14 central banks.[98] With the exception of defending the United States during wartime, no government body has deployed the country's resources in domestic affairs with such speed and independence.

Takeoff #3. Congress and the president battle over taxes and spending—the normal tools of what is called "fiscal policy"—and elections and voters hold them to account for their choices. Beginning in 2008, the Fed blasted through its normal operations to grab the authority and discretion of elected officials and "fiscal and monetary policies have become more alike."[99]

The Fed's astonishing assumption of fiscal power was executed like a two-step dance. In the first step, the Fed committed taxpayers to risky ventures. It abandoned its stringent policy of only supplying short-term, modest lending to a small group of rock-solid deposit-taking institutions that supplied impeccable collateral and posed very low risk. Instead, it made a series of Olympian decision to extend credit to failing nonbanks, limited liability firms—Bear Stearns and then the American International Group (AIG)—and to guarantee credit for a host of new purposes including mortgages, credit cards, consumer debt, and student loans.

In exchange, the Fed accepted dubious collateral and the substantial risk of loss. Congress's independent panel investigating the financial crisis complained that the central bankers "weren't sure they understood the extent of toxic assets on the balance sheets of financial institutions—so they couldn't be sure which banks were really solvent."[100] The effect, according to a flummoxed former Fed governor, was to stock the Fed's balance sheets with holdings that posed significant risk of losses—an astonishing turn of events by what had been the stringent lender of last resort.[101]

The Fed's second step was establishing itself as a fiscal agent. It captured gains for the Treasury and itself—if its loans panned out.

The Fed's qualitative shift responded to the partisan discord in Congress that stymied the use of fiscal policy and deficit spending to boost the economy—despite the pleadings of a broad swathe of economists. Fed actions to dull the Great Recession simultaneously tempered the depths of the economic downturn and wrote a new chapter in its historic transformation into a Goliath of domestic government power. The dysfunction in Congress created a need and an opportunity that the Fed unilaterally seized to extend its responsibilities from long-existing routine actions (altering the money supply and interest rates) to novel new programs that targeted businesses far outside the banking system.

Reassuring cooing from the Fed and its allies does not mask the transformation. The Fed, according to prominent economists, usurped "the authority that the Constitution reserves for Congress" by "taking fiscal action and invading the territory of the [elected] fiscal authorities."[102] Put another way, the Fed outwardly demands an exception to Madison's system of accountability to manage supposedly technical matters of money supply free of politics while practicing the art of politics—selecting some firms for government credit while denying others.[103]

Concealed Advantage

Debate over health care reform since 2009 has been intense, sustained, and highly public. President Obama devoted his first

15 months in office to barnstorming the country and browbeating Congress to pass the reform. After the president signed the Affordable Care Act (ACA) in March 2010, the public drama then shifted from Washington to state lawmakers and to judges who scrutinized the ACA for years. Following five years of national acrimony, about two-thirds of states refused to implement its insurance exchanges and 20 turned down its expanded program for low-income Americans. Bottom line: a fiery public debate revealed sharp disagreements over philosophy and interests and produced a much different program than if it was entirely hatched behind closed doors by an Obama White House or agency.

The public conflict that engulfed health reform is similar (though more sustained) to the battles over reforming immigration, Social Security, and taxation. Public contestation is not an aberration but a predictable—and indeed often heralded—feature of the US Constitution's invitation to rivalry and checking. The result is an enduring pattern of "deadlock and delay."[104]

Did You Know?

What stands out about the Federal Reserve is its evasion of the normal public conflict and institutional checking *before* policy is made. It commits more US assets than many normal legislative bills that are signed into law, and yet receives far less searching scrutiny. The spotlight on the Fed only occasionally pops on (often with the Fed controlling its presentation) and even then only fleetingly *after* it has changed interest rates or other policies.

Here's a test: Did you know that the Fed's loans and guarantees during the Great Recession equaled *half* of the value of everything produced in the United States in 2009?[105] That's a monstrous commitment, and you may be reasonably wondering: How did I miss that? Good question.

But the huge rescue in 2008–2009 merely highlights standard procedure.

Strategies of Concealment

The Fed has a repertoire of strategies to obscure and camouflage its decisions and to dodge intense, sustained scrutiny by elected officials, the press, and social media. It debates and implements policy in secret and then masks its picking of winners and losers in the nap-inducing jargon of technocrats and in vague pronouncements about "market forces."[106]

Secrecy and the stonewalling of requests for information from journalists and lawmakers is another strategy. One reason that few knew the magnitude of the Fed's commitments is that it refused to give a straight answer. It took an intensive investigation and a court case by the global media powerhouse Bloomberg News to figure out that the Fed funneled upward of $7.7 trillion as loans or guarantees.[107] The Fed also withheld the names of the firms that were helped on the pretense that secrecy was necessary to save the broader system; releasing names would destroy the good reputations of firms—assuming, of course, that their reputations and financial strength were intact and believed.

By the way, the European Central Bank (ECB) doled out $638 billion in 2011 to lenders in the eurozone *and* disclosed the identities of the firms taking the aid.[108] One financial analyst stripped bare the Fed's effort to shield from public view its catering to financial interests: "The perceived stigma attached to central bank borrowing has not prevented euro-zone banks from making extensive use of the ECB's offer."[109] Fed secrecy shielded it from public scrutiny and enabled overstretched or insolvent US financial firms to masquerade as healthy and, in some cases, to elude bankruptcy.

You may be wondering, doesn't the Fed release a steady stream of information? Fair enough. The public testimony of its chairs has catapulted them into celebrities among geeks and newshawks. It now provides transcripts of the Open Market Committee meetings and reports (though several years after the meeting).

The selective release of information, however, is hardly tantamount to transparency. The Fed continues to control how and what is released publicly. Public airing of who wins and who loses are, in effect, quarantined from public airing.

The Fed's Game Plan

The Fed conceals its policymaking for two reasons. The first is to mute the kind of searing public and congressional debate that marked nineteenth-century populism. Where health reform featured dueling gladiators in the modern coliseum of media coverage, the Fed's momentous decisions of 2008–2009 were preceded by near public silence. This is one of the most remarkable nonevents in all of American politics.

Stealth decision-making is quite potent in depressing the public's awareness and ability to size up the Fed. In late 2009 over 40 percent of Americans were unable to evaluate the work of Fed chairman Ben Bernanke, even though he served as chair as the seeds of financial crisis were sown by the central bank's lax oversight and bumbling response during the previous year or more.[110] When sporadic and incomplete reports about the government's bailouts were forced into public debate, the public recoiled—confirming the bank's distance from the country. Public discussion of the Fed's help for the supersized insurance company AIG piqued the interest of Americans—about two-thirds followed the news on it—and split the country.[111]

The Fed's suppression of information also handicapped members of Congress as they drafted the Dodd-Frank reform—preventing them from pursuing a more thoroughgoing reform and further reducing the Fed's powers.[112]

Even when the Fed does release information, it does so in a form crafted to fit its public relations campaign. The nonpartisan watchdog of the government's rescues criticized a pattern of "misleading" public presentation about what it did and how that "risks . . . the public's trust."[113]

The second reason for secretive Fed policymaking is to privatize decisions. The most crucial monetary decisions are reached by the Federal Open Market Committee, which consist of the Board of Governors (who are appointed by the president and confirmed by the Senate) and by the presidents of five of the 12 private regional banks. Although this governing structure precludes any one bank from monopolizing policy, its decisions are cordoned off and are made by representatives of one industry and by appointees who (after being filtered through the executive and legislative branches) consistently embrace the Fed's general mission. Put simply, the process of making monetary policy confines who participates to narrowly organized and particularistic sets of interests—finance.

American politicians are skilled at "submerging" policies that favor the few.[114] Take tax policy: deductions for home mortgage interest payments and the health insurance premiums paid by employers are huge programs, and yet few think of them as government benefits. That's a nifty trick.

The Fed's insulated decision-making is more diabolical. Submerged policy must survive the normal legislative process, and it is possible (though uncommon) for lawmakers and the press to scrutinize them in public and to get policy changed. The Fed's advantage, however, is substantially greater. Its decision-making over the 2008–2009 rescue and economic stimulus (also known as "quantitative easing") was immune to both the normal public inspection and checking.

New York Times columnist Gretchen Morgenson looked back over the four years after the 2008 crisis with amazement at the Fed's effectiveness in favoring the banks.[115] The answer is that the Fed's operations are designed to blunt public inspection and the accountability it propels.

REFORMING THE FED

The Fed's responses to the 2008–2009 crisis elevated its power to new heights and its favoritism of finance but at the cost of eroding its already fragile legitimacy as an independent, apolitical institution that expertly served the public good. Despite the Fed's labored efforts to conceal its operations, press and independent investigators did excavate information about its mistakes that contributed to the crisis and extraordinary unilateral steps to rescue Wall Street—though not without significant delays and gaps. The Fed originated during the early twentieth century in a drive to depoliticize central banking, but its interventions in 2008–2009 "overpoliticized" its preference for private capital markets and institutional dependence on them. The new scrutiny fuels public and congressional interest in reforms to restore the accountability that is the bedrock of America's constitutional system.

The Fed's Legitimacy Deficit

Reservations about the Fed's legitimacy and lack of accountability are animated by three sets of concerns—concerns that have gravitated from the margins of public debate toward the center of American business and politics.

Misgiving #1. One set of questions strike at the heart of the Fed's claims to technocratic rule—expertise. A number of leading economists worry that the Fed's interventions are generating another bubble economy by artificially manufacturing low interest rates and pumping up the stock market and other assets through quantitative easing. Ronald Reagan's head of the Council of Economic Advisors and Harvard economist Martin Feldstein warns that the Fed's high-risk commitments may stick taxpayers with substantial losses. Meanwhile, others point to evidence of a steady, consistent (though not rapid) improvement in hiring and the broader economy.[116]

Another line of criticism is that the Fed's interventions will encourage future risk-taking. Why not speculate if you expect the Fed to step in when your gamble flops?

Good time for a pause. This is a burning topic that is draped in jargon about "moral hazards" (translation: bailouts make financial speculation safe and therefore encourage them) and "too big to fail"—mega-banks and investment firms pose such gigantic risks to the US financial system that they compel bailouts and, of course, they expect that. Buried in the arcane verbiage is a telling question: Why are US regulators so persistently unable to prevent speculative recklessness in the first place? American lawmakers jump to how they will respond to the next financial crisis—imagine lemmings heading for the next cliff and unable to turn back. Canada has, for instance, preempted the problem of rewarding failure by preventing it in the first place through coherent and aggressive regulation of finance.

The big picture: divisions among prominent and influential economists and the uncertainty about the Fed's unprecedented actions have dimmed the central bank's once bright technocratic glow and its ability to induce deference from ruling circles in government, business, and civil society. Deference has been replaced by caution and doubts about the Fed's ability to prevent and manage financial crisis. The independent congressional investigation of the 2008–2009 crisis reached a sober verdict: the collapse was "avoidable" and was the "result of human action and inaction, not of Mother Nature or computer models gone haywire." The investigation particularly singles out the Fed for its "pivotal failure to stem the flow of toxic" securities before 2008 and catalogues its poor judgment and execution in responding to the crisis.[117]

Misgiving #2. A second and widespread apprehension is that the Fed engages in favoritism. Influential voices within finance question why it allocated credit for certain financial firms (and not others) and for certain types of credit—auto and student loans—but not housing mortgages held by millions of Americans. Picking winners and losers, these critics warn, are political choices about fiscal policy.[118]

The Fed's ties to finance are so deep that efforts to break free backfire. The Fed and a conservative Republican administration decided not to rescue Lehman Brothers in fall 2008 because of growing grassroots opposition to government bailouts for banks and philosophical beliefs about minimal government. The consequences shook the global financial system and froze America's financial system: banks and other financial institutions struggled to honor requests of depositors for withdrawals, to pay contracts, and to supply credit for ordinarily safe mortgages, auto and business loans, and credit cards.

Misgiving #3. The Fed's deviation from America's democratic accountability and favoritism stirred intense opposition. The nonpartisan Financial Crisis Inquiry Commission compellingly distilled an unsettling contradiction: "Actions, inactions, and misjudgments" by the Fed, banks, and others left the country exposed to "the total collapse of our financial system," and yet taxpayers were left "to stabilize the system and prevent catastrophic damage to the economy."[119]

Broad public unease about the Fed has stirred, but the greater concern to Washington politicians are the Tea Party and the "liberty movement" on the right and Occupy Wall Street and Massachusetts senator Elizabeth Warren on the left. These disparate political forces share an intense distrust of the Fed as illegitimate, undemocratic, and unfair. Scrutiny of the Fed is worrisome to the political establishment because the nomination processes in the Republican and Democratic parties are driven by activists on the left and right. Crossing either faction on their demands to rein in the Fed carries the political risk of public anger and political backlash that members of Congress and presidential hopefuls can no longer ignore.

Why America Needs a Properly Designed Central Bank

The deficit in the Fed's legitimacy is an urgent threat. Financial turmoil is coming but the Fed will be compromised by distrust among citizens, policymakers, journalists, and economists. Future Fed responses—including prudent interventions—will face more opposition than in the past, and perhaps crippling resistance.

Yes, We Need a Central Bank

The Fed was enacted in 1913 after persistent and debilitating banking crises during the nineteenth and early twentieth centuries. After its founding, America shed its internationally infamous track record of nearly decennial panics and dysfunctional monetary practices—highly variable interest rates and chaotic and unreliable payment exchanges among thousands of often unstable state-chartered banks. Although severe financial crises did not disappear (as evident in the 1930s and the early twenty-first century), the Fed ushered in a more sound and efficient system for facilitating payments and sustaining credit during periods of heightened uncertainty.

The Fed's responsibilities have expanded in today's "no-borders" financial system. Gone are the days when US businesses routinely met the payroll by handing out envelopes with cash in them. Today, many large employers rely on short-term credit that allows them to wait on incoming sales and other forms of revenue. And the business of banking has been entirely transformed since the days when the bank at the corner held on to your mortgage; today, they trade it to earn a better return. The Fed facilitates the millions of financial transfers and payments that define modern commerce by serving domestic banks as well as US and foreign governments. All of these—and other—routine financial practices are part of a fast-moving flow of money across America and its borders. Going back to the nineteenth century of corner banks is as make-believe as the idea that central banks are unnecessary.

As international finance has grown, the Fed has taken on greater responsibilities—working alone and in concert with other central banks—to respond to periodic jolts to the global markets and facilitating the circulation of capital on a global scale. To protect the US economy and the financial system that American businesses and consumers depend upon, the Fed intervened abroad when the Mexican currency sharply devalued in December 1994 and when the steep decline in Thailand's currency and finances in July 1997 triggered a chain reaction not only in Asia but around the globe.

Withdrawing from the international economic system is not a feasible option. It is the equivalent of financial survivalism, and would threaten the standard of living of many everyday Americans. A disciplined central bank is necessary to facilitate and stabilize the domestic and international financial systems and to foster economic prosperity—the growth of wages and savings and the efficient allocation of resources to spur innovation.

The problem, then, is not the presence of a central bank. The problem is the Fed.

Congress Channels the Distrust of the Fed

The flaw of the technocratic perspective is to view the Fed primarily as a self-contained conglomeration of technical skills rather than as an integrated component of a system of governance and set of norms about democratic accountability. The Fed's vulnerability lies in its isolation as a mutant outcropping in a system of checks and balances that favors finance.

How will future Republican members of Congress react to requests to approve a program like TARP or the application of the Fed's emergency powers to rescue finance? Any doubts that they will ruminate on the punishment delivered to their predecessors for supporting or tolerating these policies? News flash from the halls of Congress: the "TARP martyrs" loom large—Senator Robert Bennett (R-UT), six-term Republican congressman Bob Inglis (R-SC), and more.[120] On the Democratic side, support or even suspicion of coddling the Fed and finance risks battles for renomination and searing scrutiny from progressive populists in Congress—Senator Elizabeth Warren and others.

The Fed may be one crisis away from facing an effective congressional coalition to change its legal framework and substantially rein in its authority. Ron Paul's jeremiad against the Fed as "immoral, unconstitutional, impractical," and a threat to "liberty" spotlighted the idea of "ending the Fed" and returning to the gold standard—a cause of the Great Depression of the 1930s, in Paul's view.[121] The once fanciful proposal to tame the Fed is receiving broader attention within Congress as well as among a sizeable group of Americans. One out of six Americans approves ending the Fed, according to a 2010 Bloomberg poll; an additional 39 percent wanted the central bank held more accountable to Congress. Do the math: 55 percent supported a thoroughgoing reform.[122]

Lawmakers channeled the Fed's damaged position when it enacted the Wall Street Reform and Consumer Protection Act of 2010—better known as "Dodd-Frank," after its sponsors Senator Christopher Dodd and Representative Barney Frank. The effect of the reform is contradictory. On the one hand, Dodd-Frank is the most wide-ranging reform since the Great Depression and ratcheted up expectations that the Fed would prevent the next financial crisis and, if it occurs, expeditiously resolve it. On the other hand, the weak confidence of lawmakers in the Fed's stewardship prompted them to refrain from giving the central bank the practical power to act effectively to meet new responsibilities. Dodd-Frank sets a trap: it keeps the Fed as the public face of financial management but withholds the power to deliver. Who set the trap? The Fed—its secretive and biased actions drained trust in its effectiveness and legitimacy. Congress expressed the legitimacy deficit created by the Fed.

America's Path to Effective Financial Management

America will battle with the next financial monster without an effective financial manager. If you are not worried, you should be.

The choice facing America is not whether it needs a central bank. It does. The question is how to restructure the Fed to regain credibility within America's system of accountability and to create effective financial management that not only serves as a last resort during crisis, but successfully prevents or mutes their emergence in the first place. Reform is not an option. It is an urgent priority.

What can be done? We need a new direction that focuses the Fed on monetary functions and builds a consolidated financial manager that is subject to democratic governance.

Reform predictably provokes age-old warnings by defenders of the Fed that reform courts financial hell—soaring inflation and nineteenth-century-like cycles of financial disaster. Time for an inspection. First, the central bank and regulatory system in Canada is effective and more accountable. Second, the knee-jerk Fed apologists distract from the real menace—the Fed's frayed legitimacy and eroded ability to intervene in the financial system. The experiences of Canada demonstrate that central bank efficacy in managing the 2008 crisis coincided with stronger accountability than the Fed currently demonstrates.

Here are two directions that we explore in more detail in the closing chapter.

Concentrating Fed on Monetary Policy

For starters, the Fed needs to be shorn of its ever-lengthening portfolio of regulatory and even fiscal responsibilities; it should be returned to its essential function of managing the supply of money. As part of a move to improve its accountability, the sway of private banks and financial investors needs to be dimmed and the role of authentic public stewards introduced. It is time to make the deciders within the Fed true stewards of the public interest.

Dodd-Frank began as an effort to claw back the Fed's regulatory and fiscal functions, but the powerful alliance that defends the Fed prevailed in protecting the central bank's role and authority. Reformers responded by shifting tactics—functions that the Fed conducted alone in the past were now shared by independent agencies. Result: the Fed's ability to act alone has declined.

Building Consolidated Financial Management

Here is a fascinating contrast of two broadly similar countries: the United States is caught in a loop of crisis, but Canada's brushes with disaster have abated over time. Canada warded off a deep recession in 2008–2009 and was not compelled to go to taxpayers for massive direct bailouts. Answering this riddle of American incompetence and Canadian effectiveness is a priority.

Canada—a country with striking political, economic, and cultural similarities to the United States—offers a compelling model. Canada's crisis produced enduring change by largely limiting the Bank of Canada to monetary policy and by creating a new regulatory institution known as the Office of the Superintendent of Financial Institutions (OSFI). After financial crises in the 1980s, the Canadians consolidated the disparate regulatory oversight and policing of banks, capital markets, and insurance into a powerful new comprehensive independent agency. OSFI's transparent and accountable mission of policing risky speculation and standing guard of the overall financial system is internationally recognized for its high performance and standards for best practice. Canada's eagle-eye focus on financial scheming has also earned the public confidence its regulators need to deter challenges from lobbyists and their allies. This formidable public and administrative presence serves as a bulwark against mission-creep by the Bank of Canada—a tendency that opened the door for Fed institutional ambition.

Dodd-Frank's response to the Fed's unilateralism curbed some excesses (including rip-off loans), but it came up short in taking the necessary constructive step of finding a replacement. Dodd-Frank's unease with the Fed's favoritism and growing prerogatives prompted it to temper the Fed's unilateralism, which left America without the capacity to regulate and manage finance. An essential and neglected step has been missed: building a new, independent capacity for financial management.

BREAKING THE SILENCE ON THE FED

Our journey into the innards of the Fed and its subterranean power centers in government and finance is mostly uncharted and certainly treacherous.[123]

How the Fed Tames Debate

Complicit silence has suffocated scrutiny of how political arrangements favor finance and engorge the Fed's institutional appetite. Why are the interests of finance consistently advanced by the Fed? Why do US private markets operate with more abandon than in Canada—a country that shares a cultural uneasiness with government, a celebration of individual self-reliance, and a federal system? Why does the US government accommodate finance after a history of speculative disasters while Canada learned from its financial meltdowns and now pursues aggressive intervention to rein in risk-taking? How has the Fed managed to jump the rails of accountability to erect the Taj Mahal of government capacity and autonomy?

Unfortunately, what we know about the politics of the Fed is scarce. Political science—a discipline geared to studying government institutions and their ties to special interests—has largely ignored the Fed (with notable exceptions).[124] The discipline's last encompassing study of the Fed was published about three decades ago.

The neglect of the Fed has occurred even as researchers have turned to American government's lopsided favoritism of business and the superrich in important books like *Winner Take All Politics* and *Unequal Democracy*, and in the American Political Science

Association's task force to investigate inequality and American democracy.[125] One can comb these and other leading studies of inequality and find not a single reference to the Fed. The silence is glaring. It leaves our understanding of inequality incomplete and perpetuates the Fed's deception as operating beyond politics.

Another problem perpetuating silence—cooptation. Academics earn prestigious positions, higher wages, and opportunities for advancement by vigorously jousting in scholarly circles, which spills out into media news reports, opinion pieces, and government policy deliberations. Not so in the world of the Fed. Of course, there are disputes over interest rates and the risks of inflation, but more striking are the missing debates on the appropriateness of Fed deference to private markets and its institutional empire-building.

The Fed has wrapped three potentially suffocating tentacles around the necks of researchers and analysts (mostly trained in economics) who are best positioned to disrupt its power and to question its alliances with finance.[126]

- *Tentacle #1*: Fed invests about $400 million a year in researchers who might raise meaningful challenges. Who bites the hand that feeds them?
- *Tentacle #2*: Editors and members of the editorial boards of the premier publications on Fed policy simultaneously get cash from the Fed and decide what articles get published and whose career moves forward—or shrivels.
- *Tentacle #3*: The Fed controls the lifeblood of research—supplying data and bestowing the status necessary for advancement by extending conference invitations, visiting positions, and lucrative contracts.[127] Think: Mean Girls.

Bottom line: offending the Fed is a recipe for career failure, and the Fed uses that dependence. "Manipulating the size of staff and the activities for which they are rewarded or penalized," a prominent economist explained, equips Fed officials to "shape the agenda of contemporary economic research on monetary policy."[128]

Not a pretty picture. The least obnoxious possibility is that economists who work on monetary policy are "susceptible to capture."[129]

Another possibility is harsher and is spelled out by three disturbing words: "conflict of interest." Think of a researcher who is paid by a pharmaceutical company to test its new drug and also serves as editor of a leading outlet for authoritative research that guides the decisions of regulators and doctors. Now read this from a journalistic investigation: "It is common for a journal editor to review submissions dealing with Fed policy while also taking the bank's money."[130]

The Fed has erected a kind of intellectual minefield. Economists who dare break ranks to investigate the organization of America's political economy that the Fed considers settled face the risk of ostracism and punishment—papers rejected by respected journals, invites withheld, and contracts no longer extended. The economists who play ball receive rewards, and in exchange grind out research accepting the Fed's organizational foundations (accommodation of finance deference and autonomy) and deliver Fed-friendly testimony to Congress and judicial panels.[131]

Eyes wide open. The Fed uses the dependence on its largesse and sway over markers of prestige to steer research by economists and other analysts of monetary policy toward "safe" issues.

We are engaged academics who apply serious research to ignored questions of public import. We are not beholden to the Fed or to addled academic theories. We call out the Fed's deviance from James Madison's system of governance and its implication for generating inequality and favoritism. We jettison the all-too-common hermetic language of academia in favor of candor and directness. "Words ought to be a little wild," John Maynard Keynes counseled, "for they are the assault of thoughts on the unthinking."

Three Types of Evidence

Our straight talk is backed up by extensive evidence, which is documented in the endnotes. Our analysis is rooted in careful studies of historical, institutional, and political economic developments.

We draw on three streams of evidence to make sense of the Fed despite its secrecy.[132]

Stream #1: Show and Tell. We rely on concrete observations of the behavior and preferences of the Fed and its partners through speeches, interviews, and reports from journalists, the Financial Crisis Inquiry Commission, its online materials, and other sources; studies of the central bank's balance sheets; and surveys of public attitudes. These bodies of evidence spotlight intent and action—what the Fed and finance want, what resources they possess for political action, and in what ways they succeed or fail.[133]

The history of the Fed—as told by its senior officials as well as lawmakers and their staff—occasionally reveals its agenda to expand the agency's independence and capacity. Commenting on the series of steps that the Fed chair Marriner Eccles undertook in the 1930s to enlarge the central bank's powers, the congressional leader Carter Glass described him as driving to "absorb every federal agency he can lay his hands on."[134] A later Fed chair (William Martin) pressed Congress to allow it to take actions that were "insulated from direct political pressures."[135]

But wait: the written record is not enough. Important aspects of Fed policymaking and its relations with finance are out of sight—deliberately so. We need to do more than beg for empirical crumbs or retreat from investigating Fed power.

Stream #2. It's All about Relationships. Individuals are not just discrete isolates. They react to each other, which puts a premium on how relationships are organized, who is favored, and what kind of identities, interests, and capacities people form as they interact with each other.[136]

In the eyes of Fed officials, billionaire bankers and hedge fund high-flyers define "success."[137] In this relationship, the white guys with cash (and, yes, they are mostly guys and mostly white) enjoy "cultural capital" and high status, and it follows that folks at the Fed tend to look up to them for knowing capital markets. These relationships of power and subordination exist—even though we may not be able to observe private interactions and the intention of each set of players.

Stream #3. Loading the Dice. Individuals have come and gone at the Fed for a century, and yet its policies have consistently favored finance and itself. Why? Part of the answer is the hard-wiring or structure of our economy and society in a global system of private markets and asset ownership.[138] Even a chair of the Fed who publicly recoils at its acceleration of inequality—Janet Yellen—is compelled to accept and accommodate global financial markets because of the concrete demands of their institutional position to defend and promote the central bank. Fostering a favorable investment climate and economic activity is not an option on a menu—it is a requirement for sustaining the systems of credit and investment on which American society and the Fed depends. Look at Europe, Japan, and Canada—separate countries, varied central banks, and yet they share with the United States a predictable pattern of relying on private finance and, to differing degrees, accommodating it.

Researching Favoritism

How can we separate the Fed's promotion of itself and finance from its claims to be serving the public interest and taking the "only option" to save the country in 2008–2009? Here are three proven approaches.

The first uses comparisons with earlier periods in US history and other countries to demonstrate the Fed's developmental trajectory to 2008–2009. The Fed began a century ago tethered to regional banks, subservient to the US Treasury, and operated for decades with relatively limited powers. That helps form a baseline in Chapter 2 for marking its transformation toward monopolizing monetary policy and becoming a growing force on fiscal policy.

Another approach is to leverage contemporary comparisons with the policies of central banks in other affluent democracies to assess the extraordinary scale of the Fed's powers, its favoritism of finance in 2008–2009, and its inaction to aid everyday Americans. Were the Fed's interventions the only alternative, as the Fed alliance claims?

• How could it have saved the financial system without obsequiously favoring rich? Look to Canada, as we will.

- How unusual were the Fed's rescues in 2008–2009? Chapter 3 looks closely at their terms and finds that they were unnecessary giveaways when judged against US allies.
- What could the Fed have done for millions of homeowners faced with foreclosure instead of sitting on its hands? Britain supplied favorable terms to vulnerable banks, and in exchange required them to extend loans to support mortgage lending. Why was the Bank of England able to design a program to tackle the mortgage crisis rampaging through its towns while the Fed did not?

A third approach is to consider "what if" scenarios.[139] What might have happened in America, for instance, if the South had won the Civil War? Competing accounts project a more confident South striding toward modernization and freeing the slaves on its own accord or, more soberly, the long persistence of slavery and violent resistance.[140] This approach is helpful in spotlighting key drivers (e.g., the North's win at Antietam in September 1862).

Considering alternative histories of the Fed's responses in 2008–2009 raises a series of intriguing possibilities.

- What might have happened if the Fed's response in 2008–2009 lacked the massive concessions it made to finance? Chapter 3 picks this up.
- What if the United States, which shares Canada's cultural suspicions of big banks and its federal form of government, had also agreed to establish and sustain reliable regulations against speculative booms and busts before the 2008–2009 crisis? Why did financial crisis propel strict regulatory controls in Canada and not in the United States? The last two chapters return to these questions.

These types of thought experiments can help us tease out alternatives to the Fed's giveaway to finance and the impact of its own historical mission of empire-building.

The Fed's suffocating tourniquet on research is, quite intentionally, starving debates about how to move America forward to better achieve effective and accountable financial management. This book disrupts the silence on the Fed's political economy to raise fundamental, unaddressed maladies in the United States— the Fed's institutional imperialism and favoritism.

FROM FIERY POPULISM TO ACQUIESCENCE AND DOUBT

It is tempting to think of the Fed and financial markets as seamlessly following a master plan of empire-building. The reality is quite different. They are the drivers of "creative destruction"— the Fed and financial market have "incessantly revolutioniz[ed] the economic structure from within, incessantly destroy[ed] the old one, incessantly creat[ed] a new one."[141] The history of the Fed has produced monumental changes and jarring disruptions: it was handmaiden to toppling US regional financial markets a century ago; birthed new systems of credit and monetary policy that enormously strengthened its powers and elevated Wall Street into a global financial capital; and introduced political and financial pressures that threatens its very accomplishments. The Fed's actions are both cleverly strategic in plotting a stunning rise to power and potentially self-defeating.

Fed Power weaves together four themes. First, the Fed's origins in the flames of late nineteenth- and early twentieth-century populist politics set it on a tenuous path: depoliticize monetary policy by moving it off the front pages into the cloistered halls of banks and government and, by effectively doing so, set it up to repoliticize the government's accommodation of banks and private investors when its actions regain salience. Over the course of its century of development, policymakers and Fed officials repeatedly expanded the central bank's authority and administrative capacity in the elusive hope of resolving political and global financial tensions, which in turn reset the search for solutions. Chapter 2 delves into the Fed's dual process of creative growth and disruption since the nineteenth century.

Second, the tumultuous Great Recession reignited the process of creative destruction. Chapter 3 zeroes in on the Fed's steps to capitalize on the 2008–2009 crisis in order to inflate its authority, administrative capacity, and independence to unprecedented levels. The Fed deployed its extraordinary new resources to deliver astonishing benefits for finance—and not everyday Americans— that were concealed in the details of rescue programs. The Fed's interventions to rescue finance revolutionized central banking; they also threatened to repoliticize their interconnections by returning them to the front pages.

Third, the Fed's institutional surge unintentionally sowed seeds of potential disruption. The Fed's interventions in 2008– 2009 profiled its favoritism for finance. Chapter 4 reveals shifts in public opinion and the deficit in its legitimacy as an authentic public steward.

Fourth, America is heading into the next financial implosion without a trusted crisis manager. The Fed's actions eroded its legitimacy, and the Dodd-Frank reform deepened its predicament by putting it in a no-win situation—higher expectations without the practical power to deliver. Chapter 5 explains the paradox of Dodd-Frank and debunks the false choice of accepting unaccountable Fed power or consigning America to financial catastrophe. We present a reform agenda to establish effective financial management and democratic accountability by building on the experiences in the United States and Canada.

2

The Rise of the Fed State

ONE OF THE most extraordinary features of American politics during the nineteenth and early twentieth centuries is that financial crises precipitated and defined the terms of conflict. A century later, the financial crisis was—given its scope and devastation— remarkably apolitical. The financial upheaval and the Fed's unprecedented responses featured in few Republican primaries and was largely bypassed by President Barack Obama and Republican Mitt Romney during their 2012 general election contest. This is a fundamental political development. Monetary policy and the favoritism of finance were defining public issues and preoccupied the debates among dueling presidential campaigns 120 years ago, and are no longer.

The Fed has been ushered out of the bright lights of public debate and political conflict by banking and government elites who were alarmed by the politicization of finance during the late nineteenth century, and by the Fed's strategic maneuvering after 1913 to capitalize on new crises and changes in finance.

The Fed's operations have been not only depoliticized, but also empowered to an extent that would astound late nineteenth-century observers. As it transitioned to becoming a "safe issue," the Fed transformed itself from humble beginnings to an exceptional institution—one that deployed enormous resources to intervene in the US economy and financial system and distribute selective benefits to one industry. This breathtaking trajectory is as much political as economic.

This chapter traces three themes in the origins and development of the Federal Reserve since the nineteenth century. First, the Fed's structures embody a "mobilization of bias" that favors organized, well-connected financial interests at the expense of disorganized, poorly resourced, or diffuse individuals and businesses.[1] The Fed's bias was publicly contested during the noisy politics of the nineteenth century when presidential campaigns and congressional votes on monetary policy related to currency and the banking system inflamed the country and ignited fiery battles between political parties and economic factions of workers and businesses. The historic removal of monetary policy from the front line of public attention and political dispute and the building of a bias for finance are neglected themes in contemporary American politics.[2] Over time, the Fed created processes to distribute its benefits narrowly to finance, evade routine public scrutiny, and elude even the modest checks by regional banks, US presidents, or members of Congress that its founding legislation designed. By the 2008 crisis, the Fed exercised more power while enjoying less meaningful transparency and checks than applied to monetary policy a century earlier.

Here's what you'd see if this were a slideshow.

First set of slides: Faded images of panicked runs on banks, which occurred every 20 years from 1819 to 1907, interspersed with pictures from around the country of poor farmers locked out of shuttered banks and denied credit and taking to the streets to protest.

Second set of slides: Grainy photos of white men with black top hats bobbing in and out of closed-door meetings with wealthy bankers and government insiders as they design the Fed and chart its passage in 1913.

Third set of slides: Crisp shots of a grim-faced Fed chair Ben Bernanke in a white-walled congressional hearing room as he somberly recounts the severity of the financial run in 2008–2009 while practicing a strategy of obscuring the magnitude of aid to specific firms. Missing (with a few exceptions): sustained organized protests across the nation.

The second theme in the Fed's history is its initially limited and then rapidly expanding national administrative capacity and authority. This transformation enabled the Fed to protect and give shape to swift changes in global finance and to advance its institutional interests to monopolize the monetary system in ways that were unimaginable at its origin. The Fed was both a product of America's financial system, reflecting its interests and imperatives, and a driver, steering America to serve as a reliable hub for global finance.

Third, the process of change that produced today's Fed was both intentional and structural. It resulted from the calculated strategy of its leaders and allies to expand the Fed's budget and authority as well as impersonal forces that defy any one person's ability to direct. It is too simple to reduce the Fed's development to all-seeing visionaries at its founding in 1913 or later critical junctures. What initially appears as a minor design choice by lawmakers unintentionally truncated certain paths of institutional change while opening new trajectories for later policymakers to develop in response to fresh circumstances.[3] Over the course of the past century the Fed was repeatedly remade, but not according to a clear roadmap. Its administrative resources, independence, and mission were constructed and reshaped in reaction to financial crises, institutional self-interest to exploit opportunities for reinvention, pressures from well-connected banks and investors, and the shifting circumstances of the global economy. Changes at one point in time would later backfire, take on greater significance than intended, or get fundamentally redirected in response to new pressing circumstances.

This chapter argues that the end of mass mobilization over monetary policy and the enlarging of the Fed State were connected, representing a critical feature of American political development. It begins with public conflicts over banks and monetary policy, and then proceeds to trace the interactions of organized finance, institutional ambitions, and America's changing economy in a global system.

THE RAUCOUS POLITICS OF NINETEENTH-CENTURY MONETARY POLICY

The Great Recession of 2008 staggered the US economy, propelling mass layoffs and wiping out life savings to a degree not seen since the Great Depression of the 1930s. Imagine catastrophic economic crises as a regular occurrence, rather than as an every-other-generation shock. That was life in the nineteenth century.

Economic Calamity

Chaotic and decentralized banking exposed nineteenth-century American banks to recurring breakdown. The United States was populated with an extraordinary number of independent, local banks (about 30,000 by the early 1900s). Most banks were on their own, unable quickly and effectively to pool resources to stave off runs. Deposits were often held in stocks and shares at another bank that was rarely nearby.[4] By contrast, nineteenth-century banks in Europe normally carried little cash in their vaults because they could rapidly access emergency funds from their central bank.

The infamous bank robberies of nineteenth-century America reflected a unique feature of US banks—they carried exceptional amounts of cash in their vaults to meet the risk of a run that would destroy them. Take the infamous bank robbers Jessie and Frank James, and their February 1866 heist of the Clay County Savings Association in Liberty, Missouri. They reportedly made off with $60,000 in cash and bonds.[5] That's equivalent to nearly $1 million today, or fifty to one hundred times more than the cash reserves of a contemporary suburban bank or credit union.[6]

Nineteenth-century American banks were sitting ducks not only for bank robbers, but for calamitous cycles of euphoric booms and nightmarish busts. The War of 1812 sparked a boom that was followed seven years later by the first significant peacetime implosion of banks. Panics became depressingly regular: rumor or credit crunches would spook farmers and laborers and businesses to withdraw their deposits, and then they would discover

that banks were unable to meet their requests and would literally close their doors. You don't have to live this cycle more than
once to fear for the safety of your deposits and put you on edge to
anticipate the next crisis. Banks turned to local and regional clearinghouses, such as the New York Clearing Association, but the
hoped-for protection often proved ineffective in quenching the
desperate thirst for cash and credit.[7]

The runs on banks triggered a destructive chain reaction in
the country's finances and economy. Bank panics froze credit
and sparked stock market crashes or outright collapses. The fear
over lost deposits and investments then swept over the country's
economy and froze it—not for a week or two, but for years. The
panic of 1873 stretched five and a half years to March 1879—the
longest recorded economic downturn in US history. The panics of
1884, 1890, 1893, and 1907 were shorter in duration, but they
suffocated the country's economy for prolonged periods.

Farmers and everyday people bore the brunt of the financial
rollercoaster. Panics wiped out farmers and families or pushed
them to the brink of financial ruin, which in turn intensified
their struggle to find credit (at jacked-up interest rates) to borrow
for planting and paying their old debt.

Fiery Debates over Monetary Policy

Bank panics, however, were rarely only financial; their origins
and impacts were often political. The political distinctiveness of
nineteenth-century financial tumult poses striking contrasts with
the twenty-first century's Great Recession.

Nineteenth-Century Contrast #1. The bank panics of the nineteenth century ignited incendiary debates over winners and losers.
In our time, banking and monetary policies are relatively invisible
or arcane compared to the searing political and economic divisions
that enveloped them in the nineteenth century.[8]

Bank runs and the ensuing disaster fueled intense scrutiny of
banks and more general suspicions of monopolies and concentrated
economic power. Andrew Jackson toppled the political machine

of the early nineteenth century and catapulted himself into the White House as the seventh president by mobilizing masses of Americans behind his populist outrage against elites, and, especially, banks and the government's Second Bank of the United States. Jackson and his supporters blamed banks and political insiders for capturing government power to enrich themselves and for putting a chokehold on credit that hit everyday people and fueled foreclosures. Jackson's populist rage crystalized in his veto of the congressional reauthorization of the Second Bank in 1832 and his charge that the "rich and powerful...bend the acts of government to their selfish purposes." Evoking his reputation as a war hero, Jackson brandished his veto pen to "take a stand against...any prostitution of our Government to the advancement of the few at the expense of the many."[9]

Jackson's populist rage against high-and-mighty elites reverberated into the last decades of the nineteenth century and infused the seemingly technical issue of whether gold alone or gold and silver should backstop America's currency.

The debate over the US currency sparked divisions between regions and among the classes. Banks, merchants, and other creditors pressed for gold. Its preciousness checked governments from printing money of little value and boosted the value of their assets and loans. By contrast, the advocates for silver coins were miners of the precious metal in the West as well as farmers and other debtors, who relied on a larger supply of money to boost prices for crops and reduce debt by lowering the interest rates for borrowing.

Farmers were especially vulnerable to the vagaries of banks and credit. They borrowed for planting and then repaid at harvest. High interest rates made it difficult, even after working the fields for months and persevering through volatile weather, to avoid losing money, going further into debt, and risking the loss of their property. The threat to farmers worsened after the Civil War. The seemingly good news of renewed growth ended up driving down prices for many goods, including agricultural products. To keep more currency in circulation and stay ahead of their debts, farmers in the 1870s favored Greenbacks—the paper money printed by the North during the Civil War to pay soldiers and military suppliers and infrastructure (including the transcontinental railroad).

> The domestic turmoil over monetary policy in America was intensified by global capital markets. Germany's decision, in particular, to fully switch from silver to the gold standard in 1871 to improve the value of its currency contributed to America's topsy-turvy financial markets. Its move fuelled a global flight from a swelling pool of cheap silver and reinforced uncertainty about the dollar's stability and value. Even when America's economy strengthened during the later nineteenth century, its ability to trade internationally was handicapped by its unattractive currency and backward financial markets.[10]

Nineteenth-Century Contrast #2. In 2008–2009 the Federal Reserve often acted out of the public eye, and most Americans were unaware and disinterested. Debates over banking and monetary policies were cloistered away behind closed doors or in obscure government offices.

By contrast, hard-hit farmers, silver miners, and their allies succeeded during the nineteenth century in launching a sustained noisy, nationwide campaign against wealthy creditors and monetary policy. The relatively arcane issue of whether silver or gold should backstop the dollar was fought out in communities across America as well as in Congress. Loud voices dominated and made it hard to ignore. Everyday Americans followed the debates, and many were motivated by the tumult to engage in campaigns. Winning elections often required a well-considered position on monetary policy.

Think of today's most riveting issues in political debate—health reform, taxes, or government spending and deficits. That hot seat was held by gold and silver in the nineteenth century, and never more clearly than in the 1896 election between the Democratic firebrand populist William Jennings Bryan and the establishment Republican William McKinley. McKinley, who was the sitting governor of Ohio and had been an influential force in Congress, championed a conservative monetary policy and opposed "easy" currency based on silver.

Bryan mobilized southerners and westerners to topple conservative easterners, electrifying them with his infamous speech for "free silver" that concluded the 1896 Democratic Convention. "Having behind us the producing masses of this nation and the world, supported by the commercial interests, the laboring interests and the toilers everywhere," he said, "we will answer their demand for a gold standard by saying to them: 'You shall not press down upon the brow of labor this crown of thorns; you shall not crucify mankind upon a cross of gold.'"

Bryan's "Cross of Gold" speech epitomizes the in-your-face debate over monetary policy. It propelled the 1896 Convention to adopt a platform that ranked the "money plank" as its top priority and to nominate Bryan as its presidential candidate on the fifth ballot. "The money question is paramount to all others," the platform trumpeted. The platform stridently declared the Democratic Party "unalterably opposed to [gold] monometallism" and harshly denounced Goldbugs as "not only un-American but anti-American."[11]

Nineteenth-Century Contrast #3. The bailouts in 2008–2010 inspired the Tea Party and its vivid demonstrations of raw frustration with government and its favoritism. On the left, the Occupy Wall Street protests contrasted the vast wealth of the 1 percent of America against the stagnating or declining circumstances of most other Americans. As compelling as both were, the Tea Party and Occupy rarely seized the center stage of American life; they struggled to sustain their challenge; and neither expressed a compelling alternative to what they did not like.

By comparison, populists in the nineteenth century produced a cogent critique of elite governance and roadmaps for building alternative financial and economic structures. They anticipated the kind of secretive policymaking in favor of wealthy interests that the Fed would later establish and they articulated an alternative scenario that culminated with economic democracy. Where the Fed established substantial autonomy, populists insisted on establishing strong accountability through elected representatives and national government initiatives to support farmers and sponsor local economic growth.[12]

The Muting of Populist Opposition to Banks and Monetary Policy

Here is one of the most striking features of the election of 1896: it was followed by near silence on monetary policy and banks after decades of red-hot disputes. The Jacksonian revolt and populism defined potent traditions to inspire challenges to the Federal Reserve Act and later policies, but they failed to pose a serious threat and the protest that emerged was sporadic. Where did America's populist outrage go?

The short answer: populism was defeated.[13] The establishment of the Federal Reserve in 1913 was the populist Waterloo, and it was preceded by one-sided battles that shifted America to the gold standard with the 1873 Coinage Act and the 1875 Specie Resumption Act.

The move to gold was propelled by new political and economic circumstances, and, in turn, it ignited a cascade of reactions. America's conversion reflected a global shift to gold, growing industrialization in the United States, and rising commerce abroad, which put a premium on an internationally valued stable currency. But the action created a reaction. The conversion of the dollar set off a scramble for scarce gold, boosting interest rates and shrinking capital and credit. Banks and creditors were winners. Farmers and silver miners were the losers.

The economic reverberations of the gold conversion sparked ferocious political reactions against the "Crime of '73." Congress tried—unsuccessfully—to quell the populist insurgence over monetary policy by passing the Bland-Allison Act of 1878 to partially restore silver currency. Populist response: empty gesture. The move from silver confirmed the populist critique: farmers and many working people interpreted it as a betrayal of wage earners to advantage the financial elite.[14] The "1873 demonetizing of silver," the Democratic Party's 1896 platform declared, occurred "without the knowledge or approval of the American people" in order to enrich "the money-lending class," while creating "the prostration of industry and impoverishment of the people."[15]

Rather than producing the next Jacksonian rebellion, the populist backlash was largely tamed after the 1896 election by political and economic elites who exploited the new circumstances. Banks and large businesses evolved into a more coherent and organized political force that mobilized its resources to blunt populism and its agenda to reorganize economic power. Walter Dean Burnham and E. E. Schattschneider famously identified the "System of 1896" as a critical juncture defined by the emergence of a coalition of "corporate capital...broadly united [to]...defend against the mass pressures" and to "insulate industrial and finance capital from adverse mass pressures."[16]

Following the defeat of Bryan, the Democratic and Republican parties redrew their battle lines. Fights over economics, monopolies, and monetary policy fell in importance. The Republicans won two presidential elections (1896 and 1900) and improved their strength in the US House of Representatives. The Democratic Party responded to Republican gains by renovating its platform for the 1900 election. It renominated Bryan and downgraded monetary policy in favor of profiling imperialism and other issues that it expected to play better with voters and its allies.[17] By the 1912 election, the party's platform made no mention of gold or monetary policy. Its position on banking reform was buried in the thick middle section on a laundry list. Only months away from passing the Federal Reserve Act of 1913, the Democratic Party replaced the strident language of populist rebellion against banks with turgid technocratic prose: "our country will be largely freed from panics and consequent unemployment and business depression by such a systematic revision of our banking laws as will render temporary relief in localities where such relief is needed."[18] Monetary policy had begun its long slide from the top of the country's agenda and it soon lost its potency for mobilizing Americans.

How monetary policy was governed also changed. The nineteenth century's headline-grabbing public debate and decision-making in Congress and presidential campaigns disappeared. The direct and salient role and influence of democratically elected government officials declined, and economic power was further concentrated in the hands of broadly based elites. The new coalition of business interests and its allies pushed through new administrative structures and bodies to quiet public debate and empower dominant stakeholders and the experts they respected. Control over monetary supply, which had been the jurisdiction of Congress and subject to public debate, was now stripped from democratic control and shifted inside a distant and insulated agency.[19] The effect was to dull the threat of reform to elites and to expand federal control in the name of reform while tightening the domination of an insulated elite.[20] American monetary policy was on its way to becoming what Jackson and populists feared.

REMOVING MONETARY POLICY FROM DEMOCRATIC POLITICS: THE FEDERAL RESERVE ACT OF 1913

Today's Federal Reserve Bank monopolizes monetary policy with relatively little accountability or transparency. It is both a sharp departure from America's history of spurning central banks and far from the outcome intended by the chief sponsors of the Federal Reserve Act of 1913. The Fed's unexpected path is an outgrowth of an ambiguous elite compromise: surprisingly wide bipartisan support for routinizing monetary policy less than two decades after the stormy 1896 slugfest, and crucial modifications of the original design that laid the foundation for the later creation of a new centralized government entity. This compromise was necessary to win passage of the Fed's founding legislation in 1913, and initially appeared relatively inconsequential. Over time, however, the modified design took on unintended significance as the Fed weathered economic crises, adapted to the transformations of global finance, and, most striking of all, developed the independent will and brawn to enlarge its powers.

The Ruling Banks Did Not Rule

Was the Federal Reserve Act of 1913 designed by and for the country's most powerful banks based in New York City? Fair question. After all, the fingerprints of the ruling banks are easy to detect.

Banker Fingerprints #1. The unruly financial disruptions that culminated in the banking runs of 1907–1908 woke up private bankers to the limits of their power to manage crisis. The tycoon J. Pierpont Morgan personally directed Wall Street's response to the runs on the big New York banks—especially the Knickerbocker Trust Co.—as well as to calming the resulting economic collapse that drove down the GDP by over 10 percent from 1907 to 1908.

While grateful to Morgan's intervention, private banks and allies in government appreciated that relying on one aging businessman to size up the solvency of individual banks and arrange loans to the failing firms was not a viable long-term strategy for a country of increasing international significance. The agenda of change opened as elites started to explore options for replacing recurrent crisis and reliance on individual intervention with a routine and enduring solution—a new monetary authority that served as a backstop to banks and investors.

Banker Fingerprints #2. Bankers helped design the 1913 legislation. True to form, they met in secret with other power brokers in an exclusive hotel, which was appropriately known as the Millionaires Club. The meeting in late November 1910 took place on the remote Jekyll Island in Georgia. It brought together Nelson Aldrich (Republican senator, chair of the Finance Committee, and, arguably, a preeminent Washington power) along with Wall Street bankers and premier financial authorities: Morgan's partner Henry Davison, international banker Paul Warburg, National City Bank president Frank Vanderlip, Assistant Secretary of the US Treasury A. Piatt Andrew Jr., and the later president of the prominent Federal Reserve Bank of New York, Benjamin Strong.[21]

This cast of characters instigated a coalition of elites for what later became the 1913 legislation. They appreciated that creating a durable central bank in the United States would need to overcome a cursed history: Alexander Hamilton's First Bank of the

United States in 1791 was terminated by 1811 in the wake of a popular backlash, and the Second Bank of the United States was closed when Andrew Jackson vetoed its reauthorization. Warburg worked assiduously to build the case for revisiting America's troubled history with central banks; he had an acute understanding of international finance and the anxiety among US business about the advantages of British and French bankers who used their central banks to prosper in the global trade in sterling and the franc.[22]

Senator Aldrich was the ringleader. He understood the domestic and international issues and was respected in Congress as an authority on finance and banking. The senator had begun in 1908 to coalesce bankers and their supporters (especially Republicans) behind the Aldrich Plan, using a process of congressional hearings and reports.[23]

The key payoff of the Jekyll Island meeting was to form a coalition of business and government elites to back the Aldrich Plan and to set in motion plans to build support for its passage. Most of its participants used the newly created National Citizens' League for the Promotion of Sound Banking—funded by $500,000 raised from banks—to lobby lawmakers and voters to support a central bank, distributing close to a million free pamphlets advocating the Aldrich Plan.[24] Warburg played a particularly active role campaigning to win public and congressional support.[25]

Banker Fingerprints #3. Large banks and investment firms have their fingerprints all over the drive to establish the Fed, and they were rewarded. Their biggest payoff from the 1913 Federal Reserve Act was to establish the dollar in international financial circles as the dominant currency. For large New York Wall Street banks like Morgan's, this was a golden brick road to international business and great profits.[26]

The advantages for US banks in establishing the Federal Reserve are compelling and help to account for surprisingly broad elite agreement on creating a new monetary authority. They are not, however, sufficient explanations. Attributing the Fed to Big Banks falls short and leaves us unable to account for later developments that were not anticipated by Aldrich and his clique.

Political conflict and institutional design interrupted the plans of bankers and delivered setbacks that would take on enormous importance. While the incendiary battles over banks and currency receded after the 1896 election, strong distrust of New York banks by voters as well as banks and businesses in other regions continued. The election of Democrats in 1912 ensured that the unease with New York banks would not be ignored. Persistent political resistance to the Aldrich blueprints and relatively small modifications of it set the stage for unforeseen but consequential later developments.

The Compromise of 1913

Legislation authorizing a central bank in 1913 passed with broad political acceptance, crossing the rubicon that had bedeviled America for a century. Previously, the United States lagged well behind early industrial powers that had created a central bank—Britain in 1694, Sweden in 1668, France in 1800, and Germany in 1876.

By 1913, however, the century of wide and fiery divisions over a monetary policy and banking was replaced by broad acceptance among Democrats and Republicans of the need for a new authority. The differences narrowed to design features. The shift toward accepting a central bank was demonstrably driven home by its political sponsor—the Democratic Party that formed in reaction to elite rule and the rage against banks. The Democrats enacted America's first sustained central bank after the 1912 elections put them in control of the White House with President Woodrow Wilson, and in majorities in Congress. The decisive action by Democrats in 1913 underscored its shift from the perfunctory incantation of dated dogma—"we oppose...the establishment of a central bank"—that lingered in its 1912 Platform.

Agreeing on the Big Plan
The basic objectives and construct of the Federal Reserve Act of 1913 included three features that Democrats, Republicans, and banks and other businesses supported. First, elites agreed on the

linchpin of the 1913 act: to "provide for the establishment of a Federal reserve bank." The establishment of a new monetary authority was an historic breakthrough for American elites.

Smarting from ad hoc and delayed responses that had met past financial contagions (think J. Pierpont Morgan), business and political leaders supported a new central bank as institutional scaffolding to stabilize the country's banking and monetary system and, by extension, the broader economy. The core aim of the 1913 law was to create a system for adjusting the supply of money, and, in particular, to correct for the perennial failures of individual banks by heading off and relieving shortages of money and credit.[27] The tools of the new monetary authority were to change the money supply and to aid banks in need of additional funds by allowing them to use loans and other assets as collateral. The rudder for directing the supply of money was the Fed's new national powers to set and change the interest rates paid by member banks that borrowed funds, or the rates they received when they made deposits.

The second area of agreement is that both political parties as well as business elites supported a decentralized system. The new authority was anchored in 12 regional branches spread out around the country. Dispersing control to regional banks was intended to put reserves of cash within a night's train ride of any bank manager facing a panic-driven run.

Third, elites accepted that banks and private business would exercise substantial influence over the new monetary authority. In contrast to America's general system of representation in which elected or appointed officials stood for citizens, the Federal Reserve Act stipulates that private banks and businesses directly participate in the new system's decision-making and assume considerable responsibilities for its operations. Writing private business into the governing of the money supply and the operation of banks is akin to assigning foxes to guard the chicken coop. Banks were granted—with broad bipartisan support—direct and unparalleled governing powers over their industry.

Perhaps the most political aspect of American politics—who controls the economy and the money supply—was ceded in important respects to banks and investors.

Tactical Disputes on Details

Fundamental elite agreement on the defining features of the Federal Reserve Act framed what were tactical differences over how to achieve shared objectives. Partisan politics and populist resentment toward banks influenced what were (at that point) marginal tweaks of the fundamental objective (establishing a new monetary agency).[28]

Two design elements received particular attention and were altered by Democrats in 1913. Amid general elite agreement on creating a new monetary authority and granting significant autonomy and responsibility to regional banks that were geographically dispersed, there was a tussle over organizational details about the degree of decentralization and private control. The Aldrich Plan called for an organizational structure of 15 regional district branches and one privately controlled reserve bank—the National Reserve Association—that would print money, supply emergency loans to member banks, and serve as the government's fiscal agent.[29]

After Democrats won unified control over the White House and Congress in the 1912 elections, they tweaked its organizational design. Democratic congressional leaders (especially the chairs of the House and Senate Banking and Currency Committees, Representative Carter Glass and Senator Robert Owen) and President Wilson continued the Aldrich Plan's emphasis on the 12 regional banks and granted them significant autonomy—a sharp turn from populism. They did modify the plan, though, by replacing the private association with a new government agency based in Washington, DC—the Federal Reserve Board.

A second (and related) quarrel was over the extent of private sector control. The Aldrich Plan and the Carter/Owen compromise with Wilson agreed on ensuring significant participation by banks and businesses in the operation of the Federal Reserve System. Where banks welcomed Senator Aldrich's proposal for nearly full private control and a small public role, Democrats assigned presidents the power to make seven appointees to the Board of Directors for the new public entity (the Federal Reserve Board in Washington), designated the new Federal Reserve note as an obligation of the

US Treasury instead of private banks, and mandated nationally chartered banks to become members of the new monetary authority instead of having the option to choose.

The modifications by Democrats would take on later importance, but at the time their value appeared to be largely symbolic—gestures to soothe the party base with little practical effect. For some time, banks and regional businesses did dominate as the Aldrich Plan and the Jekyll Island cabal hoped. The new presidentially appointed Board of Directors was impotent, subordinate to the powerful presidents of regional Federal Reserve Banks. The board's appointees lacked experience in financial markets and training in rudimentary economics, and they were deliberately paid substantially less than their regional counterparts as a signal to the ambitious and skilled to stay away.[30] What was supposed to be the Fed's key power—setting discount rates—was wielded by the regional banks. Later commentators understandably concluded from the immediate aftermath of the 1913 legislation that its designers "did not intend to create either a central bank or a powerful institution."[31] Another observer referred to President Wilson's national office as a "limited agency."[32]

Lacking immediate practical effect, the quarrels over institutional design did not ignite debilitating political division as they had previously. Congressional votes broke along party lines: Democrats were supportive and more pro-business Republicans tended to oppose it, though some voted for the act.

In short, the squabbles over the Federal Reserve Act's organizational design were framed by broader and deeper convergence. Pitched and enduring battles on par with the protests against the Crime of '73 did not break out. Instead, legislative quarrels in 1913 quickly gave way to bipartisan pragmatism. Republican leaders accepted the Fed. The fiery anti-bank populism of William Jennings Bryan, which had defined the Democratic Party in the 1896 presidential election, was replaced in 1913 by another Democrat, Woodrow Wilson, who heralded the bank-friendly Federal Reserve Act as a landmark accomplishment. President Wilson boasted three years after the passage of the new law that it made it possible for America to "take her place in the world of finance and commerce upon a scale that she never dreamed of before." The Federal Reserve created the "equipment...[to] assist American commerce, not only in our own country, but in any part of the world."[33]

THE MAKING OF THE FED STATE

The Fed was an accidental behemoth. The central bank established in 1913 was an institutional pigmy in comparison to regional banks. Further diminishing the Fed's stature, the initial limits on the Fed intensified after its enactment.[34] Signaling its lowly rank, the board was housed in the Treasury for decades after 1913.

How did the Fed develop the capacity and autonomy to monopolize monetary policy from its modest origins? We trace the Fed's astonishing path through a series of pivotal junctures when American policymakers faced changes in domestic and global markets for capital and trade that posed grave risks to the United States and they responded, often at the Fed's invitation, by expanding its capacity and independence. Each revision set the stage for future expansion and reconfiguring, which in turn moved the Fed further from its limited and impotent beginning in 1913.

Three changes course through the Fed's development after its establishment. First, the Fed centralized and established vast capacity. Authority and decision-making shifted from the decentralized regional banks to the Washington-based board. As central authority took hold the Fed cultivated an increasingly skilled staff, enhanced the prominence and credibility of its chair as one of the country's leading economic authorities, and constructed a widening spectrum of monetary tools for its policymaking body, the Federal Open Market Committee (FOMC).

Second, the Fed attained a degree of autonomy that finds no parallel in America's system of checks and balances—nor in central banks in Western Europe, Canada, or Japan. Over time the Fed separated from the US Treasury, resisted White House direction, and acquired unrivaled powers, codified in section 13(3) of its revised statutory authorization. These and other steps were linked together by the Fed's growing sense of its own interests and drive to advance them with vigor.

Third, the Fed exercised its administrative capacity and autonomy to protect and advance the interests of US finance. Attentiveness to finance is not new, of course. What changed is its source—direct pressure from specific banks was augmented by a growing realization by the Fed that it helped itself by serving finance as a whole.

The Takeoff: Fed State-Building, 1913–1952

The Fed's power grew as it started to stake out its institutional position, and global financial transformations and economic upheavals created opportunities for the central bank and its allies to showcase the Fed's potential to respond.

First Comes Centralization

The jolts of the Great Depression and the two world wars precipitated intense scrutiny of the decentralized regional banking system established in 1913 and, eventually, produced a conviction that an effective centralized monetary authority was needed. Although Democrats attempted to water down the control of banks that the Aldrich Plan envisioned, the banks did retain a vital source of influence: the Fed relied on the financial system for revenue and received no government funding. The need to pay expenses instilled in the Fed a realization that a stable and prospering financial sector served its institutional interest.

In the Fed's first decade, the drive to generate revenue focused the new authority on securing interest income first from loans to banks and then from purchasing government securities in the open market. Driven initially by their need to raise revenue and to establish fiscal self-reliance, the regional banks came to appreciate the efficacy of market trades as a quick and powerful monetary tool to change short-term interest rates and the supply of money and credit. By 1923 five eastern regional banks led by the New York Reserve Bank created a coordinating body—the Open Market Investment Committee—to coordinate their purchases and sales of government securities in order to improve policy efficacy and boost revenue. These modest steps toward greater coordination left standing a system that remained largely decentralized; some regional banks still claimed the right to act autonomously in the open market. What originated from institutional self-interest to raise revenue led to new policy instruments and greater coordination.

The stirring of the Fed's institutional hunger merged with a broad realization of the frailties of the 1913 compromise and the promise of a centralized system. The Great Depression revealed the 1913 system as an ill-coordinated hodge-podge that was incapable of preventing the run on banks and stemming their cascading effects after 1929. The collapse of smaller banks outside the Federal Reserve System sapped consumer confidence in banks and froze up credit markets. "Startling incompetence" describes its performance.[35]

Franklin D. Roosevelt's New Deal is most commonly associated with programs to alleviate poverty and joblessness, including Social Security, unemployment insurance, and public works. But the New Deal's first priority and wave of legislative actions was geared to the financial system. After three months in office Roosevelt signed the Banking Act of 1933, which was followed by another banking reform in 1935.

The New Deal banking reforms stripped control over monetary policy from the regional banks that had formed the backbone of the 1913 legislation, and initiated a process of centralization that triggered long-running institutional battles for institutional position and power. Faced with more fully integrated and dynamic national and international markets, the New Deal prohibited regional banks from conducting open market buying and selling and stripped them of other sources of discretion. Power shifted to Washington and the FOMC, where decisions were reached by the seven members of the presidentially appointed Board of Governors. The position of reserve banks on the board was reduced—only five of its 12 presidents were allowed to vote. The once dominant New York branch of the regional banks was also undercut and reduced to a subordinate position.

Building National Administrative Capacity

Financial crisis inspired the establishment of the Fed in 1913: New Deal laws empowered it to break the damaging cycle of bank runs, which closed over 4,000 banks by the mid-1930s. The 1913 compromise, which had deferred to banks and enfeebled the Fed system, opened the door during the first third of the twentieth century to the proliferation of hundreds of small retail banks. These banks prospered by merging the accounts of depositing customers (think James Stewart in *It's a Wonderful Life*) with their investments in corporate bonds and other securities. Banks used the savings of their customers to speculate. The crash in 1929 revealed the risks: as security investments bombed, banks lost the savings of depositors and were forced out of business, wiping out everyday Americans and triggering bankruptcies. The Glass-Steagall Banking Act of 1933 stepped in. The law prohibited banks from mixing the deposits of their customers with speculative trading or investment, creating a wall that stood for nearly seven decades.[36] At the same time, the new Federal Deposit Insurance Corporation (FDIC) guaranteed savers' deposits.

Crises and policy conflict prodded Congress (under Glass-Steagall) to open the door for the Fed to centralize power and to widen its authority as a regulator of banks and securities. This underscores a recurrent theme: calamity created opportunities for building the Fed State.

World War II and the political push for conservative fiscal policy hatched more opportunities for the Fed to step into new territory. The US Treasury sternly opposed raising taxes during the war, making the government dependent on the Fed to sell bonds and securities. While the Fed did not support the Treasury's policy of borrowing heavily (unparalleled among American allies), it welcomed the new authority and expectations to purchase large quantities of Treasury bonds and short-term certificates. As the Fed accreted new capacities, it began to articulate and press with greater insistence the distinct policy views of bankers and creditors who worried that the Treasury's war financing would increase the money supply, generate inflation, and swell government debt. The Fed would lose its skirmish with Treasury over interest rates during the 1930s and 1940s, but its support for cautious monetary policy was winning a following and positioned the central bank to prevail in pushing for lower inflation after the war.[37]

The takeoff in the Fed's centralization and capacity during the New Deal and World War II fueled a growth in its staff and the recruitment of trained economists and experienced investors. As the central bank expanded its skilled personnel, it also strengthened its credibility for technical expertise—trends that would continue to accelerate.

Going Independent

Independence was another big step in the Fed's development. The first hurdle was gaining separation from the regional banks in order to form and pursue distinct policies. The statutory recognition in 1935 of the Fed chairman as an "active executive officer" and Roosevelt's appointment of Marriner Eccles as its first leader created a single prominent public face for monetary policy. A skillful chair was able to use the Fed's public platform and authoritative position to champion the central bank's distinct policy views and institutional interests.[38] Reflecting the chair's new assertiveness, Congressman Carter Glass openly marveled at Eccles's forceful and strategic expansion of the Fed to "absorb every federal agency he can lay his hands on." According to Glass, the Fed chair "wants to be everything except President and he'd like to be that if he can."[39]

Even with the Fed's advancing independence, it faced running skirmishes with the US Treasury and the White House.[40] Before the 1930s the Fed, according to an important study, was a "subordinate" and "captive of the Treasury" in its everyday operations.[41] But New Deal legislation that administratively bolstered the Fed also loosened—but did not remove—the US Treasury's grip by ending the secretary's position as chair of the Federal Reserve Board and "ex officio" membership on the FOMC. Gaining leeway from the Treasury's tutelage enabled the Fed to fashion and promote distinct views about monetary policy that privileged low inflation and raising interest rates to smother it at the cost of higher unemployment.

The Fed–Treasury tussle over interest rates escalated after the New Deal. An accord during World War II set a "peg" that fixed low interest rates for Treasury bills and short-term certificates. A fierce battle broke out after the war between the Fed's insistence on higher rates to depress inflation and the Treasury secretary, under pressure from his political boss in the White House, who pressed for low rates to make credit less expensive and to encourage economic activity.

President Harry Truman grasped at what seemed like an easy solution to imposing low rates and stimulating the economy: he pushed out Eccles. Far from signaling the Fed's defeat, Truman's move against Eccles revealed the central bank's new institutional imprint. It had succeeded in formulating and advancing a distinct policy, exercised independence and defiance of the political Olympians in the White House and Treasury, and forced the president to revert, as a last resort, to pushing out a respected Fed chair. The result was not good for Truman. The president's standing among investors and the business community was damaged, and he feebly tried to mollify Eccles by (oddly) promising to keep him on the board as vice chair—an invitation that Eccles eventually turned down.[42]

The rub for Truman is that his extreme step failed: the Fed continued to push for higher rates and refused to fall in line with the administration's position led by the Treasury. Future presidents who failed to learn from Truman's experience suffered even higher costs, but most appreciated the Fed's new institutional position and accepted the new limits on their power over the Fed (see Table 2.1, which lists the modern chairs of the Fed).

Truman's ineffective move to quell the Fed's persistence in pressing for low interest rates precipitated another flash point—one that drew in Congress. The continuing strife between the Treasury and Fed led to an accord in 1951 that was featured in congressional hearings the next year. The peace treaty conceded control over bond rates to the central bank.[43] The compromise registered another step in the Fed's progression toward fuller independence in pursuing low interests and taking a leading role in managing financial markets.[44]

TABLE 2.1. Chairs of the Modern Federal Reserve System

Federal Reserve Chairs	Years in Office	President Nominating Chair
Marriner S. Eccles	1934–1948	Franklin Roosevelt
Thomas B. McCabe	1948–1951	Harry Truman
William Chesney Martin	1951–1970	Harry Truman
Arthur Burns	1970–1978	Richard Nixon
G. William Miller	1978–1979	Jimmy Carter
Paul Volcker	1979–1987	Jimmy Carter and Ronald Reagan
Alan Greenspan	1987–2006	Ronald Reagan
Ben S. Bernanke	2006–2014	George W. Bush and Barack Obama
Janet Yellen	2014–	Barack Obama

The Trojan Horse of Emergency Powers

The most radical dimension of Fed autonomy was initiated in the 1930s as a result of the familiar mix of economic crisis, political deadlock, and institutional positioning. As bank panics spread across America following the stock market crash of 1929, President Herbert Hoover accepted congressional actions in January 1932 to create a new government entity—the Reconstruction Finance Corporation (RFC)—to make loans to financial institutions, and especially banks and credit unions. But the conservative Hoover resisted further-reaching reforms, vetoing legislation in July 1932 to expand the RFC's authority to lend to individuals. The Fed was the beneficiary of the ensuing interbranch bargaining. Hoover signed new legislation that expanded the Federal Reserve Act by adding an extraordinary power: Section 13, paragraph 3. Although 13(3) was created to expand lending to individuals, its radical step was the autonomy it granted the Fed to act as it chose "in unusual and exigent circumstances." Absent an improbable uprising of the Board of Governors—five of its seven members were required to approve the use of 13(3)—the new emergency powers cut loose America's central bank from the system of accountability and transparency that routinely stymies its three branches of government. In a delicious historic irony, Hoover's bid to limit government ended up empowering the Fed to decide, on its own, the magnitude and form of credit to supply, who to help, and what type of collateral to accept.

The extraordinary wild card introduced by 13(3) was rarely used before the twenty-first century.[45] In the 1930s, only 123 loans (totaling about $23 million in today's dollars) were made to individuals and businesses.[46] The Fed became even more reticent about using its emergency powers until its massive deployment after 2007. As we discuss in the next chapter, the Fed exercised 13(3) to extend credit and guarantees on its own and to a degree that was unprecedented in the history of the US and western central banks.

The economic crisis of the Great Depression created an opportunity for institution-building, triggering the emergence of a central bank with the administrative capacity and independence to form distinct monetary policies and to press them effectively. The Fed's budding stature as a hub of monetary policy was cemented in a new home (it moved out of the Treasury in 1937) and a fresh name: the Board of Governors of the Federal Reserve System.[47]

Organizing Finance, 1952–1979

In postwar America, institutional promotion and crisis management mingled. The Bretton Woods agreement in 1944 stabilized global commerce and monetary policy for three decades by creating new international organizations and by encouraging the world's leading economies to harmonize monetary policy and currency by tying them to the gold-backed US dollar. The International Monetary Fund (IMF) bridged temporary imbalances of payments among trading countries. The Fed became, in effect, the chief operating officer of global financial interactions and domestic macroeconomic policy, lowering interest rates to reverse recessions and increasing them as inflation threatened.

By 1970, however, economic growth in Japan and Germany reduced US dominance, while the costs of the Vietnam War and Great Society swelled US government debt and triggered inflation. These challenging domestic and international conditions fueled a monetary tsunami: the value of the dollar declined, and leading economic powers left Bretton Woods and demanded that America exhaust its depleted gold reserves by converting their dollars. In a sign that pragmatism trumped ideology, Richard Nixon abandoned Bretton Woods in 1971 and ended fixed exchange rates in 1973. A more anarchic system resulted with currencies freely floating. The new uncertainty was intensified by the onset of the oil price shock and high inflation.[48]

The collapse of Bretton Woods and the long post–WWII expansion translated into institution-building opportunities for America's central bank. The Fed assumed primary responsibility for stabilizing global markets threatened by credit crises, runs on currencies, and other threats. The Fed also enlarged its domestic position, taking the lead to stimulate growth and to police against inflation. During the 1970s inflation accelerated and merged into "stagflation"—a perplexing combination of inflation with sluggish growth and high unemployment.

Seizing the Opportunity of Crisis

The push/pull of crisis and response widened the Fed's control of monetary policy. The training and skill of the Fed's monetary team grew markedly.[49] Adroit leadership and policymaking exploited this technical base. The FOMC gradually accumulated power, concentrating the Fed's activity on buying and selling Treasury bills and finalizing the shift of power from regional banks and the powerful Federal Reserve Bank of New York. The Fed's new centrality was distilled in the broad public attention that came to be devoted to the decisions of the closed FOMC meetings. The FOMC blossomed into a kind of Board of Trustees of finance.

The Fed's growing national administrative capacity and institutional confidence was reflected in the behavior of two board chairs, both of whom owed their ascent to the president who appointed them and then rewarded that sponsorship with defiance. One was William McChesney Martin, whom Truman installed to promote economic growth through low interest rates in the belief he would return the favor. Truman's hope sprung from Martin's earlier success as the Treasury's lead negotiator in pressing the Fed to lower rates during World War II. After Martin's appointment in 1951, however, he became a legendary advocate for the Fed, forcefully articulating its positions and expanding its capacity.[50] Foiling yet another Truman gambit to control the Fed, Martin outlasted the president, becoming the longest serving chair by the time he retired in 1970.

The other presidential turncoat was more surprising and revealing: Arthur Burns. With Republican loyalties stretching back to his service as chairman of the Council of Economic Advisers under President Dwight Eisenhower, Nixon expected loyalty from Burns, quipping at one point: "I respect Burns's independence. However, I hope that independently he will conclude that my views are the ones that should be followed."[51] In practice, Burns deferred to the White House on occasion, but more striking, he defied Nixon to advocate the Fed's position. Burns opposed Nixon's 1971 decision to impose controls on wages and prices to combat potential inflation, but expressed more public defiance over interest rate policy: Nixon pressed for low rates and a looser money supply to boost sagging economic growth (as well as his prospects for re-election after Republican setbacks in the 1970 elections). But under Burns, the Fed resisted.[52] Institutional loyalty trumped party loyalty. Burns, and Martin before him, signaled the Fed's institutional presence by defying their presidential sponsor and then outlasting them. Burns served until 1978, long after Nixon's ignoble departure from the White House.

Presidents flailed around searching—unsuccessfully—for tactics to foster smoother relations: scheduling formal and informal meetings, planting loyalists by meticulously screening appointments to the Fed, and so forth. None transcended a basic conflict: presidents were keen to advance their political interests and policy goals, and the Fed came to harbor its own institutional preferences to fight against inflation by adjusting interest rates and to defer to orderly markets. As the Fed's capacity, performance, and reputation grew, presidential retribution became less of an option.[53] Removing the Fed chair risked market confidence (think: big stock market drop) and stability, as well as a political counterattack by US finance through Congress, the press, and campaign contributions for rivals.

Here's another irony. Modern presidents proved incapable of chaining the Fed to White House interests, but it was the sharp expansion of executive power since Roosevelt that created the precedents and cover for the Fed's rise. Growing demands on government, international challenges, and congressional dysfunction prodded Roosevelt to propose a major reorganization of the executive branch to satisfy his conviction and that of his advisors that the "president needs help," and to generate more freedom for unilateral White House action. Subsequent presidents steadily carved out and expanded their office's prerogatives and the capacity to sustain them. Nixon's run-ins with Democratic congressional majorities inspired him to develop administrative tools to circumvent Congress by using executive orders and the writing of regulatory rules to achieve what he could not do legislatively. The swelling of the presidency crimped the policy initiative and oversight that Congress had traditionally exercised.

The Fed was not a tool of the presidency, but it flourished in the institutional crevice between retracted legislative engagement and the broad expanse of executive policymaking.[54] Building administrative capacity and, especially, the technical skill to conduct advanced analytics equipped the Fed with the know-how and confidence to pursue independent policies and to justify its claims for leeway to conduct policy without interference.[55]

The Fed's technical capacity grew substantially as it became a fixture in Washington. It attracted a sizeable staff with doctoral training in economics, numbering eventually over two hundred in Washington, a similar number in regional banks, and perhaps another hundred working as consultants. In addition, it built a latticework of relationships and pipelines to researchers within the discipline of economics through funding, organizing visiting positions, and convening large and prestigious conferences.[56]

Acting Independent

Over time, the central bank publicly and aggressively took actions that were, Chairman Martin insisted to Congress in 1956, "insulated from direct political pressures" whether coming from the White House or the Treasury, which it now openly treated as a coequal instead of its superior.[57]

Independent sources of revenue formed the foundation of the Fed's autonomy from Congress—and its tie to finance. The Fed's funding separated it from most other government agencies that compete in Congress for a budget allocation and face the scrutiny that often accompanies the annual appropriations process. The routinizing of its revenue sources firmed up the foundation of the Fed's finances and boosted its confidence to act independently.

Knowledge is power, and one of the Fed's shields is to dim congressional knowledge about its operations. Well before the Fed hid information about its 2008–2009 rescues, it undermined the kind of transparency that is routine in government. The central bank succeeded in carving out exemptions from the Sunshine Act of 1976 and persistently diluted congressional efforts for more accountability.[58] Apart from the Supreme Court's private deliberations, few government bodies are as effective in preventing public access to its deliberations leading up to decisions.[59]

One of the Fed's most intriguing institution-building strategies was to welcome and then channel congressional oversight as a means to neutralize the White House and Treasury. On the one hand, the Fed worked with legislators to establish new lines of targeted oversight to compete with pressure from the White House. A series of congressional actions in the mid-1970s regularized testimony by the chair—inflating his public prominence—and expanded central bank reporting to Congress on its economic projections and targets for interest rates and monetary supply.[60] Lawmakers also offered broad policy direction by passing the Humphrey-Hawkins Act to reaffirm its dual mandate, first enunciated in the 1946 Employment Act: maintain price stability and stoke employment.

On the other hand, the Fed worked with Congress to design the new oversight to avoid intrusive interference with the making of monetary policy. Although some lawmakers raised the prospect of setting specific interest rate targets for the FOMC and imposing other restrictions, the Fed maintained the freedom to set monetary policy and negotiated limits on what information was released and when. Organized labor and Democrats cheered the objective of fuller employment in Humphrey-Hawkins, but it exerted little consistent practical effect; Fed policymakers treat it (with congressional acquiescence) as one among several competing goals and choose to subordinate it to what they define as their principal anti-inflation mission.

The Fed's cooperation with increased congressional reporting coincided with strong and perhaps greater Fed independence as it established itself as a "fourth branch of government." Fed chair Martin insisted to members of Congress that "central banks should not, in my judgment, be in politics."[61] "The Fed's job," he explained in a more lively off-the-cuff comment, "is to take away the punch bowl just when the party gets going." The Kansas City Federal Reserve approvingly quoted the stern warning of its German counterpart: "A [central] bank has to be independent because one cannot really trust the politicians—they are a rotten lot and any of them might seek to get out of a hole by printing money."[62]

New Policy Frameworks for Fed Activism

The Fed's development as the independent arbiter of monetary policy by the mid-1970s was reinforced by the emergence of monetarism. Roosevelt's response to the Great Depression established government intervention—and, specifically, government spending—as an effective policy tool for managing the economy. The crux of this policy framework (known as Keynesianism) was using government to increase the demand of consumers and lift employment.[63]

The 1970s, however, posed a perplexing challenge to Keynesian policy: the sharp rise in unemployment *and* inflation in the wake of the 1973 oil shock (stagflation). Keynes had a policy prescription to lift employment (government spending), but it also worsened inflation. This policy conundrum created an opening for a new macroeconomic framework known as monetarism, which

relied on changing the money supply and interest rates to stimulate or contract economic activity.

Monetarism's proposed response to stagflation offered a clear
alternative to Keynesianism—push down interest rates and accept
higher unemployment as unavoidable costs until the economy
bounced back.[64] When the tight money policy of Fed chair Paul
Volcker (1979–1987) reduced inflation, monetarism gained credibility among policy elites. For the Fed, monetarism provided a
cogent (if contested) intellectual rationale for its role as dictator
of the money supply.[65] The arrival of monetarism also further elevated the economics profession into secular oracles, trained to read
the tea leaves of economic and financial data to chart Fed policy.

Institutional Independence and Advancing Finance

As the Fed crawled out from under the thumb of regional banks
and then the US Treasury, it developed a mission and set of policies defined by engaged independence—advancing its own interests by serving those of finance as a whole. Stabilizing and
advancing US finance served the overall interests of the industry
while also garnering the Fed revenues and political support to
fend off rival institutions. Although the Fed is literally separate
from any one firm, its development was anchored in finance.

Fed Anchors in Finance #1. The personnel and mindset of Wall
Street and other parts of the industry are literally present in the
Fed. This was baked into the Aldrich Plan and the 1913 law by
the inclusion of banks and businesses in its governance and the
expectation that the Fed would be "of" finance. The revolving door
of senior Fed officials back and forth between the central bank
and lucrative private positions, along with routine communica-
tions, cements the original plans.

Finance's "in" within the Fed is poignantly portrayed by Paul
Volcker—one of the Fed's most influential chairs. President Carter
appointed him, according to a senior advisor, "because he was
the candidate of Wall Street. This was their price."[66]

The personal stakes of looking out for finance inside the Fed were
vividly conveyed by Neil Barofsky (the first watchdog of TARP

spending). Barofsky was invited out one night early in his term by Herb Allison (the affluent former Merrill Lynch president and presiding boss of TARP). In the guise of offering friendly advice, Allison warned him that "you're doing yourself real harm" by issuing hard-hitting reports and proceeded to draw the connections between Barofsky's official conduct and his future payout in the financial industry. His pitch started out by reminding him of the stakes: "You're a young man, just starting out with a family, and obviously this job isn't going to last forever." Then, Allison hit home by warning Barofsky that "there are consequences for some of the things that you are saying."[67]

Fed Anchors in Finance #2. The Fed developed a dependence on finance that did not require the personnel of finance to literally serve as staff or to lobby. The interests and needs of the Fed as an institution imprinted the perspectives of finance on senior leadership and staff.

The Fed literally relies on Wall Street and private banks to do its job—from generating revenue to sharing needed information. One of the cogs in the Fed's structural tie to finance is its reliance on the New York Federal Reserve Bank, whose president serves as deputy chair of the FOMC. The Fed in Washington uses the New York Bank to conduct its securities trading, and the Manhattan branch counts on Wall Street to runs its operations. Institutional dependence creates power and influence.

What makes most sense to the Fed as it surveys its interests helps finance. Sustaining the health of the industry also feeds revenue to the Fed and rewards banks and investment firms for their active support in Congress through lobbying and campaign contributions.

THE ERA OF FINANCE AND THE FED'S MONOPOLY OF MONETARY POLICY

The Reagan presidency marked the ascendance of the Fed over monetary policy. The earlier decentralized system that left power with regional banks had ceased. The Treasury's competition to set interest rates had been settled. And presidents had come to accept the reality of Fed independence—if not happily, or without intermittent efforts at interventions. New directions in global financial markets and America's financial deregulation both solidified the Fed's monopolization of monetary policy and vastly complicated its responsibilities.

The New World of Global Finance

Finance has been global for centuries, but the scope, speed, and penetration of capital markets qualitatively changed with the 1970s. The Fed was not only an able strategic actor plotting its rise, but it was also buffeted by the changes in domestic and international financial markets.

The closer integration of US and global finance coincided with a key political development after the 1970s: the political parties became increasingly polarized on domestic issues of taxes and spending, but agreed to open America's doors to international finance and to roll back New Deal regulations. Few acts of Congress rivaled Glass-Steagall for embodying the regulatory crackdown on financial speculation and the spectacle of bank panics during the Great Depression in the 1930s. In 1999, after numerous failed efforts over the previous decades, President Clinton signed on to toppling the wall Glass-Steagall had erected to separate the safe world of retail banking from the more risky world of investment banking.

Clinton's partnership with a Republican-controlled Congress not only removed the firewall between commercial and investment banking; it also eroded the remaining regulatory structure by splintering responsibility. The Securities and Exchange Commission (SEC) was assigned to police security and brokerage operations of investment firms, and the Fed was left with commercial operations. That was not all. Clinton teamed up with Republicans in 2000 to strip the New Deal's Commodity Exchange Act of the power to regulate derivatives and credit swap dealmaking.

Legitimized by his Democratic predecessor, President George W. Bush proceeded to topple still more bulwarks against financial scheming and invite a frenzy of speculation. The Securities and Exchange Commission (SEC) withdrew regulators from large investment banks in favor of a new voluntary code and targeted periodic audits. Firms were given the choice to opt in (or out) in exchange for exemptions from earlier requirements to keep more capital in reserve. (Later investigations prompted SEC chairman Christopher Cox to concede that the supervision system was "fundamentally flawed" and that the SEC failed to regulate the firms.[68]) The rolling back of regulations, combined with low interest rates after the 9/11 terrorist attacks, encouraged banks to pursue greater profits and accept greater risks by expanding credit and reducing how much it kept on hand to protect against unexpected losses.

The bipartisan political agenda in the United States to pull down New Deal regulations of banking and finance were key pieces of a more encompassing agenda that were embraced by "new Democrats" and conservatives. This new intellectual consensus (known as "neoliberalism") energized a search for opportunities to broaden the role of the private sector in the United States and abroad through free trade, reduced government spending, and far-reaching deregulation.[69] The bipartisan receptivity to deregulation and the intellectual imprimatur of neoliberalism drew lobbyists as bees to honey; the Washington muscle for finance went to work pulling down the scaffolding of US and international protections.

The new political climate and neoliberalism unleashed a speculative mania in financial markets and gave the green light to the takeoff in the unregulated shadow banking system. The decisions of lawmakers to dismantle the protections against excessive risk-taking bear some responsibility for later financial and economic turmoil.

Neoliberalism and deregulation not only recast US financial markets and the Fed's responsibilities, but also introduced three changes in international markets that altered the global context of American finance. First, America rose in prominence as a hub of international finance. The flow of international capital into US money markets steadily increased during the 1970s, and then accelerated in the 1980s and 1990s. The attraction was the growing leniency created by deregulation as well as the Fed's strategy during the 1980s of strangling inflation by imposing high interest rates. Investors moved aggressively into US markets to cash in.

Second, the domestic economy and banking shifted toward marketing securities (whether stocks, bonds, or other assets that are traded). As the Fed adopted unusually low interest rates during the 1990s, banks cajoled consumers to refinance existing mort-gages while credit card companies widely distributed accounts and encouraged Americans to run up debt on cheap credit. Low-income Americans were peddled subprime mortgages that they could not afford through come-on pitches that showcased initially low interest rates. Hispanics and African Americans were also targeted for subprime loans but were charged far higher rates than whites of similar or even weaker financial circumstances.[70]

Instead of finance serving as a means to generate the produc-tion of goods and services, it became the ends. Banks and in-vestment firms championed the "innovation" of derivatives, credit swaps, and the conversion of traditional securities (such as home mortgages) into something known as "securitization": the bundling of subprime loans and other consumer credit into pack-ages that were then resold in financial markets.[71] The short-term returns were off the charts. Banks and investors (especially in the United States) increasingly drove domestic economic growth and elevated the shadow banking system.[72]

The enveloping of the US economy in the seaweed of financial-ization affected not only credit and security markets. It also seeped into workplace compensation. A coalition of employers, parts of the financial industry, and Democratic and Republican lawmakers converged on policy changes to improve tax incen-tives to subsidize retirement savings in 401(k) plans and IRAs. Tax exemptions circumvented the liberal–conservative fight over government programs by relying on the private sector, and re-quiring workers to save for retirement. The result since the 1970s is that Wall Street took on new importance to Americans whose lifeline in retirement was tied to the performance of the equities that composed their pensions.

Third, America's economy became increasingly contorted by the drive to churn out interest, dividends, or capital gains. As finance came to account for a growing source of profitability, the drive to capture mammoth profits skewed the economy away from job-producing industry.[73]

Domesticating Modern Finance

Neoliberalism and financialization spawned a new generation of opportunities for the Fed to exercise and expand its capacity and independence. The high inflation that had set in during the 1970s imperiled President Jimmy Carter's re-election drive in 1980 and made the taming of inflation an urgent priority. Carter's testy relations with Chairman Arthur Burns and his successor G. William Miller renewed the tensions between the White House and the Fed over conflicting policy prescriptions. Faced with the damaging impacts of inflation on the economy and his re-election prospects, Carter appointed the president of the Federal Reserve Bank of New York, Paul Volcker, to aggressively use the Fed's tools.[74] Volcker dramatically increased rates to 20 percent in 1980–1981 and choked the money supply by elevating the capital reserve requirements for banks and pursuing other measures to impose strict monetary targets.[75]

Carter's expectation of Fed aggression and the response of Volcker and his successors marked an "historic shift in operation procedures."[76] What had become the Fed's traditional tool of interest rate adjustment was now—at the urging of political elites—joined with aggressive controls over money supply.

No doubts remained about who held the steering wheel to the US economy. Greenspan continued Volcker's approach by vigorously steering the money supply, tightening it when inflation threatened, and expanding it to pour billions into banks when shocks created the risk of a run or a seizing up of credit markets.[77] The result were striking shifts: the FOMC under Greenspan moved interest rates higher to keep inflation low, and then reversed course to stimulate the economy after the October 1987 stock market crash, the bursting of the dot-com bubble, and the 9/11 attacks.

By the twenty-first century, the Fed was competing with law-makers as the country's macroeconomic policymaker and often taking the lead when fiscal policy fell victim to partisan deadlock. As partisan and ideological polarization put a stranglehold on lawmaking, the Fed stepped in to use its capacity to act independently and aggressively to steer the economy by altering interest rates and the money supply and to prevent financial turmoil.

However, the widening scope of Fed responsibilities generated new threats. As the Fed dominated monetary policy and financial markets as never before, the risk of serious breakdowns persisted and increased. Troubles partly grew from its success in welcoming financialization and deregulation. Volcker's high rates in the early 1980s took aim at squelching inflation. But his policy also set off a veritable stampede by overseas investors to pour their cash and capital into US money markets to take advantage of the high returns. The Fed's subsequent adoption of low rates under Chairman Alan Greenspan, combined with lighter regulation of banks, fueled securitization. It lured Americans into purchasing risky subprime mortgages and enticed everyday people and businesses to assume greater debt under the illusion that credit would remain cheap.

Asset bubbles and market crashes resulted. The sharp declines in the stock market in 1987 and 2000 were not unexpected, but the risk that large investment firms would overreach, collapse, and threaten the broader financial system contradicted the myth of Fed control. A decade before Bear Stearns and Lehman Brothers became household names, an extravagantly overextended hedge fund (Long Term Capital Management) threated to trigger disaster in 1998. The Fed stepped in to rescue its investors, demonstrating not its mastery of the new financialized system but rather foreshadowing its fundamental vulnerability. The incident exposed a contradiction that would burst onto the front pages a decade later: the more that was expected and delivered by the Fed, the more financial crisis revealed the shortcomings of its operations. The Fed's institutional success in advancing its position and power spotlighted its limitations and vulnerability.

The Fed's direct, public interventions to rescue—or, more commonly, to steer the economy and foster financialization—became increasingly incongruous by the twenty-first century with its claims to independence and serving the overall public good, as opposed to serving Wall Street. The strains on the Fed's legitimacy were aggravated by the widening realization that its policies paid off for banks and investment firms far more than they did for the average person, whose economic well-being started to decline in relative terms after the 1970s. Financialization ballooned the debt of American households, and the largest payoffs of stock market surges were concentrated among a small proportion of Americans. Its encouragement of 401(k) accounts and IRAs chased out the more secure defined-benefit pension systems during the last two decades of the twentieth century.[78]

While the Fed operated largely unimpeded from the shadows of government for much of a century, its growing public prominence drew scrutiny and eroded its credibility for independence. As we discuss in Chapter 4, the Fed finds the anchor of its legitimacy (impartiality) undermined by what it must do directly and publicly to sustain finance. What it does of necessity strips bare its deference to finance.

PAST AND FUTURE

The Fed's past casts into relief several seminal developments. The Fed State that now stands astride America was never intended or even envisioned in 1913. Well-connected banks and investors pressed for the founding of a central bank at the turn of the century, but today's Fed was not their design.

The Federal Reserve is exceptional from the perspectives of its founders as well as the framers of the US Constitution who designed a system of governance anchored in accountability. Financial crises, new economic pressures, and the infirmities of America's deadlocked policy process prodded a century of policymakers to move the Fed far from its origins. Reforms that appeared to fend off financial or economic stresses at one point in time were repeatedly reconsidered in the face of subsequent crises and challenges. The consistent theme is that the Fed's responsibilities were expanded or redirected to take on new purposes.

The Fed now enjoys extraordinary capacity to manipulate economic activity through its control over interest rates and the money supply. Although lawmakers retain the authority to reorganize the Fed (which it does on occasion), no government agency of comparable power is as free of public accountability. The Fed's routine policy decisions are, in practice, shielded from the scrutiny of Congress, presidents, and Treasury secretaries, and yet the central bank dictates monetary policy and is the dominant force in steering the economy.

A second development stands out from our examination of over two centuries of debate over finance and central banks: the vibrant and widespread resistance to the rise of a financial goliath is gone. No need for romanticism. The particular critiques and prescriptions launched by Jacksonian Democrats and populists are unsuited to our times.

We have lost, however, something more enduring and important to American democracy: vigorous public debates and insistence on active accountability. The public fights over monetary policy unnerved elites in the nineteenth century, but they also instigated mass mobilization and engagement with charting alternative policies to maintain democratic control over America's financial system.

In the mainstream of public life today, the once heated debates and fervent organizing rarely confront the Fed State. The Fed has nestled in as a powerful vested interest. With little sustained scrutiny, it raises revenue and builds support among elites to expand its personnel, budgets, and authority. It is a revealing indication of its success that the notion of the Fed as an impartial, public good is widely embraced among elites and those who make a living studying the Fed.

That's not all. Compared to the Jacksonian and populist scrutiny, there is today an acquiescence to the Fed's favoritism. Absent the stinging rebuke of a president (like Andrew Jackson) against the "rich and powerful," the Fed sustains finance in order to aid the central bank's own continuation and growth. The once raucous public commotion has been decapitated by a submerged policymaking process. Private, insulated decisions exclude the voices and influence of broad publics and their political and organized representatives.

Pure triumph is not the consequence, however. The Fed's rise both created an unparalleled empire and lit the fuse to new threats. As we discuss in Chapter 4, the swelling of the Fed's activism has eroded its credibility as a steward of the public good.

3

Concealed Advantage

"IT IS A matter of days before there is a meltdown in the global financial system." That is the hair-raising report that the normally unflappable Fed chair Ben Bernanke privately delivered to congressional leaders during an unusual evening meeting on September 18, 2008.[1] In calm reflection months later, Bernanke reiterated his message that the trajectory of the "crisis" was toward "calamity" and "catastrophe."[2]

"Herbert Hoover time" is how Vice President Dick Cheney described the approaching economic implosion.[3] "Armageddon" was the reaction of Republican senator Mel Martinez, a member of the Banking Committee, after privately meeting with Bernanke and President Bush's Treasury secretary Hank Paulson during this period. Martinez confessed to being "frightened"—"even with them asking for extraordinary powers, they were not at all assured that they could prevent the kind of financial disaster that I think really was greater than the Great Depression."[4]

The alarming reports of senior government officials captured the devastating turmoil sweeping finance in the United States and abroad during 2008. The stock market's Dow Jones registered its worst losses in 75 years—it plummeted 40 percent in the year after October 2007 and 22 percent during the first week of October 2008. American business magnate Warren Buffet warned that America faced "economic Pearl Harbor."[5] The director of the International Monetary Fund sounded the alarm that financial disruptions around the world were "pushing the global financial system to the brink of systemic meltdown."[6] Surveying the charred landscape, a Goldman Sachs executive privately emailed Fed officials in mid-September an SOS—the situation was "pretty scary and ugly" and "spinning out of control."[7]

The dread of policymakers marked a rare occasion in American politics. Dire warnings were not exaggerations—though their diagnosis of the source and solution of the financial crisis were incomplete.

Penetrating the hero worship of the Fed and its strategies for perpetuating massive favoritism is the focus of this chapter. We begin by revealing the specific nature of the crisis facing America in 2008–2009. The Fed's exceptional actions in response were not an aberration (as claimed by the Fed and its apologists), but rather extended and accelerated a mutant path of institution-building that had been forming for nearly a century. We focus in particular on dissecting a set of unparalleled new programs that the Fed created unilaterally—its favoritism is encased in the details of these programs.

THE BREAKDOWN IN MODERN FINANCE

Fed officials worried about the "dangerous" and "harmful" impacts on business confidence of signaling "our panicking."[8] Their alarm accurately conveyed the breakdown in the gear-shaft of modern Western economies: gaining credit and sharing risk. You and I need a mortgage to buy a house. Normal operations by businesses and banks need quick, inexpensive credit to meet payroll and cover other expenses; they often turn to "commercial paper"—a kind of IOU with interest or a fee.[9]

The New Brave World of Debt

Business as usual, however, took an ominous turn in the early twenty-first century as debt became a wildly profitable business. A swelling "shadow" bazar outside normal banking and regulations converted loans and other forms of credit into new financial instruments and then traded them around the world. In the old days, debt sat in the bank and then you repaid that bank; before 2008 investors were making lots of money by trading debt. This meant that your mortgage was no longer literally held by your local bank where you signed papers, but instead was sold and traded around the globe. This new industry of trading loans (think, mortgages) goes by the convoluted name "collateralized debt obligations" and the even more mysterious acronym CDOs. Here is the big deal in the brave new world of turning debt into securities and trading them: it ballooned by more than fourfold to $1.4 trillion between 2000 and 2007.

With global markets trading debts, investors worried that they faced potentially large risks that the loans would go bust. Banks and other firms stepped up by expanding insurance for investors to reduce the risk of loan defaults. The mind-numbing label for this industry is "credit default swaps," or CDSs. The size of this market exploded from $6 trillion to $62 trillion between 2004 and 2007.[10] To put the enormous size of the CDS market in perspective, it was four times larger in 2007 than the *entire* US economy, which was the largest in the world.

Credit default swaps have been vilified for the 2008 crisis, but they began innocently enough in the 1990s with banks helping safeguard low-risk investments such as loans to municipal governments to build roads or sewers. Credit default swaps took a dangerous turn in the early twenty-first century. The traders of debt started to ring up impressive profits, and competition for investors tightened and spread from safe municipal loans into risky new areas. An industry with a reasonable beginning gravitated toward the most notorious financial fiascos—mortgages to lower income, unstably employed families (the inartfully labeled "subprime mortgages"). Debt traders packaged these risky mortgages into commodities to sell (here's more jargon: "mortgage-backed securities" or MBSs) and invaded the CDS market with them.

The merry-go-round of investors and traders buying credit default swaps and mortgage-backed securities cranked out profits as long as the economy and subprime mortgages were healthy. The fun screeched to a halt, however, when homeowners were unable to make payments and investors discovered that the sellers of the CDSs—the so-called insurance on bad loans—were unable to pay them for defaults. The Fed was slow to see that the fun times had ended. Even during the first half of 2008, the Fed continued to be enraptured by the good times and eerily detached from reality. Three months after Bear Stearns failed in March and three months before the collapse of Lehman Brothers nearly toppled the global system, Fed governors cooed that "the risk of the national economy sinking into a serious recession has receded" and congratulated themselves that "the worst outcomes stemming from financial market turmoil have failed to materialize thus far."[11] Although a few Fed governors worried about dark clouds, the prevalent view— as summarized by Bernanke—was the worry "about inflation and my [Bernanke's] belief that the time might be relatively soon" to fight it by tightening the money supply.[12]

As the second half of 2008 unfolded, however, the rising threat of systemic failure dawned on Bernanke and other central bank leaders, whose usually shrouded calculations were revealed by the public release of conversations in the Federal Open Market Committee. They talked with increasing urgency about "the possibility of a systemic event" (June 2008), frustration that "we've been in this now for a year" and "we keep on having shoes dropping" (July), and resignation by October that "market conditions continue to deteriorate" despite unprecedented interventions.[13]

The bottom line is that Bernanke and other senior government officials were unnerved in fall 2008 by the unthinkable. Their alarm was not simply provoked, however, by the washing out of a greasy corner of finance (subprime mortgages)—as is often assumed. The size of the subprime business was significant ($7 trillion in 2007) but manageable, and partially offset by the collateral for loans (actual property). What opened the gates of financial hell was the devastation that subprime mortgages wreaked on credit default swaps and the broader financial system. Faced with a substantial demand for payment, the insurers of the debt were unable to make payments to firms holding mortgage-backed securities. Think dominoes: the failure of credit default swaps sapped the confidence of investors in the monumental credit default market and the trading of debt, which in turn triggered a credit crunch and froze the economy in the United States and other parts of the world. Businesses and individuals could not get loans even if they sported sterling credit histories and could offer rock-solid collateral as a guarantee of repayment.[14] If you could find a firm that would lend you money, the cost of borrowing skyrocketed.[15]

The Problem with the Fed

The most publicly scathing government criticism of the Fed's decision to intervene—Ron Paul's—contends that the Fed's interventions were unnecessary (the costs would only be temporary) and destructive (it fed asset bubbles and diluted economic value). The basic outlines of the 2008 crisis resembled the perilous panics that had cursed nineteenth-century America—"hot money" in subprime loans and other toxic assets stampeded depositors and investors to run away from even strong assets out of spooked misgivings about their value. But the situation was worse in 2008. Finance was globalized, its markets more varied, and the opportunities to coordinate responses more elusive and difficult. The ingredients for a massive global depression were perilously close. Not intervening was a recipe for a decade or more of massive unemployment and misery on the scale of the Great Depression. By contrast, stepping in to supply money in frozen credit markets avoided the dreadful consequences of a full financial collapse—unemployment, business failures, and housing foreclosures that far surpassed the dreary Great Recession that afflicted America and Europe.

The problem with the Fed's action was not that it intervened (as Ron Paul and others claim) but *how* it intervened and *who*

benefited most. The Fed reached decisions in private that channeled tens of billions to a select few private businesses while ex-
cluding homeowners and many other businesses who were also
scrambling for affordable credit to avoid foreclosure and bankruptcy. The Fed's agenda was driven to advance its institutional
interests and to save big finance. Reducing the stranglehold of
household debt on the broader economy and designing comprehensive mortgage protection never showed up as a serious concern.

Drum rolls of the looming financial disaster and mayhem that
faced America in 2008 are usually paired with a celebratory parade
singing the praise for the Fed's success in "getting it right" and
putting the national interest above special interests.[16] But hero
worship of the Fed and its alleged public-spiritedness and fairness is inappropriate.

Three features of the Fed's primary interventions in 2008 and
2009 undercut the hagiology that has been erected around its
actions.

Mistakes Instead of Mastery

First, the Fed's pretensions to technocratic mastery are dented
by its mistakes before and during the crisis. Crediting the Fed
with saving the country is, with only some exaggeration, akin to
praising an arsonist who called the fire department. The Financial
Crisis Inquiry Commission concluded that "the crisis was avoidable and was caused by... widespread failures in financial regulation, including the Federal Reserve's failure to stem the tide of
toxic mortgages."[17] The straight-talking Sheila Bair—head of the
Federal Deposit Insurance Corporation (FDIC)—was equally scathing in blaming the Fed: "For decades it had been at the fore-
front of the deregulatory movement that had given us the crisis."[18]
The Fed accorded banks too much leeway, failed to adequately
monitor risks or to supervise subprime lending (even when alerted
to its scale and inherent fragility), and neglected to raise capital
requirements to meet the growing potential of substantial downturns. Alarms about these and other problems were sounded well
before the crisis.[19] The Fed would later concede its "mistakes" in
producing the crisis of 2008–2009.[20]

After the financial monsoon swept over Americans, Fed mistakes and inconsistencies continued to mar its handling of the crisis. It flooded Citibank, for instance, with emergency loans that Bernanke insisted were only intended for "sound institutions," while internal Fed reviews classified the bank's circumstances as "marginal."[21]

One of the most serious errors by the Fed (and the Treasury) was to misdiagnosis the nature of the financial crisis, and therefore to devise a flawed prescription that catered to Wall Street and other investors. For all of the terror unleashed by the financial crisis in fall 2008, the panic was reversed and confidence returned to banks, Wall Street, and credit markets in 2009. Here's the hitch: the economy we experienced—especially, jobs—remained stuck in the doldrums. The remedy hatched by the government technocrats—calming the panic and stoking Wall Street and the investor class—worked, and yet the economy did not roar back.

A key drag on the economy was the huge private debt that American households took on because of the hawking of subprime mortgages to families that could not afford them, and other factors.[22] What was the Fed's response to this first-order cause of America's sustained economic malaise? It focused on funneling massive and cheap credit to big finance. Relieving the credit crunch strangling everyday people failed to register as a pressing problem.

Implication: confidence in the Fed as an infallible force is dangerously misplaced.

The Fed Stands Up for Itself

Second, the Fed was not a disinterested bystander. Its actions and strategies advanced its institutional interests to expand its independence, resources, and administrative capacity. As the 2008 crisis hammered America's economy and finance, the Fed burst from its long-standing confines—relying on interest rate calibrations to alter the money supply and working with a relatively small number of cautious banks. Instead, it revolutionized its operations. The Fed invoked its sparingly used emergency power—known as section 13(3) in its founding statute—to create nine programs (labeled "facilities") that started "a fiscal, not a monetary operation." The Fed also transformed who it worked with, throwing open its doors to commercial banks, investment firms, insurers, credit card and student loan firms, and others.[23] And it did all this unilaterally: neither Congress nor the president approved— or even knew about the Fed's extraordinary actions.

The 2008 crisis was unnerving, as well as an opportunity for the Fed to launch interventions of unimaginable proportions. The Fed's loans and guarantees amounted to *half* of the value of everything produced in the United States in 2009.[24] The $7.77 trillion that the Fed had committed was 10 times larger than the Troubled Asset Relief Program (TARP).

The gargantuan proportions of the Fed's interventions reflected the extent of the 2008 crisis. It also created an occasion for institution-building. The Fed exploited the 2008 crisis to accelerate its century-long drive to produce a government agency with unparalleled domestic authority, reach, and resources.

Favoring Finance

Third, the Fed and Treasury may have engaged in the most lucrative favoritism in American history. Clandestinely writing checks to the big banks and investment houses—from Goldman Sachs to Citibank and others—is part of it. But the part that continues to elude scrutiny is the Fed's generous design and operation of its facilities to distribute selective benefits to particular firms and markets in finance. In a spectacular outburst against former colleagues in government, Sheila Bair rips the Fed for "the trillions of dollars" it had "seemingly willy-nilly lent...completely on its own," without "an explanation of why the programs were needed, how eligibility was determined, and most important, who was profiting and by how much."[25]

In the privileged world that the Fed created for the chosen few, normal market rules did not apply. In much of America in the desperate days of 2008 and 2009, homeowners scrambled to find relief as foreclosure loomed; small- and medium-sized businesses frantically searched for scarce credit, and, if they found it, paid exorbitant prices. For the chosen few, the Fed supplied free loans (as low as .01 percent). "Gift" is how truth-speaking economists and former

Fed officials described loans and guarantees with virtually no interest charged. Another cherry from the Fed: its anointed few were allowed to keep assets and inflate their books instead of selling them to pay investors and depositors. And as a kicker, no limits were imposed on executive compensation, even as taxpayers stepped in.

What did Fed handouts mean for the anointed? It saved some firms from certain collapse—AIG leads the list—and enabled them to retain supersized pay for executives whose firms were rocked by their failed investments. The privilege of borrowing at absurdly low rates reaped $13 billion in income, according to analysis by Bloomberg News.[26] The take for the country's six largest banks was $4.8 billion.

TARP fuelled popular outrage and insurrections from the left and right—the Tea Party and Occupy Wall Street. The Fed's subterranean facilities provoked, however, little public reaction even though they doled out more. That was no accident. The Fed designed a concealed operation that cloaked the facilities from public notice and debate. Technical jargon and processes unfamiliar to most Americans—or lawmakers—created an almost impenetrable force field. Then there was the Fed's outright defiance in requests for information: the magnitude of the facilities only came to light—years later—after lawsuits and congressional investigations forced disclosures.

The Fed's effectiveness registers in polls. About eight out of 10 Americans told pollsters that they were aware of the TARP program and about six out of 10 disliked it as a bad idea, unnecessary, and a poor model for helping other banks and businesses.[27] No polls detected the same level of public awareness and antipathy when it came to the Fed's specific programs. This disinterest and unfamiliarity was manufactured.

DESIGNING BIAS

The severity of the 2008–2009 crisis pushed the Fed to act, but what explains the content of its policy and who benefited from it? We know impressively little about why the Fed designed its policies to favor some and not others, and how this was done. The cloud over the winners and losers in Fed policy has not been penetrated by most media and research accounts, which has focused on the origins of the 2008 crisis and the size of the Fed's response.[28]

The Fed is a cloistered black box—a striking contrast with Congress. Journalists, lobbyists, and experts routinely scour the recesses of congressional bills for the favors and earmarks that are tucked away for well-connected insiders. They are able to identify who drove congressional decisions and most benefited by turning to public hearings to see who testified, studying the activities of lobbyists, and closely analyzing the votes of lawmakers.

Not so with the Fed. Most Fed watchers settle—like observers of the conclaves to choose a new pope—for scrutinizing plumes of policy announcements for their Delphic import. Many accept the fairy tale that the Fed's decisions are guided by objective truth and technocratic expertise. The result is that we stand nearly empty-handed in scrutinizing its discussions.

Time for a change. We have been busy beavers assembling extensive and diverse types of evidence to explain the Fed's actions. A major component of our analysis is a close inspection of the detailed features of the Fed's new programs in 2008–2009; we find in their meticulous designs a consistent pattern of favoritism. We also incorporate the explicit statements by Fed officials about their intentions in speeches and minutes; scrutinize the Fed's organizational ties to finance and deference to the cultural capital of Wall Street and other investors; and examine the Fed's institutional imperative to foster a favorable investment climate that sustains its budgets and political standing. In addition, we rely on comparisons to the decisions of contemporary central banks in other democratic affluent countries as well as what-if scenarios in order to situate the extraordinary scale of the Fed's powers and favoritism of finance. There were alternatives to the Fed's particular interventions in 2008–2009 that would have more effectively responded to the financial run without the scope of favoritism to finance and itself that it demonstrated.

We find that the Fed seized on the dire circumstances of 2008 to accelerate its long-standing development. Helping finance and selected businesses helped the Fed advance its budgets, autonomy, and capacity. By privileging firms in finance, the Fed activated and used their intense support for its policies and institutional position during turbulent and potentially threatening times.

Engineering Dependence and Loyalty

One of the most striking features of American politics and policymaking is the degree of nonparticipation. Only a fraction of eligible voters cast ballots in midterm elections, and only a bit more than half typically turn out for presidential candidates. Engagement in policymaking is thinner. Rampant withdrawal has often been attributed to the flaws of citizens—laziness, ignorance, and irresponsibility. But let's be candid: citizen detachment in the United States is often engineered and encouraged. Elite fears of "too much democracy" are a familiar theme not only in the nineteenth-century battles over banking, but also in our own time.[29]

The Fed Activates Finance

How government officials design benefits invites some groups and individuals into the policy process while leaving others with little interest, motivation, or resources to participate.[30] Older Americans are today's supercitizens, and the reason is telling. Our contributions to Social Security through payroll taxes and the checks we and our families get back upon retirement were devised to invite the perception of "earned right." "With those taxes in there," Roosevelt explained, "no damn politician can ever scrap my Social Security program" without motivating a backlash from those who have already contributed.[31] As planned, Social Security has spurred seniors to see their stake in the program and stimulated a large dues-paying organization (AARP), which equates its future to informing and activating seniors. The result: voting participation among seniors is now at exceptionally high levels in order to protect and expand programs that serve them.[32] Seniors have a reason to vote, and politicians are leery of proposals to reform Social Security that may ignite a backlash and cost them their jobs.[33] Before Social Security, the turnout by seniors at election time was similar to other groups who were also unsure of their immediate and large stakes.

Policies designed with little visibility to the broad public often produce—not surprisingly—underutilization or indifference among the general public even while attracting the loyalty and support of its selected winners.[34] Tax exemptions and tax credits subsidize the cost of housing, employer health insurance, and other services. They are salient to business groups and their allies that benefit and support them, but are often invisible to most Americans (especially the less affluent) who are understandably indifferent.[35]

The Fed designed its operations to generate dependence and fierce loyalty within finance while submerging its visibility to the broad public. Its initial architects held out the carrot of stabilizing the US monetary system and establishing the dollar as a trusted international currency to activate Wall Street political investment in passing and supporting the legislation that created the new central bank.[36] Over time, the Fed's control over the supply of money and the terms of its use remained a powerful inducement to finance to cooperate and support its operations.

The pattern of enticing finance to expect and therefore press for Fed support continued during the 2008 crisis through the central bank's close consultations with banks and equity firms and its search for remedies to restore credit markets. According to internal documents during the summer and fall of 2008, Fed staff closely monitored the system's "god-awful mess" in which there were "no good options"—the "market is locked up and investors are moving to Treasury funds" in a "flight to quality but these funds are no longer taking additional [business]."[37] Their alarm escalated as they projected that the struggles of major firms would impose "serious adverse effects on domestic economic conditions and financial stability."[38] Regulators sized up the potential collapse of one firm (Bank of America) to spark a damaging domino effect that would "shake market and consumer confidence in financial institutions, resulting in spillover effects that could include deposit runs on perceived weaker institutions," dislocations in credit and investment markets, and "a disruption in global payments."[39]

"Can we help?" became a familiar refrain as the Fed and its New York branch shuttled among Wall Street banks struggling to find credit to cover commitments.[40] On cue, Citigroup and other banks submitted requests to the Federal Reserve for help, and Fed staff tracked the building storm—the rising "risk profile," "deteriorating liquidity," "poor asset quality," and the prospects of "major systemic effects."[41]

The Fed's conciliatory and supportive relations with finance greased the skids to shift from information collection to massive and direct aid to private firms. In the summer and fall of 2008, Fed staff moved into high gear to "avert a widespread loss of confidence" in key credit and investment markets,[42] and to "alleviate concerns about market functioning and further boost confidence."[43] Responding to the avalanche of reports from firms that were "not sounding good at all,"[44] the staff accelerated their efforts to develop new programs to "head off a massive run" and "prevent a loss of confidence in [one firm] ... from triggering a broader loss of confidence."[45] When pressed by the intensifying crisis in late 2008, the Fed staff entertained the possibility of supplying "*unannounced* financing backstops" to banks with the intent of supporting "market confidence" by permitting them "to face the markets in a business as usual manner" and to "continue the smooth functioning of the market" (emphasis added).[46] Among the options were radical options to "step into [the] ... shoes" of failed firms or entire markets.[47] As the credit market seized up because firms were pulling away from providing credit, staff floated proposals to "step in to provide overnight financing" and to replace "the credit provided by the clearing bank[s] during the day."[48]

The Fed's obsequiousness and activism was an extraordinary departure from the ethos of minimal government and self-reliant private markets that the Fed and its chairmen had long espoused. While the circumstances of the crisis required action, the scope and unilateral nature of the Fed's interventions were exceptional within the context of American government and the practices of other central banks.

Conservative ideology took a backseat to the Fed's institutional mission. The Fed equated the well-being of finance with its own.

The Lehman Boomerang

Lehman Brothers stands out as an exception to a long-standing pattern of Fed interventions to aid finance. But in this case, inaction created a boomerang that ended up reinforcing and accelerating the interventions in 2008 and 2009.

Before Lehman's collapse, Fed officials accurately anticipated that its demise would "cause dislocations (of unknown severity) for a fair number of investors and market players."[49] The Fed took the lead in organizing a consortium of banks and investors to "explore whether they can jointly come up with a credible plan to recapitalize [it]...to enable an orderly winding down."[50]

As the Fed mobilized to follow its established routine of backstopping major firms, it ran into something new and unexpected: political interference. Republican lawmakers and the top of the Bush administration chose Lehman to take a (last) stand for drawing the line on government activism to save big finance. The result was arresting: the efforts of Fed officials to salvage Lehman through government intervention were scuttled on the ragged rocks of conservative ideology, and the collision was an event.

The reaction to Lehman's collapse ended up reconfirming and strengthening the norm of government activism to protect and advance finance. Within the Fed's shrouded inner sanctum (the Federal Open Market Committee), Bernanke confirmed in early October 2008 that its failure triggered an "extraordinary situation": "virtually all the markets—particularly the credit markets— are not functioning or are in extreme stress...[and are] creating enormous risks for the global economy."[51] Lehman unleashed anarchy, or, according to New York Fed president William Dudley, a "massive coordination problem" among the global financial system's institutions and governing bodies.[52]

The lesson learned by Fed officials and senior officials in Treasury and Congress, however, was that inaction was potentially calamitous.[53] Investors froze credit markets and sent the stock market plunging 500 points. The Fed and Treasury adopted a mantra of "never again."

Lehman showcases the boomerang of ruinous inaction that propels unprecedented initiatives by the Fed that broke from long-standing practices and initiated a new phase of institution-building. Fed intervention, as Lehman vividly demonstrated, was necessary to meet the central bank's responsibility to serve as a last resort. The issue is *how* the Fed responded: slavish accommodation of finance that exceeded what other central banks found appropriate and apathy toward the credit crunch hitting everyday families.

Behind the Cover of TARP

As the financial crisis deepened following Lehman's bankruptcy, Bernanke, together with Treasury Secretary Paulson, pressed Congress to step in by passing TARP. House Republicans initially defied the expectations of finance that they would approve a massive rescue; they were greeted by the largest single-day plunge in stock market history. Lawmakers reconsidered and responded by enacting a $700 billion emergency bailout to "buy toxic assets" from the balance sheets of banks (as Bernanke put it). Performing ideological summersaults President Bush signed TARP into law on October 3, 2008. His approval of the biggest market intervention since the Great Depression demonstrated that the political and economic pressure wielded by finance and the expectations of government support trumped the ideology of deregulation and privatization. TARP renewed the industry's expectations that the government would rescue it and accommodate its needs as necessary.

The design and direction of TARP fortified the government bulwark against financial crisis. It also advanced the Fed's drive to bolster its institutional interests. The Treasury Department took the political hit for passing TARP, but the Fed pulled its strings from the shadows.[54] A former chief economist at the New York office candidly explained that "the Fed was really behind the scenes engineering [TARP]" by determining which banks received help and how much they were allotted.[55] Bernanke worked with

Paulson—as one senior Treasury official put it—to "design [TARP's] authority" to provide "ourselves maximum firepower and maximum flexibility... [and] allow us basically to do whatever we needed to do."[56]

Years after TARP's passage, it would become clear that the Fed had worked with Treasury to redirect much of the funding away from the purpose promised Congress (to aid homeowners and those facing foreclosure) and toward ladling money to banks.

The Fed targeted TARP funds to the biggest banks. TARP paid out $45 billion to Bank of America (BOA) and Citigroup—each.[57] The Fed also selectively directed its own loans and guarantees to them, doubling TARP's outsized support in direct loans to BOA and Citigroup.[58] The Fed's coordinated giving did not stop there. In September 2008, the Fed secretly funneled $107 billion in loans to Morgan Stanley—this staggering amount was enough to pay off a tenth of all of the delinquent mortgages held by banks. Another $10 billion was later shuffled along from TARP.[59]

As Social Security's benefits for seniors energized them to organize and fight to protect the program, the selective aid by TARP and the Fed reinforced and escalated the motivation of finance to defend and support the central bank.

Hiding America's Most Powerful Domestic Policymaker

An important source of power wielded by government officials and agencies, Max Weber famously explained, is "keeping their knowledge and intentions secret."[60] The Fed built secrecy into its operations. Outright suppression of information was one tactic. The shroud of secrecy enveloped the $1.2 trillion that the Fed distributed to banks on one day (December 5, 2008) and the $460 billion it doled out to the country's six largest US banks at other junctures. Digging up these rudimentary facts required a battle royale by one of the world's largest global media organizations, Bloomberg News, which went to court to enforce the Freedom of Information

Act.[61] The Fed eventually complied by releasing 29,000 pages and 21,000 transactions between 2007 and 2009, but it succeeded in making its releases piecemeal and stretching them over many months. Without the sustained, encompassing waves of media coverage that grab and hold the attention of Congress and voters, the Fed preempted public scrutiny and potential protest.

Another Fed tactic was to disguise its operations in jargon and in the tangle of technical adjustments in interest rates, guarantees, and other actions. While public announcements herald final decisions over interest rates and other crucial issues, the Fed deliberates and reaches decisions in private. Even for prying eyes, the process for making policy is encased in technical jargon about money supply (do you follow the M1 and M2?) and the economy. It would be difficult to design a government agency more foreboding to everyday citizens and lawmakers and more effective in shielding the Fed from scrutiny.

The Fed also dissipated intense public interest by fragmenting its aid. Its help was often staggered over time.

The Fed supercharged its capacity to act in secret by exercising a little-known authority far beyond anything anticipated. In 1932, the Fed's authorizing legislation was altered to create Section 13(3) to allow it to act "in unusual and exigent circumstances." Before 2008, 13(3) was rarely used and, when it was, the action was quick and narrowly targeted. From 2007 to 2009, the Fed jumped the guardrails and used 13(3) to execute the greatest departure from domestic accountability in America's history.[62] The Federal Reserve Board's Washington staff—with the aid of the New York and Boston Fed banks—acted in near total isolation to develop sweeping new programs, as well as implement and oversee them. Sympathetic individual members of the Board of Governors cleared the staff's handiwork.[63]

There were enormous consequences.

Betting the Country's Nest Egg

The Fed's exercise of 13(3)—along with its other tools of concealment—explains how it managed to secretly leverage half of the country's wealth in 2009 on its own.

Short-Circuiting Democracy

Banks and investment firms were, of course, acutely attuned to the Fed's blitz of new programs. But where was the rowdy debate from Congress that accompanies consequential decisions? Where was the president climbing the bully pulpit to weigh in?

A massive set of new programs were concocted in the Fed's subterranean world and controlled by it. The scope and signifi-cance of the Fed's actions were disguised and largely eluded the attention of the public and lawmakers. Majorities of Americans knew about and disliked TARP, but few appreciated the give-aways wired into the Fed's new programs.

The Fed deliberately suffocated the democratic process of de-bating important and legitimate questions. The Fed untethered itself from James Madison's system of transparency and ac-countability.

The Fed's reach for 13(3) departed not only from the US consti-tutional tradition, but also from the actions of its closest allies. In Britain, for instance, the Bank of England's interventions to purchase assets (rather than relying on standard tools of ma-nipulating its rates) were anchored in explicit authorization by the Treasury, which is beholden to Parliament. Instead of acting unilaterally and in secret, the Bank of England served as an agent of the Treasury in making purchases, and the Treasury stood publicly responsible for its operations.

The Fed Helps Itself

The Fed's secret unilateral actions transformed its powers. It broke free of restrictions that had limited its operations to a narrow set of banks, and instead extended loans and guarantees across the financial system. In March it created a facility known as Maiden Lane to in effect loan JP Morgan Chase $29 billion to entice it to purchase the failing private investment bank Bear Stearns. By December, the Fed created Maiden Lane II and III to inject $85 billion of loans into the faltering insurance giant American International Group (AIG). All of these business partners were far beyond the Fed's normal parameters—and they were re-warded well.[64]

The Fed seized on its radical reading of 13(3) to stretch its purpose from the narrow mission of stabilizing the money supply to the sweeping aim of managing the financial system. "Monetary policy cannot work properly," according to the president of the New York Fed, "when there is financial instability" because of its cascading effects on bank balance sheets, credit markets, and other operations.[65] The implication, Fed chairman Bernanke reasons, is to push the Fed into a greater role in "monitoring, supervision, and regulation" as well as direct interventions to support private firms—though he omitted this critical new dimension.[66]

Establishment economists and central bank allies—including Reagan economic advisor Martin Feldstein and, eventually, seasoned lawmakers—raised alarms that the Fed's mushrooming mission pierced the limits of its authority and intruded into the domain of fiscal policy controlled by members of Congress and the president.[67] Privately, the most senior leaders of the Fed also worried about the legitimacy of their actions.[68] Grasping for a credible rationale for the unprecedented assertion of 13(3) that would calm Fed governors, Bernanke quietly commissioned a staff paper on "what we mean by 'unusual and exigent' and how we determine whether those conditions are still prevailing."[69] Geithner also directed his staff to cobble together a rationale for its power grab.[70] The Fed's awareness of its unprecedented actions did not deter it.

As the Fed swelled its purpose from manipulating the money supply to intervening in a widening array of private firms, its integration into US and global financial transactions deepened. Some Fed governors recoiled at the massive assistance to foreign central banks and the prospect of the United States guaranteeing their credit.[71] Bernanke insisted, however, with the support of most governors, that helping abroad helped the Fed and kept America at the center of global financial markets. The recipe to preserving the attractiveness of America's financial sector, the chairman explained, was to reward and sustain the "strong preference for very safe and liquid US assets" among foreign investors.[72] What was the payoff? US financial investors and American consumers continued to feast on artificially depressed interest rates for borrowing and inflated equity evaluations—and it also reinforced the Fed's position as the world's preeminent central bank and linchpin of the global financial order.

In short, the Fed's mindset and actions reflected and fueled its powers. It capitalized on its already considerable independence and administrative capacities to expand its institutional empire and to aid finance largely free from outside scrutiny. Beyond the president's national security apparatus, there may not be a domestic government body with as much independence and capacity as the Fed.[73]

FOLLOW THE MONEY

After years of hiding basic information on the identity of the private firms that received aid during the 2008 crisis and the amount they received, much of the information has been forced out. Humongous-sized loans and guarantees to large, fabulously wealthy firms (like Goldman Sachs and others) are now in public view, and it reeks. Have you seen the grimaced apologies by Fed officials, feeding frenzies of fevered news reporters, and searing formal investigations that conclude with calls for resignations and legal action? No. Revelations of undisclosed colossal deals between government and insiders have not precipitated a backlash that swept government officials from office and demolished the Fed. This nonresponse marks yet another stunning feature of the Fed's response to the 2008–2009 crisis.

Fed officials deflected charges of favoritism by claiming that the central bank's actions served the broad public interest of saving the financial system. When pressed, Fed allies and former and current officials now acknowledge the enormous advantages directly bestowed on private firms (and denied to credit-starved homeowners and Main Street businesses), but portray them as necessary to achieve their public-spirited purpose. The magnitude of the Fed's response was large, they maintain, to match the scale of the crisis. That a Great Depression did not impale America proves the wisdom of the bank's approach.

Scanning the ramparts of the Fed's defenses, just how strong is this defense? Knitting a justification from a financial disaster it enabled and then confronted is shrewd, but not persuasive. As we discuss further in the next chapter, Canada's policing of finance prevented a crisis to begin with and then put out the brushfires that leapt its southern border without massive TARP-like rescues that were funded by taxpayers.

Penetrating the Fed's airs as a well-meaning guardian requires a new approach. General critiques of inside dealing and the tabulating of the Fed's actions are valuable, but they are not adequate. The Fed swats them away with claims of serving the public good. What is needed is an autopsy of the detailed terms of the Fed's actions to reveal how private interests were served.

Finding Favoritism

Much of politics is tilting the field to favor one set of interests and giving the lame leg to others.[74] If you spend time reading legislation that creates tax policy or new programs, you can find (with the help of a trained eye) provisions that favor particular interests.

The Fed's responses to the 2008–2009 crisis was sparked by a genuine emergency and by the risk that large firms might collapse, bringing havoc to the financial system. But emergency circumstances alone did not dictate how the Fed responded.

There is a persistent bias in Fed policy during the 2008–2009 crisis that was baked into its institutional development over time, and its prodigious construction of nine new programs (or facilities) to inject credit into select firms and markets.[75] The Fed's favoritism is on display in the detailed terms of its new programs, which we now unpack.

Program-Building

The building and operation of the facilities played out over the course of 15 months—December 2007 through March 2009—as the crisis escalated demands on the Fed and created opportunities for further institution-building. As Table 3.1 shows, the

confluence of real-world crunches and Fed maneuvering produced a burst of operations in late 2007 and early 2008, and then
a pause before a second spurt of program-building a year later.

The Fed unilaterally transformed its scope of operations, re-
drawing the boundaries of who it worked directly with. Its long-
standing and frequent clients were "depository institutions"
(familiar savings and commercial banks that take deposits and
were regulated by the Federal Deposit Insurance Corporation)
and "primary dealers" (20 preferred partners, usually a bank or
brokers through which the Fed directly trades and sells the lion's
share of US Treasury securities to the public).

TABLE 3.1 Federal Reserve's New Programs to Manage
Financial Crisis

Name	Date New Program Started Operations	Target of New Program
Term Auction Facility (TAF)	December 20, 2007	Depository institutions
Primary Dealer Credit Facility (PDCF)	March 17, 2008	Primary dealer institutions
Term Securities Lending Facility (TSLF)	March 27, 2008	Primary dealer institutions
Maiden Lane I (MLI)	June 26, 2008	Bear Stearns
Asset-Backed Commercial Paper Money Market Mutual Fund Liquidity Facility (AMLF)	September 22, 2008	Depository institutions
Commercial Paper Funding Facility (CPFF)	October 28, 2008	Commercial paper issuers
Maiden Lane II (MLII)	December 12, 2008	AIG
Maiden Lane III (MLIII)	November 25, 2008	AIG
Term Asset-Backed Securities Loan Facility (TALF)	March 25, 2009	Holders of AAA, new, asset-backed securities

The Fed responded to the darkening clouds with a rapid surge of new programs and unprecedented actions. In December 2007 it invented the Term Auction Facility (TAF) to supply loans and credit to depository institutions in order to fortify them in the roiling waters. With the failure of Bear Stearns in March 2008, the central bank intervened to bolster its preferred traders (primary dealers) by easing access to credit. It created the Primary Dealer Credit Facility (PDCF) to widen the gates to overnight loans from the Fed's discount window, and the Term Securities Lending Facility (TSLF) that served up loans to primary dealers active in the repurchasing of US Treasury securities (such as US Treasury Bonds) and other financial assets.[76]

The alphabetic kaleidoscope of new Fed programs may be mind-numbing in its details, but it presented one of the most extraordinary changes in the Fed's century-long history. It transformed itself from managing the monetary supply to asserting fiscal powers to lend public funds to particular borrowers—the traditional (and constitutional) prerogatives of Congress and presidents.[77]

As astonishing as this development remains, the Fed was just getting started. It busted out of its inner circle of bank partners to reach a larger and more diverse set of discrete businesses—traders in debt (known as asset-backed securities), the already mentioned investment and brokerage firm Bear Stearns, an insurance company, and businesses sagging under the weight of consumer loans.

The Fed unleashed three programs to convert two failing private firms into sustainable operations or attractive purchases for others.

- Maiden Lane I enticed one private bank (JP Morgan Chase) to buy a collapsing bank (Bear Stearns) in March 2008 by doling out a generous 10-year loan and assuming its dubious stockpile of mortgages based on homes, businesses, and derivatives.
- The Fed resuscitated the gigantic multinational insurance company AIG in late 2008 from a risky bet on credit default swaps that went belly-up. (Credit default swaps offered insurance for traders of debt who were stuck with loans—think subprime mortgages—that went bust.) AIG hauled in large profits

from offering protection to investors in loans (helping to bal-
loon its assets to more than $1 trillion), but was unable to honor
its contracts when the loans went bad. The result was a chain
reaction: the loss of confidence in AIG provoked more redemp-
tions from investors and thwarted its ability to raise credit to
avoid default. The Fed flagged AIG's looming demise as posing
"significant systemic risks" to big investors (including banks
and retirement funds) and to the overall economy.[78] The Fed
devised two new facilities for AIG and its subsidiaries: Maiden
Lane II provided loans for the purchase of residential mortgage-
backed securities (the toxic waste of subprime home loans)
and Maiden Lane III bailed out its speculation on debt.[79]

The Fed warmed up to its new role. Tanking big banks and overextended insurance companies were joined in late 2008 by three new
sets of customers. And the Fed responded with still more programs.

The Fed devised several programs in September 2008 to stem
a run on what had been safe: money market mutual funds. The
stampede of depositors to redeem shares overran mutual funds
and overtook its ability to sell even safe securities like high quality
mortgages. The result was unimaginable—several money market
funds (including the Reserve Primary Fund) "broke the buck,"
meaning that they were unable to deliver on their promise to deliver $1 dollar for each $1 deposited. The rush out of money market
funds became a gallop with over $140 billion withdrawn in mid-
September 2008 (as compared to $7 billion the previous week and
still lower at earlier points). The Fed created the Asset-Backed
Commercial Paper Money Market Mutual Fund Liquidity Facility
(AMLF) to help money markets attract buyers of their most prized
securities by lending money to banks and other financial institutions to make the purchases. The Fed was, in effect, giving banks
a deal too good to pass up.

At the same time, the Fed concocted the Commercial Paper
Funding Facility (CPFF) to restore a casualty of the financial
implosion—the routine practice of businesses raising short-term
credit for payroll and other normal operations by issuing an IOU
with interest or a fee (what is known as the "commercial paper").

The run on money markets stopped them from purchasing commercial paper and, in turn, froze credit for a wide swath of businesses. The Fed's CPFF created a new market for commercial paper by directly purchasing from private business.

Take a deep breath: there's more to come.

The third new addition from outside the Fed's usual ambit of banks was the large business in consumer credit—loans to purchase automobiles, operate small businesses, and pursue higher education. In April 2009 the Fed created the Term Asset-Backed Securities Loan Facility (TALF) to free up consumer credit, which was aimed at reigniting consumer buying and the economy that depends on it. The purpose of TALF was to attract investors to purchasing consumer loans—another form of trading debt.[80]

Read the Fine Print

On its own and without the authorization of Congress or the president, the Fed revolutionized who it helped and how it operated. The Fed's autonomy and its capacity to write its own marching orders may be without parallel in modern domestic policy.

The Fed's unilateral actions not only expanded its scope across the economy, but also targeted benefits on finance. Its beneficiaries were not everyday Americans; they were private banks and other parts of the financial system that joined the frenzied search for profits instead of honoring their responsibilities to make prudent loans. The name of this game is: "They get the profits when times are good; we get the losses when times are bad."

Understanding the Fed's favoritism requires us to read the fine print.

The Fed's introduction of three new features tells us a lot about its exercise of power and favoritism. First, the Fed's justification for its extraordinary actions oscillated from claims to exercise its traditional authority to manage liquidity (the discount window) to assertions of its 13(3) emergency powers to unilaterally tailor its new facilities as it saw fit. Second, the Fed altered the long-standing limit on its credit to overnight advances. It agreed to unheard-of durations that ranged from 28 days up to 10 years.

Third, the Fed abandoned its prior requirements for conservative, reliable securities as collateral as the basis for receiving loans. Its new programs dramatically loosened collateral requirements; the Fed eventually accepted securities of dubious value and with uncertain prospects for being redeemed. This was an enormous change that posed great risk to the Fed (and taxpayers), and an alluring deal for investors.

An Invitation to Being Taken Advantage Of

How did the detailed features of the Fed's programs favor finance?

A peek into the Fed's most confidential meetings reveals refreshingly candid reservations about its selective generosity. As the Fed wrestled with the unraveling of Bear Stearns in March 2008, president of the Dallas Fed, Richard Fisher, pointed to the "carrot side" of the facilities that the Fed was designing and asked, "What do we get in return [for] . . . taking lesser-quality paper in return for high-quality paper?" He confided that he was *worried about being taken advantage of*" (emphasis added).[81] Charles Plosser, president of the Philadelphia Fed, agreed, pointing to a "slippery slope" of "taking assets" from other distressed investments.[82] The vice chair of the Fed's Board of Governors, Donald Kohn, reached a similar conclusion, stating that the Fed was crossing a line that sets a precedent and introduced "moral hazards" and "reputational risks."[83]

Four Features of the Fed's Facilities

What were the carrots that piped profits into banks? We trace four core features of the new programs that show increasing Fed accommodation of finance and generosity as the facilities developed from 2007 to 2009. We created ordinal measures of Fed deference and generosity to finance, which ranged from stringent rules and terms at the low end of the continuum to lavish benefits at the high end.[84]

Authorizing New Fed Interventions. We traced whether the Fed was restrained to using its traditional authority to manage liquidity through the discount window when constructing its facilities (we coded this low), or exercised its rarely used emergency powers under Sec 13(3) to generate the autonomy to cater to the industry (coded high). We also identified a middle ranking when the Fed relied on both; TSLF initially relied on the discount window operations alone, but switched in May 2008 to Sec. 13(3) authority. Greater autonomy to act expanded the Fed's discretion to tailor its programs to selected firms—from Bear Stearns to insurers, mutual funds and other private business outside the Fed's legal authority.

Targeting Financial Institutions. We examined whether the Fed restricted itself to working with its traditional set of clients that follow rigorous guidelines (depository institutions and primary dealers, coded low) or unilaterally widened its distribution of loans and guarantees to private businesses in credit markets (issuers of commercial paper were assigned a middle ranking) and, still more boldly, to firms like Bear Stearns and AIG that were far outside the central bank's purview of managing the monetary supply (coded high). The Fed's expansion of its scope translated into widening the class of firms that received generous loans and guarantees.

Lengthening Loan Duration. We tracked whether the Fed retained its traditionally stringent terms—overnight loans or 28 days in emergency circumstances (coded low); expanded the duration of loans modestly (84 days to 270 days, middle ranking); or stretched out the loans extravagantly (loans for three to 10 years were coded high). Granting firms access to low-priced capital for longer periods of time translated into an enormous, selective subsidy for the anointed firms: it enabled the fortunate few to leverage the cheap money for gain.

Loosening Collateral Requirements. We investigated whether the Fed insisted on conservative, highly reliable securities as collateral for receiving loans (coded low),[85] accepted a somewhat looser but still demanding collateral (middle ranking),[86] or dramatically loosened collateral requirements to accommodate banks, investment firms, and businesses (coded high).[87] Increasing the leniency of collateral requirements to the point of accepting instruments of dubious and uncertain value was another generous allowance. This concession, as we discuss below, occurred as everyday homeowners and Main Street businesses faced requirements for high-quality collateral, if they were fortunate enough to find available creditors.

A Pattern of Favoritism

Why were the presidents of the Fed banks alarmed at their carrots? The answer: an unmistakable and startling pattern of increasing Fed deference and generosity to private firms as the new facilities were designed in 2007–2009. Figures 3.1 to 3.4 present the over-time arc of Fed designs across four central design features: authorization, scope, loan duration, and collateral requirements.

Going It Alone. Figure 3.1 shows that the Fed began its interventions in 2007 by working within its established authority to create TAF (December) and TSLF (March 2008) before going unilateral by using 13(3) to establish new programs. In particular, the Fed broke free to create the three Maiden Lane facilities as well as AMLF, CPFF, TALF, and, over time, the rejiggered TSLF. The sharp arc toward prerogative power enabled the Fed to tailor its policies to particular industries and businesses without the encumbrance of existing rules.

Transforming the Fed's Scope. Figure 3.2 reveals that the Fed initially responded to the crisis by working with its traditional clients among depository institutions and primary dealers. It sharply

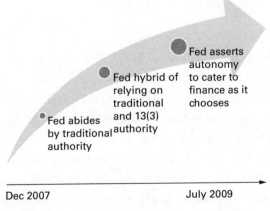

Dec 2007   July 2009

Figure 3.1. Fed Goes Unilateral to Accommodate Finance

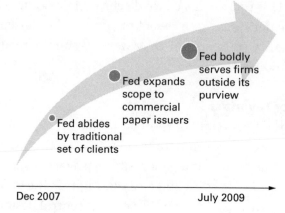

Figure 3.2. Fed Redefines the Scope of Its Generosity

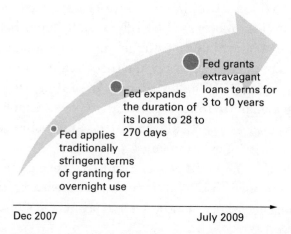

Figure 3.3. Fed Liberalizes Duration of Loans to Generously Reward Private Firms with Low-Cost Credit

changed direction, however, to crash through its previous boundaries. The Fed targeted single investment firms with Maiden Lane I (Bear Stearns) and Maiden Lane II and III (AIG), and then broadened its interventions in finance and economy with CPFF (manufacturing a market for commercial paper) and TALF (ginning up consumer credit).[88] These steps transformed the Fed's scope from its traditional purview (managing the money supply) to select firms and credit operations in the broader economy. The Fed broadened the reach of its generosity even as it targeted a few firms.

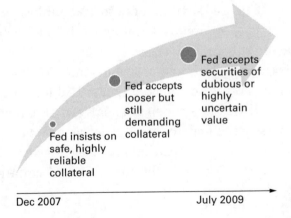

Fed accepts securities of dubious or highly uncertain value

Fed accepts looser but still demanding collateral

Fed insists on safe, highly reliable collateral

Dec 2007   July 2009

Figure 3.4. Fed's Growing Generosity to Supply Low-Cost Credit for Unsafe Securities

Liberalizing Duration of Loans. Figure 3.3 reveals that the Fed lengthened the terms of its loans from its traditional terms of offering credit for use overnight or 28 days in what was previously considered emergency circumstances—this was the case with TAF in December 2007 and PDCF and TSLF in March 2008. But with Maiden Lane I's loans to Bear Stearns and then more consistently during fall 2008, the Fed stretched the duration of its loans. It granted credit for 84 to 270 days in TAF, AMLF, and CPFF. The Fed then opened the door in Maiden II and III, and TALF to multiyear terms. The easing or near lifting of restrictions on the use of inexpensive Fed credit enabled private firms to reap substantial income and gains.

Giving Money Away. Prior to 2007, the Fed only loaned money in exchange for gold-plated securities. Figure 3.4 portrays one of the most striking abdications of the Fed's traditional, rigorous standards in the service of finance: it dramatically and consistently loosened its collateral requirements. In 2007 and early 2008 the Fed followed its traditional rules for conservative collateral for TAF, PDCF, and the initial construction of TSLF. Starting in late fall 2008, however, the Fed's Maiden Lane II and III and, later, TALF and its rejiggered TALF, accepted in effect whatever banks and investors offered—including mortgage-backed securities that were at the center of the subprime

loan bubble.[89] The Fed's willingness to take junk securities con-
stituted an unprecedented risk and put it in the uncharted territory of facing substantial losses.

In short, the Fed designed programs in 2007–2009 that lav-
ished precious credit on selected firms. Hidden in the details
of the new facilities is a consistent pattern of catering to targeted businesses: the Fed unilaterally loosened its long-standing
restrictions on which institutions it directly worked with, its
operational authority, and the duration and collateral of its
loans.

Public Good or Favoritism?

William Poole, president of the St. Louis Fed, candidly observed
in the Fed's premier policymaking body that its new terms were
gift-wrapped presents that "increase the bank's profits." Struggling
to square this payoff for a privileged few, Poole framed the Fed's
rationale: "The issue is [whether the Fed's facilities] improve the
way the markets are functioning, not whether it's feeding profits
into the banks and whether they happen to like it."[90] Despite his
later payday on Wall Street, Bernanke publicly claimed that he
"held my nose [to] stop firms from failing" for the good of the
country because they protected the unraveling of the financial
system.[91]

Absent the enticement of generous terms, the Fed and its cote-
rie of allies claim that banks and other businesses would have
turned down the free or cheap credit and the financial system
would have suffered. You might be wondering, why would a business turn down a good deal? They would be repelled, the Fed and
its allies claimed, by the stigma of borrowing from the Fed. The
president of the New York Fed, William Dudley, echoed the views
of other Fed officials when he insisted that the risk that banks
and investment firms "will be viewed as weak" would have discouraged them from taking the Fed's offers, and the financial system
would have collapsed.[92]

Helping a few, the Fed and its allies claim, helped the many. In
Yiddish, there's an ancient word for this kind of claim: chutzpah.

Let's start with the Fed's own doubts. Fed officials realized that their generosity threatened to mire Federal Reserve Banks in more "disputes," and make more firms "even more reliant on Federal Reserve support programs."[93]

Beggars can't be choosy. Firms like AIG grasped for Maiden Lane II and III as a lifeline that saved the firm and its investors from ruin. Bear Stearns and its suitor JP Morgan Chase accepted losses in exchange for a lifeline, but, unlike other central banks, the Fed was reluctant to use the desperation of banks and investors as a general rule to squeeze concessions.

What else could the Fed have done?

The European Central Bank (ECB), which was beset by crippling delays and false starts, did impose onerous conditions on banks in the (correct) expectation that desperation would trump. Like the Fed, the ECB tried to stop the credit crunch: it opened its doors to European banks by supplying cheap money and encouraging them to keep lending. Unlike the Fed, however, the ECB insisted on releasing the names of banks that received help, and banks still participated. The ECB's insistence on transparency was not popular with European banks, but the "perceived stigma attached to central bank borrowing" did not outweigh the payoff of cheap money. As one European financial insider put it, "there's almost a free lunch out there, so even banks that didn't need liquidity would be thinking, 'why not be part of it?'"[94] Why did the Fed fail to reach the same prudent conclusion?

Britain, which is home to a global financial center and shares America's philosophical attraction to minimal government and individual self-reliance, took a different and more assertive approach to the financial crisis. The British government, like its American counterpart, stepped in as a last resort to rescue its banks and other crucial financial institutions in October 2008 and January 2009, but its central bank and Treasury imposed stiff conditions. In exchange for saving the banks and building societies,[95] the Bank of England and Treasury required the operations to lend a hand to homeowners and small businesses: banks and building societies agreed to make available and actively advertise "competitively priced" loans and to "help people [who are] struggling with mortgage payments to stay in their homes." To make sure that business failure registered with investors and executives, board members were prohibited from receiving cash bonuses in 2008, dividends to investors were restricted, and compensation packages were directed to be revised to discourage reward for "failed risk taking."[96] These steps—from the stern treatment of failed financial firms to the aid to struggling homeowners and small businesses—were designed and implemented in Britain but ruled out as unworkable in the United States.

The Fed had alternatives and chose not to pursue them.

The Fed's intervention as a last resort was necessary, but again and again, what stands out is how much bounty it handed finance.[97] The Fed's free or inexpensive loans and guarantees for Wall Street and other firms did not just save them (as the public good argument claims); it generated profits and generous pay packages.

The attorney general of New York State discovered that the largest takers of TARP funding (Goldman Sachs, Morgan Stanley, and JP Morgan Chase) dished out bonuses in 2008 (nearly $18 billion) that were far greater than their net income ($9.6 billion). Here's the neat part: the bonuses were covered by taxpayers through the TARP bailouts, which totaled $45 billion to these three firms. And now some salt to rub in our wounded sense of propriety: the bonuses were directed to individuals who worked in the divisions that lost money.[98]

The secrecy that the Fed touted as a public good to avoid stigma turns out to be a friend of favored insiders, enabling banks and their sponsor publicly to disavow privileged giving while salting it away. Bank of America took $86 billion and its CEO, Kenneth Lewis, publicly promoted its success as "one of the strongest and most stable major banks in the world."[99] Not to be outdone, JP Morgan Chase CEO Jamie Dimon put on his poker face to minimize the significance of taking billions of Fed funds by chalking it up as a favor: he accepted it "at the request of the Federal Reserve to help motivate others" to use its aid. Here is what Dimon left unstated: the infusion was as an urgent step to nearly double the bank's depleted cash holdings.[100]

Why did the Fed and Treasury consider leniency and generosity essential to their success and reject the punishment that their European counterparts were willing to impose on banks and the investors that got themselves into trouble?[101] *The Fed's actions were not just discrete interventions; they reflected a long-standing mindset within the Fed that finance was a client that depended on their help and that amplified the Fed's own standing.*

The Fed's pattern of suspending its long-standing procedures to target gains to select firms accelerates an enduring institutional commitment to protecting and promoting finance. Even as the financial system shook in 2008, Fed officials continued to look up to former colleagues and financial head honchos, and that cultural capital translated into deference. They also appreciated that the unraveling of finance was a threat to the Fed's own institutional position.

THE FED'S ALTERNATIVES

While the Fed's chosen few prospered under its generous terms, other businesses, along with American homeowners, scrambled in 2008–2009 to find scarce or prohibitively priced capital to avoid huge losses, bankruptcy, or foreclosure. Could the Fed have stopped the panic, restarted the economy, and helped everyday Americans?

A quick sidebar observation: pointing to dire circumstances to justify the Fed's unaccountable power and its favoritism of vested interests is an old and potentially treacherous dodge of democratic standards. Using the ends to justify means can, without great care, lead to the abuse of power and the neglect of viable alternative policies. We focus here on the latter.

The Fed capitalized on its freedom to ignore, sabotage, or neglect policy proposals that may have dulled the pain inflicted on everyday Americans. Among the options that the Fed and Treasury bypassed were several that addressed a main source of America's economic doldrums—huge household debt and, specifically, the sinkhole of home mortgages.[102]

In 2008 alone, the whirlwind of panic and economic turmoil stripped $2.4 trillion to $19.1 trillion from residential property values and from the equity that Americans had built up and relied upon.[103] In the absence of policy by Fed and Treasury, the debt of mortgages sucked over 13 million homes into foreclosure proceedings from 2008 to 2013. For much of this period, about one of every 96 homes faced a filing for foreclosure.[104]

The Fed and Treasury behaved as if nothing could be done. The reality is that they ignored or outright resisted two policy options to intervene in the housing crisis: mortgage refinancing or "cram-downs," and the British policy of "funding for lending."

Cram-Downs

In 2009, the House of Representatives passed and the Senate defeated a reform of bankruptcy law to grant judges the discretion to reduce the principal on first mortgages for primary residences to their fair-market price and make other modifications. Here was a concrete response to the double whammy hitting many Americans—rising debt and sinking home values—and it relied on a proven approach: bankruptcy judges had a long and effective track record of exercising authority to come up with new payment plans for cars, yachts, credit cards, and more. The process repositioned debtors to pay back over time a feasible amount of what they owed—as compared to sticking lenders with abandoned homes that they sell at a steeper loss. Cram-downs, as the process was known, were expected to slow down foreclosures by providing an alternative to throwing families out of their home. It also was expected to motivate banks to negotiate feasible settlements to avoid an appearance before a judge.[105]

President Obama and the White House gave lip service to supporting cram-downs, but held back from pushing it through the Senate. Senior administration officials, including Treasury Secretary Timothy Geithner and his staff, were "personally and actively opposed to mortgage refinancing," according to George W. Bush's chief economic advisor.[106] Their objection—that mortgage reductions produced little impact—grossly underestimated the benefits of debt relief.[107]

The Federal Reserve's role was notable for its absence. Cram-downs were one of the few options for easing the stranglehold of the housing crisis on the financial system and restarting the economy in 2009. Indeed, the Fed's own research pointed to its feasibility.[108]

What if the Obama administration had pushed for cram-downs? Was it doomed in Congress, and would it have contributed to alleviating the country's financial and economic morass?

Cram-downs were not a magic bullet. They brought uncertainties and obstacles, and they also promised shrill political pushback. Mortgage refinancing, CNBC host and Tea Party instigator Rick Santelli charged, would "pay for your neighbor's mortgage [for a home] that has an extra bathroom [even though the neighbor] can't pay their [sic] bills."[109]

Of course, political and policy hurdles were hardly unique to cram-downs—after all, opposition against TARP was sufficiently strong to initially send it to defeat in the House of Representatives. Political power is what separates the two. TARP targeted Wall Street and banks that were revered within Treasury and the Fed; homeowners lacked the cultural capital and were subject to dismissal as irresponsible and ill-informed. TARP also enjoyed sustained, intense support and lobbying from banks and Wall Street; no comparable organized force backed mortgage refinancing. Its potential beneficiaries were scattered and uncertain about their stakes.

But there was a compelling case for cram-downs if the Obama administration had spotlighted the stakes for everyday Americans and rallied organized support, as it did with health care reform.[110] Charges that cram-downs rewarded irresponsible borrowers collided with the reality of bankruptcy proceedings: homeowners who received relief would be chained to a budget for up to five years that the court would monitor. Although banks and Wall Street enjoy strong cultural standing within the Fed and Treasury, many Americans faced with foreclosure were caricatured as undeserving. But many were victims who were lured into dubious mortgages by hucksters and frauds, as the nonpartisan Financial Crisis Inquiry Commission documented.[111]

Banks weighed in loudly against cram-downs, because they did not want to acknowledge the losses they suffered. But their warnings about impending spikes in interest rates and a rash of reckless borrowing were blunted by the Fed's research and the testimony of Federal bankruptcy judges.[112]

Cram-downs represented a feasible but rejected new dimension to the Fed's arsenal, one aimed at reducing the debt of American families that was depressing demand and holding back the economy. Debt relief through mortgage refinancing may well have contributed to reviving the housing sector and the broader economy.[113]

Learning from the Bank of England

England deployed several programs to reduce family debt and forestall the devastation of foreclosure that were ignored by the Fed. We have already discussed the requirements that banks and building societies help homeowners and small businesses in exchange for being saved from failure. The Fed took a pass.

The Bank of England worked with its Treasury on another program targeted at struggling homeowners: "funding for lending" to support mortgages. In particular, they supplied cheap credit and, in exchange, banks agreed to lend to households and businesses.

Funding for lending was an effective shot of adrenalin for housing, the construction industry, and the economy.[114] Compared to 2008, its effects by 2013–2014 contributed to reducing interest rates to record low levels, increasing new loans to the highest levels, and lifting housing prices to its largest annual growth rate on record.[115] With residential housing in recovery, construction in 2014 shot up to its best levels since precrisis.[116] Funding for lending was so successful in reawakening the housing sector that the government suspended the program after nearly a year and a half and bragged about its success.

Homeowners were the winners. How many times have you heard that proclaimed during America's zombie crawl through the Great Recession?

The Federal Reserve chose not to make any direct effort to tackle the mortgage crisis stalking millions of everyday people. Neither the cram-downs nor the funding for lending were cure-all remedies, but they were alternatives to the Fed's fixation on finance and they had good prospects to help. The Fed had reasonable—though not perfect—alternatives and pursued neither.

THE ERA OF BIG GOVERNMENT—FOR FINANCE AND THE CHOSEN

Dire warnings of an imperial presidency that acts alone in committing US military forces and running diplomacy have rung out for decades. Headlines and libraries are jammed with feverish warnings of the constitutional crises sparked by the unilateralism of Richard Nixon's incursions in Laos and Cambodia, Ronald Reagan's arming of rebels in the 1980s to topple the democratically elected Nicaraguan government in defiance of legislation he signed, George Bush's responses to the 9/11 attacks, and Barack Obama's expanded deployment of killer drones.[117] By contrast, a comparative silence has fallen over the enduring domestic prerogatives asserted by the Fed.[118]

Observers of American politics a century ago would have been astounded by the Fed that stood astride America in 2008–2009. It initiated actions of unprecedented size and scope that favored finance by acting alone and in secret.

The Fed's remarkable political accomplishment during the 2008 crisis was to deliver selective benefits while skirting the kind of intensive political scrutiny that was common in the nineteenth and early twentieth centuries. The protests of the Tea Party and Occupy Wall Street did prick the attention of some journalists and alert citizens, but failed to ignite a social movement that stopped Congress, staggered presidents, or threatened the foundations of American banking. This quiescence was a product of the Fed's success in cloaking the extraordinary scope and favoritism of its actions—many of which were unknown by voters and even lawmakers, or only grasped years later.

Many of the Fed's concealed advantages to finance reside in its specific design of programs. The Fed delivered its targeted support in technical operations, dispersed it over time, and tailored it to particular firms. Spotlighting the distributional consequences of the Fed's action required herculean concentration and a mind-reader's insight into hidden records.

Why did finance win so decisively? One possibility is that the Fed was "captured" by finance through lobbying, revolving doors, and the cultural capital wielded by Wall Street.[119] The direct influence of finance over the Fed is bolstered by the tightening nexus of elections and money—especially from the superrich, who have benefited most from the astronomical profits in finance.[120]

The Fed itself is an enormous force, equipped with independence and administrative capacity that is unrivaled in domestic affairs.[121] The Fed's operations during the 2008–2009 crisis reveal an institutional strategy of catering to finance in order to mobilize its support and to qualitatively expand the central bank's authority, funding, and political standing. No wonder the Fed aggressively campaigned against enhanced congressional scrutiny, as evident during debates over passing Dodd-Frank and continuing proposals for new checks. In the name of defending its independence to serve the national interest, the Fed fends for itself.

The Fed's interventions during the 2008–2009 crisis favored the interests of both finance and itself. But the very magnitude of these successes triggered tensions and reverberations that threaten the Fed's authority and capacity in the next crisis. We now turn to the most peculiar consequence of the Fed's greatest accomplishment: its future legitimacy to intervene is uncertain.

4

The Fed's Legitimacy Problem

WOULD CONGRESS APPROVE a TARP-like rescue and acquiesce in extraordinary Fed actions during a future financial crisis? Would Americans and particularly the attentive public be as detached as during 2008–2009?

These are not idle questions. Financial crisis is approaching. We don't know when or what form it will take, but the gathering storm clouds are unmistakable: real estate bubbles, run-ups in equity markets that are unsupported by economic growth, currency gyrations, persistent stagnation in Western Europe and lagging growth in China and elsewhere, the rise of global debt above the already precarious levels in 2008, the risks of central bank strategies in the United States and Europe to stimulate the economy, and the resurgence of shadow banking that accelerated the previous crisis. The last crisis originated in the leveraging of unsound subprime mortgages in the United States. The next spark may come from Western Europe, Asia, Russia, or the Americas.

The threat is not simply a new financial emergency. That's inevitable, and hardly unprecedented. The peril is the Federal Reserve's damaged legitimacy: the public, press, and political class are challenging its mutant form of governance—its secret, go-it-alone style that practices tough love for homeowners while serving up generous bailouts for insider banks and investors. Members of Congress bemoan the TARP's bailout, and then move to another level of disbelief about the Fed's free reign: "TARP at least had some strings attached," one congressman observed. "With the Fed programs, there was nothing."[1] A former Fed economist marveled: "The Fed is the second-most-important appointed body in the United States, next to the Supreme Court and we're dealing with a democracy."[2]

The next financial crisis poses a dire threat to America because the decline in the support and confidence in the Fed saps its credibility and capacity to serve effectively as a last resort. Echoing the assessments of many in Washington, former senator Ted Kaufman (D-DE) explains that "the public has no more appetite for bailouts. What would happen tomorrow if one of these big banks got in trouble? Can we survive that?"[3] The Fed's strained legitimacy handicaps its ability to rally the resources and authority necessary to stem the next run on financial institutions. After the backlashes from conservative and progressive populists, it will be more difficult for future Congresses to approve a blank check of the magnitude of TARP and to look the other way as the Fed concocts rescues to accommodate finance.

The Fed's predicament is more than a cyclical dip in confidence or a momentary venting that will recede and leave the central bank stronger and more dominant. It has built itself a self-tightening knot: as the Fed expands its prerogatives to act unilaterally, it erodes its legitimacy and degrades its effectiveness to serve as a last resort in times of genuine crisis.

The Wall Street Reform and Consumer Protection Act of 2010—or Dodd-Frank—is the most significant change to how Wall Street operates since the Great Depression. And yet Dodd-Frank came to embody the Fed's predicament. On the one hand, the central bank's dominance convinced lawmakers to ratchet up expectations that it can prevent the next financial crisis, and, when calamity threatens, expeditiously head off its worst effects.

On the other hand, lawmakers' distrust of the Fed prompted them to withhold or check the Fed's practical power to act effectively to meet new responsibilities. Dodd-Frank invites other agencies to check the Fed, encourages public scrutiny, and puts the onus on the Fed to secure congressional approval to exercise certain powers—a daunting new prospect given the long-standing difficulty of passing legislation. At the height of the Fed's powers, the hurdles to congressional action protected the Fed from meddling and gave it enormous latitude. After Dodd-Frank, important aspects of the Fed's power require Congress to act—inaction has become a check on the Fed.

Dodd-Frank's biggest flaw, however, is that it misdiagnosed the problem and missed an opportunity to initiate a new direction. The focus of Dodd-Frank was on administrative tweaks instead of restoring the legitimacy and effectiveness of financial management. The sobering reality is that America is vulnerable to another and perhaps quite severe crisis that originates in financial calamity and spreads to democratic governance.

THE FED'S DEPLETED LEGITIMACY

Why is the Fed still under fire? After all, the panic of 2008 was calmed, and the country averted a tumble into a Great Depression. In addition, significant components of the Fed's rescues have been repaid with interest, though its exposure remains substantial.[4] Former officials and finance insiders are mystified: rather than taking grief, the Fed should "take credit." Its policies were "what they had to do to avoid a much more severe macro outcome."[5]

How the Fed operated, however, damaged its legitimacy.[6] The Fed's actions punctured the standards it encouraged—that its technocratic expertise would protect against severe crisis. The Fed's failure to adequately regulate banks prior to 2008 and its later neglect of family debt and its drag on economic recovery undermined expectations about its expert performance. A second Great Depression was averted, but elites and the public were alarmed at how close America came to another disaster, and by the persistence well after 2008 of searing economic pain for people who lost savings, jobs, and homes. Years after the implosion in the fall of 2008, Democrats and progressives as well as Republicans and conservatives blame the Fed for things having "gotten worse" in terms of higher unemployment and stagnating wages.[7]

Its extensive deployment of 13(3) to take unilateral actions may have burst through its legal boundaries, and it certainly defied long-standing precedents and expectations about its operations. Independent observers are struck by the central bank's emergence as a "titan" that acts as "the primary economic policymaker in the United States, and therefore the world."[8] The claims by the Fed and its allies that dire circumstances dictated extreme measures collide with normative beliefs about American governance and the organizing principles enshrined by James Madison and the system of checks and balances. Crisis management is not a sustainable basis for legitimacy; it undermines the Fed's claims to technocratic expertise and exposes itself to searing questions about its normative justification.

Legitimacy depends on the rightful use of power. The Fed's actions, however, offended the basic rationale for its power: serving as a steward of the national interest. The Fed defended its rescues of banks and investors as restoring the financial system for everyone's benefit. But this defense did not stop lawmakers and the public from recoiling at the tilt in the Fed's policy: tough love for homeowners and help for banks responsible for the crisis. Even guarded commentators point to "the appearance of favoritism that can undermine public faith."[9] For generations, the Fed succeeded in concealing its routine operations with Wall Street and investors; its responses in 2008–2009 brought much of that into public view, along with the Fed's personal ties and its institutional dependence on finance. The Fed's claim to serve the national interest has been overtaken by the salient reality of its targeted benefits for a special interest.

The Fed has created for itself a punishing paradox. The more "help" the Fed supplies by acting alone to attempt to steady finance, the more it politicizes its mutant operations in the American system of accountable governance.

There is no clear escape. Scaling back the Fed's power is unthinkable to central bank officials after a century of amassing power. And yet moving forward is costly to itself and to finance.

The erosion of public and congressional credibility is prompting more scrutiny and legislative resistance to extending open-ended authorization. It is also making it harder for the Fed to work in the shadows and exploit its low profile to operate with little or no public inspection.

THE FED ON THE RUN

The Fed's tarnished legitimacy took several tangible forms: the decline in public confidence and support, and the backlash from members of Congress. The unraveling of public acquiescence and elite consensus, which had sustained the Fed's growth for generations, contributed to Dodd-Frank's efforts to encumber the Fed.

The Public Backlash

The general trend of public opinion about the Fed since the 1980s is downward, with a sustained drop after the 2008 crisis.[10] Figure 4.1 shows that evaluation of the job performed by the Fed chair had declined by a third since 1984.[11] From 59 percent in November 1984, approval of Chair Alan Greenspan's job declined to 51 percent in September 1988. It rose as high as the 70 percent level during the first half of the 2000s and then fell during the second half to 40 percent approval or below, with one exception in March 2007.

What might explain the sustained unpopularity of the Fed's leader? Maybe Americans just don't know enough. The proportion who indicate that they "don't know" and refuse to offer their views about the chair varies widely—from around 10 percent in the mid-1980s to 45 percent in 2007. It may be true that after Greenspan's nearly two-decade run as Fed chair the public was uncertain about who was chair, and this may have contributed to the sharply lower ratings for Bernanke after he took the helm in February 2006. This possibility, however, is contradicted by the pattern of lower "don't know" responses (and presumably greater familiarity) and the spike of disapproval in 2014.

Recessions might seem like an obvious explanation for the overall slide in the approval of the Fed chair during three decades. Perhaps the Fed chair is being blamed for bad economic news and its responses.

Yet the data don't fit cleanly. The *decline* in chair approval occurs during three out of four economic expansions. Greenspan's rating dropped during the second half of the 1980s and 2006–2007, even though the economy grew. Bernanke's disapproval remained elevated even though economists declared the recession over in June 2009.[12]

The overall cycle of the economy, however, misses who benefits and loses from recessions and expansions—precisely the issues raised by the Fed's favoritism.[13] In the economic golden age after World War II (from the late 1940s to the late 1960s), the fruits of economic expansion were widely shared, and the rise of income benefited most Americans. In statistical terms, most of the income gain was taken home by the 90 percent of wage earners who earned the least. Even as economic gain was spread around, the richest 10 percent still received well more than their share— in the range of a fifth to a third of income growth.

Times changed dramatically after 1980 as economic inequality accelerated. Income growth was largely concentrated among the richest—the top 10 percent captured three-quarters or more of income growth during the last two decades of the twentieth century and nearly all of it since 2001. The vast majority of Americans read about economic expansions in the newspaper, but did not see it in their paychecks.

Returning to Figure 4.1, the dip in approval for Greenspan during the expansion of the 1980s coincides with the sharp slowdown in income growth for most people. With a few exceptions, the general erosion of chair approval occurs during two periods of expansion that coincided with a new era of inequality in which gains were claimed by the richest.[14] In March 2006, several years before the financial crisis that struck everyday people, a solid majority (55 percent) were already convinced that the Fed failed to "help people like you get ahead in today's economy."[15]

The pattern of overall erosion of support for the Fed chair is more starkly evident when Americans are focused specifically

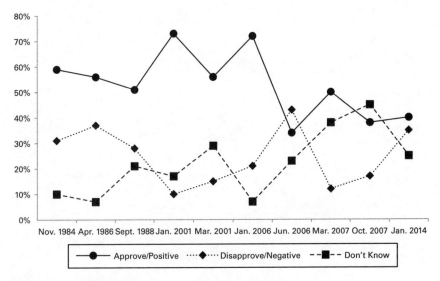

Figure 4.1. Rising Disapproval of the Fed Chair[16]

on the economy and whether they are confident in him or her to "recommend the right thing for the economy."[17] Figure 4.2 shows a nearly continuous decline from 2001 to 2014 in the proportion of Americans who express a great or fair amount of confidence in the chair. The critics who express only a little or almost no confidence more than doubles from 16 percent in 2001 to 35 percent by the crisis in 2009, and peaks at 46 percent in 2012. The disaffection abates a bit in 2015 to 31 percent, but still remains double its low and comparable to its crisis level. This elevated distrust in the Fed chair is not cured by the official end of recessions, but rather continues as the great majority of Americans no longer see their incomes rising.

Up to now we have examined evaluations of the Fed chair, and our focus has been on the performance of an individual. This may dilute, however, the public's reaction to the Fed as an institution.[18] How have Americans responded to the Fed as it aggressively expanded its interventions and the economy soured?

The public's backlash against the Fed as an institution is evident in its evaluations of the Federal Reserve Board. Figure 4.3 shows the sharp increase in the public's rating of the Fed Board as "only fair or poor"—from 38 percent in 2003 to 57 percent in 2009.[19] This severe turn against the Fed occurred as 98 percent

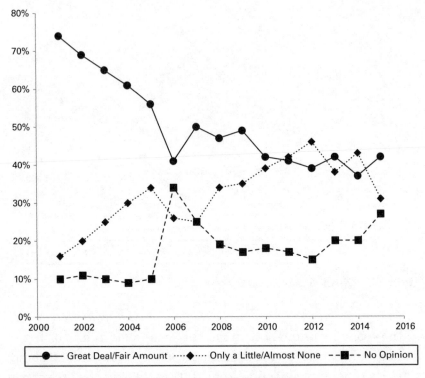

Figure 4.2. Damaged Confidence in the Fed Chair[20]

of the income gain was cornered by the most affluent 10 percent. Although the discontent with the Fed eased a bit, large majorities or pluralities continue to disparage the Fed's performance rather than rate it positively.

Another possible explanation for the Fed's sagging credibility and support is that its fate is bound up with an across-the-board collapse in political trust. While trust in government has generally declined in the recent period, the Fed's performance as an institution is judged far worse compared to that of other government agencies. Figure 4.4 shows that when the public ranked the performance of eight government bodies, the Fed ranked very last.[21] About six out of 10 Americans agreed that the Centers for Disease Control, NASA, and the FBI are doing an excellent or good job. A mere 30 percent gave the Fed that rating. How low is the Fed's standing in the eyes of Americans? The oft-derided Internal Revenue Service enjoys more respect (40 percent reported

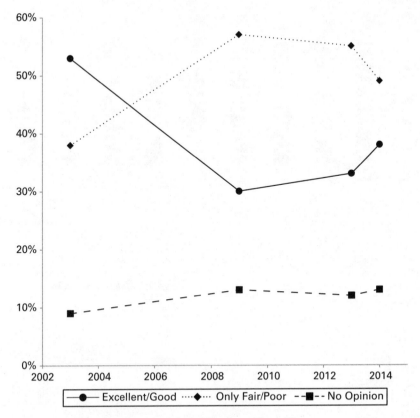

Figure 4.3. Discontent with the Fed Reserve Board[22]

that it performed an excellent or good job). Discontent with the Fed is not only a function of a general low regard for government; the Fed is singled out and scorned.

But does the public know enough to draw a sensible general assessment of the Fed and connect its policies to rising inequality? It is true that the public struggles with trivial pursuit questions about the name of the Fed chair. Figure 4.5 shows six surveys that asked Americans to identify the chair, and a plurality in two chose the wrong person. The "don't knows" were a plurality in two more surveys and close to it in still another. This is not surprising, as the public struggles with the names of other political figures, from US senators to vice presidents.[23]

Knowing the names of the Fed, however, is not a test of the public's understanding of what the Fed does.[24] The names of

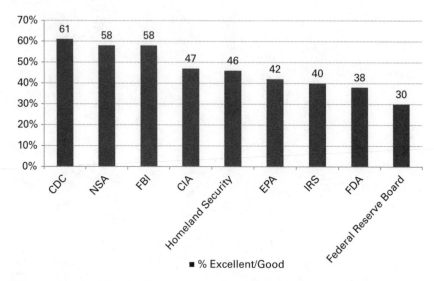

Figure 4.4. Fed Ranked Last among Government Agencies for Job Performance[25]

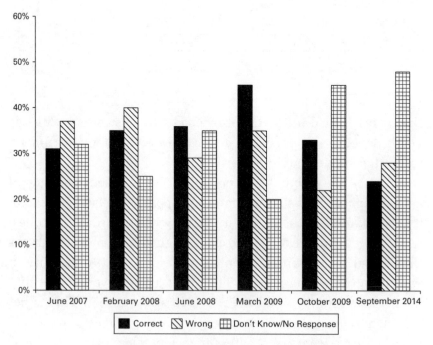

Figure 4.5. Public Confusion about Who Is the Fed Chair[26]

Greenspan, Bernanke, and Yellen are familiar to those of us who make a habit of reading the business pages of the newspaper, but they only occasionally receive coverage on the front page or on TV. No wonder they are not household names.

The public does have a strong grasp on the Fed's policy decisions and its institutional responsibilities. Figure 4.6 presents questions over the past three decades that shows majorities and, at times, supermajorities of two-thirds or more Americans who accurately describe the Fed's changes in interest rates. Similar majorities correctly know that the Fed exercises responsibility for "monetary policy" and setting the "prime rate." What's particularly impressive is that Americans are deciphering the correct responses despite being presented with a number of (incorrect) alternatives.

The public's scorn for the Fed also shows up in its support for far-reaching reforms and for changes to diminish its powers. Fifty-three percent believe that "the Federal Reserve is out of control."[27] This backlash flowed into support for significant reform, including 55 percent who supported the complete abolition of the Fed or making it more accountable to Congress.[28] Several polls found that seven out of 10 Americans or more

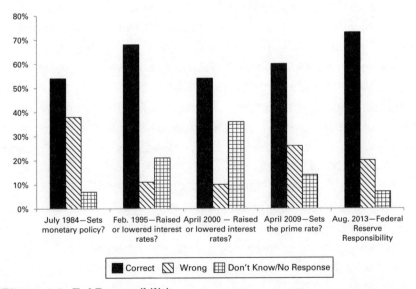

Figure 4.6. Fed Responsibilities

favored greater transparency, including a law to allow Congress to conduct annual internal reviews of the Fed.[29]

The Elite Backlash

The public's turn on the Fed fueled and reflected the unusual backlash by members of Congress, journalists, and other elites that continued years after the crisis of 2008–2009. The type of questions and challenges posed by lawmakers shifted. For years the focus was on the Fed's management of the economy and interest rates; after 2008 legislators remained concerned about monetary policy, but they also threatened its powers and ability to skirt accountability—the defining features of the modern Fed State.

"The last time we had any really severe criticism of the Fed," according to a former Fed governor, "was in the early 1980s, when the Fed was pursuing this brutally tight policy to keep inflation under control."[30]

Good comparison. Let's hit the history books to find out if the Fed faced threats to its organizational prerogatives and powers comparable to today's.

The Fed and its hard-driving chair, Paul Volcker, did face congressional pushback during the sharp recession of the early 1980s when the Fed increased interest rates to 20 percent and unemployment peaked at 10.8 percent (its highest level since the Great Depression). In congressional hearings, however, legislators targeted how the Fed used it powers, rather than its structure. The toughest questions directed at Volcker took aim at the Fed's economic and monetary management, especially its sharp increase in interest rates and the ensuing rise in unemployment. Senator Jim Sasser (D-TN) echoed the views of many Democrats when he singled out the Fed's high interest rates "as a chief cause of our current economic problems" that "are leading us to the brink of economic chaos." Volcker's responses were tailored to defending the Fed's management of monetary policy. He insisted that "excessive money and the inflation it breeds are enemies of the real savings needed to finance investment," and he predicted that tackling them and budget deficits assures "a prompt and strong recovery."[31]

The congressional pressure on Volcker to alter interest rates was intense in the early 1980s, but fit into a well-established pattern. Upticks in congressional hearings and attention to the Fed's rates are correlated to tweaks in Fed monetary policy.[32]

Today's elites—and, specifically, members of Congress—have shifted gears from the Fed's management of interest rates to direct attacks on the Fed's power. Observing the congressional salvos against the Fed's structure and prerogatives, a *New York Times* reporter dryly remarked in 2015: "Lawmakers in Congress evidently do not share Wall Street's obsessive interest in the exact timing of interest rate increases."[33] Lawmakers are "really beginning to wake up" about the scope of Fed policies, according to Paul Ryan (Budget Committee chair, 2012 Republican vice presidential candidate, and currently Speaker of the House of Representatives).[34]

The Fed as Bullseye

The new era of confrontation that the Fed has entered is not an isolated or momentary episode (as in 1982). It faces diverse and salient challenges that have persisted well after the recession was declared over.

One of the biggest changes is salience: the Fed has been pushed out of the shadows into the spotlight. Its arrival as a target was ignominiously marked by Governor Rick Perry's incendiary description of Bernanke in 2011 as "treasonous" and speculation that "we would treat him pretty ugly down in Texas."[35] Threatening the Federal Reserve chairman had apparently become "good politics" in the battle for the Republican presidential nomination in 2012 and 2016. Stiff (if more temperate) opposition became the norm, as the Fed drew heat from across the political spectrum—quasi-Socialist senator Bernie Sanders (Independent-VT) and populist progressive senators led by Elizabeth Warren (D-MA); Libertarian senator Rand Paul (R-KY); Tea Partiers senator Ted Cruz (R-TX) and former Republican governors Sarah Palin (Alaska) and Rick Perry (Texas). The antennae of establishment Republicans picked up the outrage on their right and left.

Another marker of the new ugly treatment the Fed faced was the record opposition to the reappointment of Bernanke as chair and the later confirmation of his successor, Janet Yellen, who received the thinnest margin of support on record. Opposition to Yellen was entirely from Republicans, but Bernanke (who was initially nominated by George W. Bush) was opposed by members of both parties (though by more Republicans).[36] This was just the tip of the iceberg, as members of Congress lashed out at the Fed's unprecedented assertions of authority and failed regulatory performance.

Withering Criticisms

The Fed's shield of technocratic expertise, which once induced lawmakers to defer to it, has weakened and given way to sustained scrutiny.

Bipartisan ire rained down on the Fed for failing to prevent the housing bubble by effectively regulating subprime mortgages. It was thrashed for misdiagnosing the severity of the financial catastrophe in July 2007, when it refused to lower interest rates as panic seeped from the subprime mortgages into the broader securities and credit markets.[37] Lawmakers marveled at its lax oversight that allowed big banks to mix our deposits that we count on with "enormously risky" speculation.[38]

False hope also sapped faith in the Fed's much-advertised expertise—its mistaken assessment in the spring of 2007 that the teetering housing market was "contained," its incorrect warning during the second half of 2008 that inflation was the top priority instead of heading off financial crisis, and its recurrent promises of vigorous economic recovery after 2009. The unease of legislators with the Fed's performance would have intensified if they had listened in on the Fed's private meetings; recently released minutes reveal a staggering cluelessness about the scope and nature of the crisis.[39]

Poor performance opened the door to searching questions about the extraordinary power and independence that the Fed exercised during 2008–2010. Echoing a disaffection that was shared in both political parties, Republican chair of the House Financial Services Committee Jeb Hensarling questioned the "incredible amount of discretionary power [that] has been imparted upon the unelected and relatively unaccountable." "The extraordinary measures of 2008," he concluded disapprovingly in 2014, "morphed into the ordinary measures."[40]

Being wrong eats away at claims for expertise; being suspected of favoring banks and investors is still more corrosive.[41] The Fed's rescues fanned the suspicions of congressional reformers and journalists that it was "too cozy with banks and Wall Street firms."[42] A spotlight was directed at Fed officials—including the influential president of the New York Fed William Dudley—for moving through the "revolving door" between lucrative positions in investment and the central bank. Insider connections were credited for receiving "a phone call returned quickly" and gaining entry to "the highest levels of an agency."[43]

The press and congressional committees spotlighted cases of favoritism. They lit up a regulator in the Fed's New York branch who leaked confidential information on its regulatory plans to a banker (and former colleague) at Goldman Sachs.[44] As another exhibit of the Fed's cozy ties with finance, journalists and lawmakers zeroed in on the case of Carmen Segarra, a midlevel staffer in the central bank's New York office who was fired after filing a critical report about Goldman Sachs and refusing—in her words— to "falsify my findings."[45] Senators Elizabeth Warren and Sherrod Brown (D-OH) seized on the Segarra case as more evidence that "regulators care more about protecting big banks from accountability than they do about protecting the American people from risky and illegal behavior on Wall Street."[46]

To journalists and lawmakers who were alarmed by the Fed, they charged that its conduct crossed a line. It had the power to clamp down on excesses in finance, but did not. It had an obligation to serve as a neutral public steward, but bestowed targeted benefits and gave the lame leg to the rest of America. Echoing the views of many of his colleagues, Republican senator Charles Grassley (R-IA) groused that the Fed's "benefits to Main Street have been questionable at best."[47]

Distrust and doubt about the Fed's performance fueled congressional scrutiny long after 2009. Instead of dissipating, scrutiny seemed to gather momentum. In 2013 and later, House Republicans led by Representative Jeb Hensarling (R-TX) launched what he described as "the most rigorous examination and oversight of the Federal Reserve in its history."[48] Reflecting a pattern of bipartisan discontent, Democratic senator Carl Levin (D-MI) joined in 2014 with his GOP colleague Senator John McCain (R-AZ) to investigate the Fed's weak regulatory record.[49]

A Barrage of Proposals to Strip the Fed of Powers

Members of Congress not only scrutinized the Fed, but also fired a Gatling Gun of proposals from the left and the right as well as from the common ground of bipartisanship. The barrage started in 2009 and stretched out for years.

Conservatives pushed to open up the Fed's operations to public inspection and congressional oversight—a direct assault on the Fed's secretive world. A conservative centerpiece, especially in the House of Representatives after the Republicans gained the majority in 2010, was to enact former congressman Ron Paul's once fringe idea of auditing the Fed. The thrust of the audit push was to enable members of Congress to use the Government Accountability Office (GAO) to probe Fed decisions to alter interest rates and to review its balance sheets.

Although the Fed has stoutly resisted House proposals for audits, the truth is that the GAO has reviewed the Fed since 1978. It gained new powers to examine loans, the use of contractors, and administrative arrangements since 2011. In addition, the Fed's financial statements are audited by professional accountants (which are now posted on the Fed's website).[50] Prying open the Fed is a trend that is inching toward its inner sanctum.

Another set of proposals from House conservatives aimed to restrict the Fed's discretion. One thrust was to replace the central bank's current dual mandate with a singular focus on controlling inflation (dropping full employment from its mission). Another reform was to tether the Fed's short-term interest rates to a strict formula that prioritized low inflation.[51] Its purpose, according to Republican congressional leader Mike Pence, was to "get the Fed back to its original mission on price stability."[52]

Although a number of Republicans were committed to checking the Fed, there were divisions within the GOP that slowed the most far-reaching House proposals. In particular, Republican senator Richard Shelby (R-AL), who became chair of the Banking Committee in 2015, resisted the House push for an audit (despite Senator Rand Paul's endorsement) and for handcuffing interest rates to a strict formula.[53]

The Senate GOP pushback against House conservatives and auditing the Fed mirrored the anxiety among Wall Street bank executives who were alarmed that "the once-quixotic issue is gathering more widespread support."[54] Banks and the US Chamber of Commerce remained stubbornly loyal to the Fed, convinced (according to the Chamber's chief economist) that "the degree of autonomy that they currently enjoy works well for the country" and that the "likelihood of [an audit] becoming law [was] zilch."[55]

Even as the House's most far-reaching plans to reduce the Fed's powers and autonomy was countered by finance and Republican leaders, Senator Shelby and other lawmakers did embrace reforms that, if enacted, would ratchet up transparency and congressional oversight by pressing for more and faster public reporting, as well as by trimming the Fed's independence. In a sign of the shift against the Fed and the continuing push to restrict the Fed's powers, even the cautious Shelby joined the push to rein in its authority and increase public scrutiny.[56]

Congressional Democrats share the Republican ambition to puncture the Fed's insularity and change its operations, but there were significant ideological divisions over the government's role.[57] Where Republicans wanted to scale back the Fed and government regulations, Democrats looked to strengthen the government's policing of finance as a check on the Fed's laxity. The ideological split was apparent during the legislative debates over enacting the Dodd-Frank reforms, and they continued after its passage in 2010.

Progressive Democrats led the charge in continuing to reform the Fed after 2010. Senators Elizabeth Warren and Jeff Merkley (D-OR) pressed President Obama to make "financial regulation and oversight obligations...front and central to the Board's work."[58] "The events of 2008 showed," they argued, that "when the Federal Reserve and other financial regulators failed to engage in appropriate financial regulation, the results were the worst financial crisis in 80 years."

Despite partisan and ideological differences, Democratic and Republican reformers joined forces to further diminish the Fed's power. Senator Shelby supported Democratic proposals to make the quite powerful president of the New York Fed a position that is appointed by the president and confirmed by the Senate. An odd couple in the Senate—conservative David Vitter and progressive Elizabeth Warren—jointly pushed for diminishing the Fed's 13(3) authority to act on its own and to target a few with exceptional benefits. In particular, they proposed to prevent the Fed from targeting benefits (it would need to be available to five or more institutions); its loans would be required to be 5 percentage points more expensive than Treasury bonds; and active congressional approval would be required to waive these restrictions, which of course is unlikely.[59] Sizing up these and other congressional proposals, Wall Street and its allies conceded that the Fed may see its powers limited further.[60]

The overall thrust of congressional hearings and proposals after 2008 demonstrated a sustained offensive to roll back the power and autonomy that the Fed wielded during the 2008 crisis. What stands out, according to a financial expert, is the realization by "the far-right and the far-left on Capitol Hill" that they are "in agreement" on improving transparency and accountability— despite their partisan and ideological divisions.[61]

Fed Damage Control: Too Little, Too Late

The scope and sustained nature of the congressional resurgence stirred the Fed to respond in order to contain the gathering storm.

Step #1: Humility. Bernanke and other Fed officials publicly accepted their failings, showering lawmakers with solemn sounding promises to do better.[62] Bowing and scraping is now part of the job description for Fed chair. Bernanke confided as he left office that "I had not entirely anticipated that I would spend so much time meeting with legislators outside of hearings" to calm the roiled waters.[63]

Sympathetic listening, however, works less well than in the past to coopt the public, press, and Congress.

Step #2: Goodwill Mission. Fed chairs opened a new public campaign to win back public confidence. Bernanke released more information about the private deliberations of the Federal Open Market Committee.

Step #3: Take on Critics. When humble pie and public shows of contrition failed to slow reformers, the Fed publicly took on its critics. "There have been criticisms from the right and from the left," Bernanke privately acknowledged to his colleagues inside the Fed, but he signaled that he was ready to repudiate the challenges to the Fed's power and responsibilities.[64]

Yellen arrived at congressional hearings equipped to defend publicly the central bank's powers and to confront threats to "the independence of monetary policy by bringing political pressures to bear on the committee's judgment."[65] Armed for public jousting, Yellen abandoned the convoluted language preferred by central bankers. Instead, she turned to barbed and direct warnings against making the "grave mistake" of limiting the Fed's powers.[66] Reaching for the Fed's tarnished mantel of public steward, she rebuked "efforts to further increase transparency" as a threat to the Fed's "ability to make policy in the long-run best interest of American families and businesses."[67] What the Fed discovered, though, is that its claim to legitimacy—defender of the public interest—was no longer strong enough to block reform.

Step #4: Accept Limited Change. As Fed strategies to cool the pitched battles with Congress and elude public suspicions failed, it rolled out a campaign of "soul searching" and announced inquiries by its inspector general.[68] But the effort, according to an astute observer, "looks an awful lot like damage control" and flopped.[69]

The fundamental hurdle blocking the Fed was distrust and weak credibility among a critical group of legislators. Serving the national interest became the rallying call for reformers: instead of viewing greater transparency and accountability as threatening the country (as the Fed insisted), legislators considered reform as urgent to protecting the national interest from the Fed. Reformers resentfully looked back at nearly a decade of important congressional decisions, convinced that public disclosures about the handling of TARP and the Fed's rescues "could have changed the whole approach to reform legislation." Fuller information about the Fed's activities, one senator predicted as he looked back on Dodd-Frank, "would have demanded Congress take much more courageous actions to stop the practices that caused this near financial collapse."[70] Senator Sherrod Brown and other lawmakers that supported legislation to slash the size of banks blamed their failure on the Fed's withholding of information. "Lawmakers in both parties," they insisted, would have "change[d] their votes" and effectively united "the Tea Party and Occupy Wall Street."[71] "The lack of transparency is not just frustrating," the inspector general for TARP concluded; "it really blocked accountability."[72] Even a former Fed official conceded that the Fed withheld "totally appropriate" information.[73]

Times have changed. The Fed confronts a new environment of scrutiny by the public and congressional reformers. The shift from acquiescence to public doubt and congressional oversight are not a cyclical uptick that receded after the recession ended in 2009.[74] Battle lines have also shifted: public disputes are not limited to interest rate adjustments, but extend to the Fed's power and scope of action. Restructuring the Fed to reduce its control and favoritism of finance is now on the agenda. Despite predictable partisan divisions, what most stands out is the shared Democratic and Republican skepticism about the Fed's inflated claims to public stewardship.

THE DODD-FRANK PARADOX

The Dodd-Frank reform, which was enacted in July 2010, represents the most significant reform of America's financial system since the Great Depression. "Not since the Great Depression have we seen such extensive changes in financial regulation," Bernanke observed, "as those codified in the Dodd-Frank Act."[75]

The purpose of Dodd-Frank was to prevent a repeat of the nightmarish cascade in 2008–2009 when the shenanigans of unregulated subprime mortgages and their conversion into speculative securities provoked runs on banks and investment firms, which in turn required massive government bailouts to forestall the toppling of the American financial system and a global catastrophe. The law's preamble promises to "protect the American taxpayer by ending bailouts." It pursued a dual-track approach: prevent the speculation that threatened "systemically important" financial institutions that could topple the economy and banking and, if disaster does strike, facilitate crisis management.

Dodd-Frank has reined in some of the most outrageous hustles that afflicted US finance and led to the 2008–2009 implosion, but it needed to do more than tweak regulations. It needed to restore credibility in *how* the government handles finance and, specifically, address the Fed's frayed legitimacy, which stokes the ongoing drive to scale back its powers.

Instead of solving the strained legitimacy of US financial management, Dodd-Frank compounded it by creating a snare and delusion. It lifted expectations that the Fed would forestall future crises of the financial system that put the country on the edge of another Great Depression. But in the new era of distrust, Dodd-Frank limited the Fed's authority and independence to deliver while failing to create an effective financial manager in its place.

Dodd-Frank's aim to forestall future systemic crises that would require taxpayer bailouts ended up making matters worse, in certain respects. It allowed the Fed's fundamental limitation— its damaged credibility that fuels the public and elite pushback— to fester, and left America vulnerable to the next financial tsunami.

The Fed State Grows

Dodd-Frank presents a curious historic twist: it originated as a backlash against the Fed, and yet it *expanded* its responsibilities.[76] After the Great Depression, the New Deal sought to prevent the next major financial cave-in by safeguarding consumers, individual firms, and their solvency—this is how we ended up with insurance on your bank deposits up to a certain amount, and other protections.[77] Dodd-Frank took a different approach by attempting to tame threats to the entire financial structure—what geeks refer to as "macroprudential regulation." The keywords for the new world of Fed responsibility are "systemically important financial institutions" (or SIFIs, for the insiders). The focus of regulators is on banks and nonbanks (like the insurance goliath AIG) whose commitments and ties to other firms (such as promises to make good on demands to redeem investments) have the potential to topple the financial system. Even if poor investments like subprime mortgages fail, the broader system should be able to absorb it and remain functioning.

Dodd-Frank loaded new expectation on the Fed's shoulders to protect the financial system and the result was a blizzard of new or augmented responsibilities—along with off-putting, shorthand jargon.[78] Here are three.

- *Higher capital requirements*: The Fed is charged with raising the amount of money or capital that banks and other financial firms have on hand for depositors or investors who seek to redeem their holdings. This new policy is directed at ending the bad old days before 2008: banks and other firms courted disaster by issuing massive amounts of debt while depending on inadequate stores of assets and unreliable collateral as their cushion to absorb losses.[79]
- *Stress tests*: The Fed is now expected to conduct a financial check-up of the big banks—those with assets over $50 billion (roughly the size of the Luxembourg economy)—to assess the danger of collapse. For the big banks that do tip toward bankruptcy, they need to devise "living wills" to permit their orderly unwinding. Designers of Dodd-Frank expected these steps to break from the permissiveness of the past when the Fed and other regulators (think Alan Greenspan) relied on finance to monitor itself.
- *Volcker Rule*: The Fed is charged with ensuring that banks separate their commercial activities (our savings and loans)

from their speculative investments. This is a case of going back to go forward. The Volcker rule (named after the former Fed chair) shares the general commitment of the New Deal's Glass-Steagall Act, which Bill Clinton terminated: restrict conventional banks that take our deposits and handle our checking accounts from taking on massive risks that can wipe our savings and topple America's system of finance.[80]

Dodd-Frank also elevated the Fed's responsibility for protecting consumers against the deception and abuse by companies selling mortgages, credit cards, student loans, and other financial products. The Fed houses the new task master—the Consumer Financial Protection Bureau—and is expected to work with the Bureau to stop, for instance, the kind of rip-off artists that sold the doomed subprime mortgages by determining if families could afford to make payments.

There are initial indications that Dodd-Frank's provisions are mitigating some of the most outrageous excesses. The Consumer Financial Protection Bureau appears, for instance, to be reining in rip-off loans.[81] The truth, though, is that substantial components of Dodd-Frank remain to be implemented, tested, and rigorously evaluated.

A Path Not Taken

Dodd-Frank's first salvo is to stave off systemic collapse and protect consumers. Its second is to improve the Fed's management of crisis when it hits. New responsibility is heaped on the Fed to work with banks to produce living wills that spell out their plans for recovering from a crisis and for going out of business.

The swelling of Fed responsibilities stands in stark contrast with the initial impetus for Dodd-Frank. Senator Christopher Dodd—an influential congressional leader on financial reform—began his campaign for reform with a probing question: "Why does the Fed deserve more authority when institutionally it seems to have failed to prevent the current crisis?"[82]

The efforts by Dodd and other lawmakers to scale back (not increase) the Fed's responsibilities were blunted, however, by two strategies. First, the Fed's historic effort to build alliances with finance as a bulwark against threats paid big dividends. The Fed and its allies in finance launched a ferocious campaign to swat down the structural reforms by Senator Dodd and others that would have fundamentally diminished central bank powers and prerogatives. Second, the Fed withheld damning information on the magnitude and favoritism of its rescues. This kept lawmakers in the dark and unable to fully appreciate the scope of Fed powers, though it also later fueled the backlash.

The Fed's two-pronged strategy defeated Dodd's efforts to strip its powers. In the well-known Washington game known as "turf," the Fed won—given the significance of the initial threats it faced. It also secured *new* responsibilities and increases to its budget and staff. For instance, it amassed three hundred staff to implement the 50 new rules that Dodd-Frank enacted.[83]

The Fed may have held its own during the first round with Dodd-Frank, but the fierce battle over its powers is far from settled. The Fed's sidetracking of Senator Dodd's most far-reaching plans set the stage for Dodd-Frank reforms and subsequent pushback.

The Fed Booby Trap

Dodd-Frank sidetracked Senator Dodd's initial interest in substantially scaling back the Fed's powers, but the central bank's frayed legitimacy convinced lawmakers to deprive it of the practical power to deliver on its responsibilities to stave off and resolve future financial crises. Institutional checks hamper its operations and ability to respond effectively to the next crisis.

Three factors account for the Fed's no-win predicament—more responsibility without the means to deliver.

Divide and Conquer

The suspicion that the Fed would cede new authority to benefit privileged insiders led to a familiar American pattern: the operation of new agencies or responsibilities requires the agreement of multiple, often competing parts of the sprawling Washington bureaucracy—a sure-fire way to break the kind of unilateralism that defined the Fed's responses to the 2008–2009 crisis. The Fed is required to carry out its responsibility for taming the systemically important financial institutions in conjunction with a new, multiagency body known as the Financial Stability Oversight Council (FSOC), which has 10 voting members (including some from the Fed) and is chaired by the US Treasury secretary.[84]

Will the government's regulation of systemic risk be effective and coordinated? Think of a three-legged race in which one of the legs of two people are tied together as they struggle to run. The new responsibility for consumer protection is housed in the Fed and strapped to an unwieldy structure that includes the Federal Trade Commission, Federal Deposit Insurance Corporation (FDIC), National Credit Union Administration, Department of Housing and Urban Development, Treasury Department, and potentially 50 state regulators.

The Fed is also stripped of its lead responsibility for handling failing firms. This is a break from 2008–2009 when the Fed sat as judge, jury, and almshouse for the likes of Bear Stearns, Lehman Brothers, and AIG—assessing systemic risk, crafting responses, and, if necessary, managing their demise. Dodd-Frank assigned the FDIC with the sole authority to liquidate giant, complex financial companies threatened with collapse in order to pay off its debts and obligations. This designation avoids the delay and disruption of the bankruptcy process and, over time, may erode the Fed's temptation and institutional positioning to concoct outlandish rescues. Finance insiders understandably quiver with anxiety that the shift will produce draconian changes. Instead of the Fed's luxurious paybacks to investors, the FDIC is expected to impose haircuts that punish investors and management for risks that go bad.[85]

The dispersing of responsibility extends beyond the regulation of systemic risk. Trading markets (such as the Chicago Mercantile Exchange) presented another threat that Dodd-Frank pinpointed. Fitting with a theme, the reform paired up the Fed with the Commodity Futures Trading Commission to oversee them. In still another move to disperse regulatory authority, Dodd-Frank abolished the Office of Thrift, which failed to police chartered banks and savings and loans associations. Thrift's responsibilities were sprinkled among three parts of the federal bureaucracy: the Office of the Comptroller of the Currency (OCC), the FDIC, and the Fed. Fitting with the theme of divide and conquer, the Fed's responsibility for setting higher capital requirements is not wielded alone, but is shared with the FDIC and the OCC.

Regulation of shadow banking was also split. The swelling markets outside the traditional banking and trading systems were assigned to the Commodity Futures Trading Commission in general. The Securities and Exchange Commission (SEC) took charge of still other parts of shadow banking.[86]

Dodd-Frank's reshuffling of agency turf and anointing of new responsibilities fit into a consistent pattern. It applied the familiar Madisonian principle—checks and balances. The Fed garnered new responsibilities but lawmakers dissipated its power to pursue them alone and doled out responsibility to other agencies. If the Fed attempted to widen its operations (as is its habit), it would likely bump into agencies jealous of their institutional position and primed to defend them.

Dodd-Frank's embrace of Madison invites multiple and competing lines of authority and the predictable result—agency rivalry, administrative confusion, and policy stalemate in the management of finance. In opting for division and deadlock, Dodd-Frank opted for a style of American governance that harkens back to the Fed's origins when it was hobbled by confusion and conflict.[87] Inaction was chosen over allowing the Fed to continue to use its authority unilaterally and to the benefit of the privileged few.

Shining a Bright Light

Dodd-Frank built in new provisions for public reporting to penetrate the Fed's prior strategy of concealing its operations in order to quietly dole out sweetheart terms. It is under new requirements to identify firms that are being aided to congressional leaders and its oversight committees—the House Financial Services Committee and the Senate Banking Committee.[88] Audits are another means for opening up the Fed's operations to public inspection. Dodd-Frank authorizes the Government Accountability Office to audit the Fed's emergency loans and credit facilities and, more generally, assigns the Comptroller General to audit the Fed Board as well as banks and credit institutions. "Our representatives in Congress," a former Fed official observes, need "information so they can oversee the Fed."[89] (These audits differ from those proposed by Republican conservatives.)[90]

New reporting requirements introduce a potentially significant check on Fed actions. First, it empowers searching congressional oversight. There is a long history of lawmakers ducking their responsibilities to conduct effective oversight of the Fed: "Why cause trouble?" Dodd-Frank ratchets up the cost to lawmakers who look the other way. Second, reporting requirements bring into the open the identity of the firms and people who are selected for help, and sets up a potential chain reaction. The media is likely to flag who is helped and who is not; the public has the opportunity to question the unfairness, and Congress is then on the hot seat to take action or face the prospects of irate voters.

Scaling Back the Fed's Emergency Powers

The most deviant aspect of the Fed's response to the 2008–2009 crisis was its extensive use of the 13(3) provision in its founding legislation to act alone. Fed officials seized on this rarely exercised provision to recast its powers: it extended their power from monetary to fiscal policy and acted unilaterally to create new programs and to conduct the massive buying of bonds that were unparalleled in scope—both among the central banks in other democratic countries and US domestic policy. Dodd-Frank took aim at this deviant feature of the Fed. It did not terminate the power, but lawmakers did set new boundaries, terms, and restrictions on its use. According to a disgruntled former Fed vice chair, Dodd-Frank's new curbs on the use of 13(3) created "less room to maneuver" and "tied [the central bank's] hands" in important respects.[91] Correct, as a summary of reformers' intent.

Dodd-Frank imposed three new checks on the Fed's free-wielding use of 13(3)—limits that vary in their stringency.

Number #1. It required the Fed to secure the approval of the Treasury secretary to move on policies that shell out credit. This poses the weakest hurdle given the recent close collaboration of the two. The next two checks tighten the restrictions.

Number #2. Dodd-Frank requires the Fed to restrict its unilateral use of 13(3) to a "program or facility with broad-based eligibility" (such as the credit markets used by business for short-term purposes) instead of rescuing individual banking or investment firms like AIG or Bear Stearns.[92] The scope of the Fed's emergency powers is narrowed but highly motivated officials can likely generate creative terms to reach its targets. The first two checks justify the skepticism of Jeffrey Lacker (president of the Richmond Fed Bank), who declared that it is "an open question about how constraining Dodd-Frank will be" on 13(3) powers.[93]

Number #3. Dodd-Frank pushes back against the Fed's accommodative terms. During the recent crisis, the Fed broke with its long-standing insistence on short, fixed loan periods and high-quality collateral, and instead agreed to payback periods that changed with circumstances and collateral that included high-risk instruments (including mortgage-backed securities). Moving forward, the Fed is required by law to adopt stricter standards for loan collateral and to set a fixed schedule and means for repaying assistance from the central bank. These changes narrow the Fed's degrees of freedom: repayment is more fixed, and it cannot readily accept the toxic securities that it previously accepted.

Dodd-Frank's trimming of 13(3) was passed over the objections of Fed officials and loyalists. They described the changes as "impractical" and warned that they have "handcuffed (maybe gutted)" the central bank's necessary prerogative powers.[94] The president of the San Francisco Fed Bank ominously cautioned that "the risk of runs in financial markets remains a very real concern," but that the Fed's prior capacity to "stem a full-blown meltdown of the financial system may not be available in future crises."[95]

The concerns of Fed officials and its defenders are self-serving, but they underscore a new reality: the Fed now faces greater scrutiny by Americans and lawmakers and taller barriers to action.

DODD-FRANK AS SYMPTOM

For the Fed and its acolytes, the push for reform is an ungrateful and inexplicable response to rescuing the financial system. They recoil at "blunt[ing] our last working economic tool."[96] Former Fed leader Stanley Fischer lashed out at the "big mistake" of throwing away "things that could be useful" because reformers are "worried."[97]

Dodd-Frank is a symptom, however, not a cause, of the Fed's predicament. Its problem lies not with an overreaching Congress but with itself—a mutant body that has built unprecedented independence and institutional capacity, and burst the seams of America's system of accountable governance and the country's normative beliefs about democracy. It is the Fed's own development that damaged its credibility and set in motion the search for reforms.

The combination of Dodd-Frank and the political toxicity of TARP have introduced a new institutional logic for future interventions in financial crises. Before 2008, the institutional rules favored intervention. The most significant institutional advantage for crisis managers was that the Fed enjoyed nearly unlimited freedom and capacity. Although Congress could act, its default behavior—inaction—granted the Fed wide latitude to proceed. The legitimacy of the Fed and Treasury was enough to enact TARP, though not without a hiccup or two.

After the 2008–2009 crisis and Dodd-Frank, action by Congress is now required to approve decisive interventions that the Fed favors, and new rules open the way to public disclosure of who was helped and with how much. During the next financial meltdown, the Fed's power will be more hamstrung: it will need Congress to enact new policies to grant the latitude to use 13(3) to take targeted unilateral actions to save the next AIG. The old schemes of operating in secret are threatened by new requirements for public reporting: members of Congress who support the Fed's initiatives or would like to look the other way face the prospect of intense media scrutiny and irate voters. In short, congressional inaction shielded the Fed before 2008, but now the central bank is thrust into the unenviable position of needing Congress to pass politically treacherous legislation.

Dodd-Frank and the new institutional logic of financial rescues should trigger a high-pitched warning: America lacks an effective central bank. The Fed's credibility is damaged and its ability to act is checked. What's missing is effective financial management. Will America sail into the next financial crisis with a crippled Fed, or can it build a central bank with adequate legitimacy that can be effective? We turn to this question now.

5

Preparing for the Next Financial Crisis

REASONABLE CITIZENS, LAWMAKERS, and experts following the Fed's travails are stranded in a no-man's land.

On the one hand, critics of the Fed see through the heroic iconography of the Fed as a savior deploying its unrivaled powers in domestic policy to avert the dire consequences of inherently irresponsible politicians—runaway inflation and economic downturns.[1] Instead, their attention is riveted to the mounting evidence of the Fed's favoritism and institutional self-interest and the resulting distrust that has engulfed the central bank.

On the other hand, reasonable people recoil from extreme proposals to "end the Fed," as the title of Ron Paul's book succinctly puts the case. They recognize the value of adjusting the supply of money to stabilize prices or employment as well as stepping in when the financial system is threatened by runs on credit and collapse. If a central bank did not manage monetary policy and respond as a crisis manager, these essential responsibilities would fall to private or public entities ill-suited to the job, and the economic well-being of most Americans would suffer.[2]

Thoughtful lawmakers and informed citizens are searching for an escape from the box that Fed supporters try to jam them into: accepting a flawed and unfair Fed or suffering the dire consequences of ending the Fed.[3] This dichotomy is, of course, false. Effective and accountable central banks do exist and do not require, as Fed loyalists insist, extraordinary degrees of secrecy and autonomy. It is possible both to reject the Fed's favoritism and biases and to develop a central bank in America that is effective and held to account by elected officials to serve the public good.

Of course no system is without limitations, but the idea that the Fed has cornered the market on financial management is absurd. The effective and credible central bank that America needs is already working elsewhere with more accountability and transparency than the Fed. Studies of central banking show that greater accountability and transparency produce more effective regulation in other Western democracies and guard against banking crises and massive bailouts.[4] Faced with the prospect of public scrutiny and punishment by voters, regulators are less prone to cater to special interests, and politicians are more insistent on high performance from them and are less prone to support generous bailouts. In countries with systems of accountability, banks and investors read the writing on the wall: they are less drawn to risk-taking in anticipation that wrongdoing will be salient, and that elected officials will respond to taxpayers instead of them.

Look to Canada. A smaller economy, certainly, and yet it was largely unaffected by the 2008–2009 financial tsunami and made do without TARP and the Fed's jerry-rigged interventions. How did Canada succeed where America failed? It focused its central bank on monetary policy, created a separate and effective regulatory structure, and established a tradition of regular and intrusive oversight by the legislature.[5]

Time is short, however. America lacks an effective system for financial management after the erosion of the Fed's legitimacy and the arrival of Dodd-Frank's checks on its powers. The time is now to prepare to confront the next financial crisis with structural reforms to America's central bank and financial management.

THE EXCEPTIONALISM CURSE VERSUS WHAT AMERICA SHOULD LEARN FROM CANADA

There is a feasible path forward. The first step is to accept that America's approach to financial management has failed. The second step is to learn from the best practices in countries with vibrant democratic and capitalist systems.

America Stands Out for Appeasing Finance

One of the most enduring myths about the United States is its exceptionalism as a global model of excellence. American elites are fond of trumpeting national greatness and its sources—the country's frontier history, its embrace of freedom, and "up-from-the-bootstraps" opportunity.[6]

Exceptionalism has a more ominous meaning when it comes to managing the 2008–2009 crisis. America's uniqueness was its lavish, accommodating treatment of finance in a context of deepening economic inequality.

Other affluent democratic countries pursued assertive interventions instead of the appeasement in the United States. Their stringent approach was most evident in the conditions and pricing of government assistance. The United Kingdom, for instance, intervened forcefully by nationalizing failing firms and supplying financial assistance to banks at punishing rates and on the condition of aiding consumers and small businesses.[7]

Flippant dismissals of comparative lessons often stress America's philosophical conservatism—its preference for individual self-reliance and reluctance to use government. It's a reasonable point. Assertive intervention in financial markets did occur in countries that were already familiar with government activism. French and German intervention in financial markets fit with their large roles in banking, owning (respectively) 17.26 percent and 36.36 percent of the largest 10 banks as of 1995. The United States holds none.[8]

What stands out about finance, however, is that massive government intervention occurs in countries that normally profess conservative, anti-government homilies. Britain both aggressively intervened in financial markets after 2008 and is home to Adam Smith and Charles Darwin—idols of US conservatives and their embrace of government distrust and individual self-reliance.[9] The United States itself champions free markets, and yet stands out internationally for its big government interventions in financial markets.

Size of government is not a helpful guide. What does separate the United States from its advanced capitalist counterparts is *how* government is used. Where the Fed deployed its administrative might and independence to advance its own institutional interests and those of finance, other countries intervened more forcefully to restructure and reorder private financial markets.[10]

Learning from Canada?

Canada is an enticing model for US reformers. Canada's economy pales in size to the US behemoth ($1.83 trillion Gross Domestic Product in 2013 compared with America's $16.8 trillion in US dollars). While Canada's economy is smaller overall, its financial sector—and, specifically, its banks—are quite substantial. They regularly rank as among the largest *within* the United States.[11]

There are also similarities. Both countries share federal systems of government, extensive cross-border trade (the United States receives three-quarters of its exports from its northern neighbor), similar types of business (including some that are integrated across the border), and a shared embrace of the Anglo-American legal tradition.[12]

The US-Canada similarities stop when it comes to management of their financial sectors. America is approaching a decade since the onset of the Great Recession and its horrid wreckage of lost jobs, savings, and equity. Recovery has started, but many are still feeling its effects. Eight million people are still looking for work, and half of Americans report that the country remains in recession five years after its official end.[13]

An entirely different situation reigns in Canada despite the potential spillover of the financial pandemic across the border.[14] In the past, Canada's banks were "challenged" by "systemic risk running through the whole global economy," according to testimony by a prominent economist in front of Canada's Senate banking committee. But Canada dodged the bullet of financial calamity in 2008–2009 by developing a "better banking system": it stuck by stringent regulations and steered finance away from the kind of speculation that was rampant south of its borders.[15]

Each country's handling of deregulation and Glass-Steagall illustrates a more general pattern. The United States responded to global markets and complaints by finance that government mandates unnecessarily hampered innovation and were excessive given the industry's rigorous self-policing: Democratic and Republican lawmakers embraced deregulation and abandoned the New Deal's Glass-Steagall Act prohibition on banks mixing their speculative investments and cautious handling of deposits. By comparison, Canada also responded to global pressures by allowing banks to engage in investments, but unlike the United States, it continued to insist on rigorous public oversight.[16] In particular, Canada paired the termination of its equivalent to the Glass-Steagall Act with the maintenance of stringent rules against excessive speculation and new oversight of banks and security dealers. One result is that Canada insisted that banks and other firms hold more capital to make good on their commitments.[17] (After the 2008–2009 crisis Dodd-Frank did require higher capital buffers from large banks and systemically important nonbanks, but lobbyists are scheming against them.)[18]

That's not the only way that Canada stands apart from the United States. Canada's central bank and regulators insist that the capital held on hand meet high standards—in fact, the highest standards for quality among the major advanced Western economies. By contrast, US firms often used flimsy securities, such as those based on subprime mortgages that could not be redeemed in 2008–2009 and which then precipitated the financial crisis.[19] "One of the reasons the Canadian system did respond so well and weathered the storm as well as it did," the Bank of Canada's governor boasted to Parliament, "was that our main institutions were adequately capitalized, even for a shock as severe as the one we experienced. However, the global system was insufficiently capitalized."[20]

Mortgages distill the cross-border contrast. With the Fed and other government bodies deferring to finance, US firms treated mortgages as investment opportunities. Lenders pressed subprime mortgages on low-income families and then converted these risky mortgages into securities and churned out enormous profits—for a while.[21] By contrast, Canadian rules encouraged banks to treat mortgages as assets to be held: their mortgages required larger down payments from borrowers than in the United States. And the Canadian Mortgage and Housing Corporation conducted regular assessments of the ability of homeowners to make their payments. Bottom line: the proportion of mortgages that could be sold as securities by 2008 was far lower in Canada (25 percent) than in the United States (60 percent).[22]

The long list of US–Canada differences reveals a fundamental divide. The United States welcomed a financial system that ran on high risk in the pursuit of supersized profits;[23] Canada's government put a priority on preventing crisis, minimizing risk, and establishing an expectation of banks as "managed prudently and sufficiently capitalized."[24] If there is a tradeoff between stability and profitability, there was no doubt about Canada's choice. In a decisive step that remains unfathomable in the United States, it stalled the trading of securities (such as subprime mortgages) by creating—and enforcing—rules that limited the securitization boom.[25] Its reward, according to the World Bank and other experts, is that it achieved "relatively low exposures to various structured products such as collateralized mortgage obligations, structured investment vehicles and credit default obligations."[26] For years before and after the 2008 crisis, Canada's banks were ranked by the International Monetary Fund (IMF) and the World Economic Forum as the most sound in the world.[27]

Are we sure, though, that Canada's vigorous policing accounts for its evasion of the recent crisis? Perhaps Canada's good fortune was owed to the infusion of funds from its petroleum business.

But 2008–2009 was not the first financial contagion that Canada fended off. Robust financial regulation helps explain why neither the Asian crisis of 1997 nor the dotcom bubble implosion in 2000 devastated Canada (as it did the United States) despite its exposure—its six largest banks earned half their earnings from international activity.[28]

You may be wondering about the regulatory tourniquet on the Canadian economy and the competitive disadvantages. After all, Americans are habitually warned of just these effects. The Canadians achieved stability, but how much did their economy suffer from "over-regulation"? Strap yourself in. Canada's economic growth, household spending, competitiveness, and returns to investors all stood out for their strength between 2008 and 2011.[29] More news: no taxpayer funds were needed to rescue insolvent or illiquid private sector banks or other financial institutions. TARP-like government bailouts did not happen in Canada.[30] Canada "weathered a very violent storm," a senior official at the Bank of Canada recounted, but "arrived safely in port."[31]

In short, what stands out about Canada and its central bank is its organizing principle: it intervened to structure markets to serve the socially desirable purposes of financial stability and protections for businesses, consumers, and workers. The Canadian pattern is evident in the content of its regulations (directive rather than deferential to finance), enforcement (consistent instead of irregular and accommodative), and socially consequential with regard to the operation of financial and economic systems. Canadian regulations create transparency and hold firms and government officials to account for their performance.[32]

Here is one of the most significant consequences of the financial management by the central bank and other regulators in Canada: public confidence. Instead of the Fed's strained legitimacy, Canadian lawmakers and citizens express general confidence in the Bank of Canada. When polled, Canadians overwhelmingly rate their banks highly for stability and soundness. Supermajorities of 63 to 90 percent of Canadians express confidence in the Bank of Canada's ability to safeguard the country's financial system and to protect their personal finances and economic well-being.[33]

A MODEL FOR FINANCIAL STABILITY AND EFFECTIVENESS

Why does central bank deference to finance endure in the United States despite its history of failure, whereas assertive intervention to safeguard the financial system took root in Canada?

The Political Dimension of Financial Management

Canadian central bank expert, Louis Pauly, offers one possibility: social learning from the past.[34] Canadian policymakers, he contends, learned from banking crises since the 1920s that financial disaster results from accommodation of finance, dispersal of authority, and rivalry among multiple and competing agencies responsible for overseeing finance. This recognition influenced the founding and design of the Bank of Canada in 1935 as well as the contemporary framework for policing the full spectrum of financial institutions—from banks and trust companies to investment dealers and insurance.[35]

Social learning helpfully redirects our attention from larger-than-life personalities and isolated episodes, and instead spotlights the patterns of institutional change over time. It does fall short, however, as an adequate explanation for why two broadly similar countries pursued quite different approaches to government intervention in finance.[36] American deference to finance and lackluster regulations did not result from low financial intelligence or poor learning. Indeed, the track record for learning in the United States is impressive. Like Canada, the United States responded to crisis with extensive investigations and reforms—pioneering a new infrastructure of financial protections during the New Deal and unleashing a blizzard of changes following the 2008–2009 implosion. The problem is less learning than retention—the sustaining of reforms, maintaining effective implementation, and establishing and protecting administrative capacity. The consistent pattern in the United States is that after reforms are enacted, they are eviscerated in response to significant counterpressures to repeal or blunt them. This very process, as we discuss below, is underway against Dodd-Frank, as opponents scheme to weaken it.

Another possibility is the structure of the financial sector.[37] The Canadian financial system is dominated by six banks.[38] During crises, Canada's banking industry is equipped to withstand sudden and large demands to redeem investments for cash because resources are concentrated. By comparison, America's banks are diffuse and rely on capital markets to raise and issue credit.[39] The smaller and more dispersed US banks are comparatively more susceptible to runs.[40]

Industry concentration does amass resources to withstand crisis, but this account falls short as the singular explanation for Canada's effectiveness in skirting recurrent crisis and America's instability. Oligopolies in business and politics have long been blamed for socially undesirable outcomes—driving up prices and dictating policy for narrow, selfish ends.[41] Robert Dahl's landmark studies of pluralism, for instance, argue that the distribution of economic and political resources generate political competition and socially beneficial countervailing effects; by contrast, the concentration of resources disproportionately favors the already powerful.[42]

What, then, has driven the United States and Canada in divergent directions? The history of government institutions loaded the dice to favor specific patterns of social learning and banking structure.[43] Take Canada. Its founding constitution authorized the national government to charter and to regulate banks, which over time fostered a durable pattern of concentrated, large, and nationwide banks. By contrast, the US Constitution did not grant the federal government power over banking; since the early nineteenth century, pitched battles challenged the legitimacy of government central banking, and private banks proliferated and fragmented.[44]

The lesson is that Canada has persistently invested in government institutions that facilitate the operation of its financial system and make stability a top priority. Its long-standing commitment fosters social learning and motivates financial markets to seek consistent and stable profits over boom-and-bust cycles.

Institutions: A Focused Central Bank and Coherent Regulator

The Fed enjoyed remarkable leeway in charting its most significant developments; legislative oversight of its institutional growth tended to be modest and inconsistent. By contrast, Canada nested its central bank in a dense institutional setting that routinely checked its powers. Neighborhood matters.

What Legislative Oversight Looks Like

The Fed and its acolytes respond to proposals to improve accountability with far-fetched scenarios of destructive political tampering. Canada offers a model of legislative accountability that authorizes the Bank of Canada to conduct monetary policy while appropriately hemming in its discretion.

What would accountability look like if Congress stopped acquiescing to the Fed and lobbyists for finance? Canada's Parliament conducts active oversight of the Bank of Canada and its relations with banks without micromanaging monetary policy. In particular, Parliament reviews private banks and decides whether or not they are awarded charters to operate.[45] The rigor of this inspection deters banks from risky speculation, and it also puts the Bank of Canada on notice that its performance as regulator will be scrutinized.

Legislative backsliding is another difference. Part of the Fed's troubles stems from zealous deregulation by Congress and regulatory agencies, and from the design of convoluted oversight responsibilities by lawmakers. By comparison, Canada's Parliament did not bow to pressure from finance to abandon stringent oversight (much as Congress and US regulators did). In contrast to the United States, Parliament insisted that banks continue to meet comparatively onerous requirements to backstop its loans and investments with ample assets—creating the cushion that allowed Canadian banks to absorb the crisis of 2008–2009 without a taxpayer bailout. Canada also continued to rigorously manage mortgage loans by restricting the terms of mortgages (such as the interest rates it can charge) and by requiring tests of the financial capacity of borrowers to repay loans. Typifying Canada's approach was its decision in 2008 to severely restrict subprime mortgage lending, which ravaged the financial sector in the United States. Subprime loans ballooned to 25 percent of the mortgage market in the United States, and 60 percent were repackaged into securities; by contrast, Canada's protections dramatically reduced its exposure (only 5 percent of the mortgage market was in subprime loans, and 25 percent were securitized).[46]

What Coordinated Regulation Looks Like

One of Canada's sharpest departures from the American approach to financial management is to separate the central bank's handling of monetary policy from financial regulation. Where the Fed is involved in handling both, Parliament limited the Bank of Canada to monetary policy and set up a separate body to handle regulation. Keeping the central bank out of the regulation business removed incentives for it to appease banks and other firms that it regularly relies upon to buy and sell securities.[47] And regulators have clear priorities to minimize risk and speculation.

Canada ratcheted up its regulatory oversight in 1987 by consolidating the disparate agencies charged with oversight of banks, capital markets, private pensions, and insurance into a comprehensive independent agency: the Office of the Superintendent of Financial Institutions (OSFI). The glue for integrating agencies is a chief coordinating body, the Financial Institutions Supervisory Committee, which is chaired by the OSFI's superintendent and includes the Deputy Minister of Finance as well as representatives from the Bank of Canada, and all of the federal financial regulators.[48]

The OSFI meets routinely with large financial institutions to monitor whether their operations are sound and stable. These regular meetings include visits with the governing boards of banks, which sometimes occur without the executive directors in order to invite candor. Banks that show signs of insolvency are targeted by OSFI for possible closure or are given instructions to change its operations.[49] OSFI is also stringent in overseeing brokers and investment firms; America's SEC, by contrast, is lenient in its exercising responsibility for nonbanks.[50]

How does OSFI fare in the dog-eat-dog world of agency battles over turf? The Fed offers a cautionary tale over the past century of how an ambitious institution can expand its empire and sideline other agencies. Not so in Canada. OSFI enjoys unusual protection against getting swallowed by the Bank of Canada or the Ministry of Finance. It reports to Parliament, and its superintendent is solely responsible for fulfilling its mission of minimizing losses to investors and the risks of upheaval.

OSFI also faces internal checks to bolster its commitment to stringent oversight. One of the most telling is its values and mission that staff are expected to embrace—to act "in favor of the public interest." There are also backstops. American regulators are tarnished by the seductions of the revolving door between financial regulation and lucrative jobs in finance. Much less so in Canada, where agencies heavily recruit public sector workers who lack the dual loyalties of Americans with past jobs on Wall Street or a hankering to land one. Canada also closely polices against conflicts of interests that arise from hiring personnel in the financial sector, including prohibitions against later careers that take advantage of insider information.[51]

Canada appreciates the fundamental importance of earning trust. OSFI is mandated to rigorously monitor its credibility by commissioning anonymous surveys of both "knowledgeable observers of OSFI operations" (including executives of financial firms that it regulates) and the mass public to assess its confidence in the agency's operations.[52] This requirement underscores Canada's focus on sustaining the legitimacy of its financial management, another contrast with the United States.

How does the performance of OSFI compare to that of US regulators? Let's put it this way: Canada is a regular Gold Medal winner, and the United States is not. Before the Great Recession hit, the leading international watchdog (the Financial Stability Board at the IMF) proclaimed that "Canada's financial system is mature, sophisticated and well-managed."[53] The strong marks continued during the postmortems of the 2008–2009 crisis, as the IMF praised OSFI for delivering "cooperation between relevant agencies" that was "swift and effective," and for effectively preventing defaults on home mortgages from overwhelming the broader financial system.[54]

As for the United States, it refused to participate in the IMF reviews before the crisis. When the United States did submit to an assessment five years after the collapse of Lehman Brothers, the review flagged "the complex and fragmented US regulatory and supervisory structure."[55] "Unlike their American peers," a prominent scholar observed, "Canada's regulators did not lack the authority to govern domestic institutions that can deliver bank-like services."[56]

A Tale of Two Countries

Central bank responses to the crisis of 2008–2009 distills the divergent approaches to financial management in the United States and Canada. The Fed worked under the cover of secrecy with Treasury to pass and direct TARP's rescues to a relatively few firms; it also unilaterally targeted its own massive assistance to a few firms. By contrast, OSFI helped preempt the speculative bubble that formed in the United States by imposing capital requirements and other rules on banks, and by leading the country's response in 2008.[57]

The Bank of Canada played a crucial role on monetary policy, but it did not literally run the show as the Fed did. The central bank's role was hemmed in, in important respects, by the institutional space and responsibilities of Parliament and OSFI. Pressure on the Bank of Canada by private banks and investment firms to appease them is counteracted by the oversight of Parliament and the administratively formidable OSFI.

But do Canada's assertive regulations disrupt the ability of financial markets to work and poison its relations with finance? No. Canada has developed cooperative relations based on clear institutional incentives. The Bank of Canada and Parliament steer its interactions with big banks from conflict over priorities toward collaboration to stabilize their operations. Government–industry relations are organized, in effect, by cooperative oligopoly—regulations privilege stability over profits, while banks are favored through charters that limit entry to the industry. From the perspective of banks, their incentives are to err on the side of compliance with regulations. They appreciate that the exposure to risk that their US counterparts accept could be quite costly to them if Parliament punishes them by refusing to grant them another charter.

THE BATTLE FOR REFORM IN THE UNITED STATES

America faces a momentous choice: invite future financial turmoil, or choose a new direction that puts a priority on financial stability and real economic growth. The short-term prognosis is alarming: finance and its allies are working overtime to weaken government regulations and open the door to financial scheming and the next crisis. The old model of acquiescence and appeasement of finance is resurfacing but it is also producing strains that create opportunities for transitioning toward credible and administratively effective financial management.

More of the Same

America did not learn its lesson from the 2008–2009 crisis and is instead repeating three patterns that open the door to the next one.

Administrative Incoherence Remains

Dodd-Frank set out to protect against reckless speculation and overreaching by the Fed, and yet its approach had the effect of further dispersing authority. Students of American political history could predict the response: turf battles have broken out among government agencies in Washington and in the states as they share oversight of banks, credit unions, and trust companies. The consequence, according to the Fed's inspector general, is "gaps in supervisory coverage or duplication of efforts."[58]

Meanwhile, special interests are not sitting by idly. Lobbyists for finance are skillfully playing off contending agencies and exploiting areas where regulatory authority is uncertain or contested. The insurance industry, which spawned financial giants capable of torpedoing the financial system (think AIG), is regulated by states. No federal agency polices it. Good news for finance and its lobbyists in the short term, even though America is vulnerable to speculation and the next AIG-type implosion.[59] The security brokers and exchanges, which have a checkered history of ripping off consumers and businesses, are largely outside effective state or federal government oversight. Private associations of members are trusted to self-police, putting the foxes in charge of guarding the hen house.[60]

Meanwhile, the Fed continues its lackadaisical oversight of finance. The "London Whale" incident starred Bruno Iksil in the London office of JP Morgan Chase, who single-handedly placed enormous bets in 2012 that evaded detection by the much ballyhooed internal checks and suffocating regulators. The failure of oversight incinerated $51 billion of shareholder value and stuck JP Morgan Chase with losses ($6 billion) that were three times larger than CEO Dimon's initial tally.[61] Where were the regulatory police that Wall Street is complaining about? According to the Fed's Office of Inspector General, it was not that the Fed fell asleep at the wheel. It was worse: the New York Fed office identified risks in the London branch of JP Morgan Chase, but failed to step in.[62]

The inspector general's stinging reports on the Fed's mishandling of the London Whale and other incidents fit into a familiar pattern of excessive deference to finance.[63] Again and again, the reports point to Fed regulators making discoveries and failing to investigate or crack down. Old habits and mistakes have returned and administrative incoherence remains.

Delay and Sidetrack Dodd-Frank

Stalling is another familiar pattern. Wall Street lobbyists and their congressional allies are working hard to delay implementation of new rules and to strangle Dodd-Frank provisions before they were even released as new regulations.[64]

One of the snafus in the United States during 2008–2009— and one that Canada avoided—is that banks and investment firms (think Bear Stearns, Lehman Brothers, and others) borrowed to fund their speculation with little capital backing up their bets. Having $1 for every $40 invested is a recipe for disaster, because even a relatively small dip in asset value will overwhelm the firms.

Dodd-Frank directed regulators to make sure that financial institutions had ample cushions by increasing the capital backing up their loans and investments. Guess what has happened? Soon after President Obama signed Dodd-Frank into law, a battle broke out over the rules that the Fed was designing. By the time the Fed released these rules, informed observers hit the fire alarm. The rules failed, they reported, to create adequate cushions. Worse, the Fed created "incentives for banks to manipulate their financial statements, hide risks, and engage in dysfunctional strategies—much like those that doomed Lehman Brothers and brought the financial system to the brink of collapse." Inviting firms to operate—once again—on thin margins is an "impending blunder": firms will be unable to cover the losses, and taxpayers and regulators will be asked to step in again.[65]

Gutting Dodd-Frank

Looks bad, right? The situation may become more precarious.

As the drama of 2008–2009 recedes, finance and its lobbyists are gaining traction to repeal or water down Dodd-Frank provisions that curtail their freedom to speculate.[66] After profiting from government succor during the crisis, JP Morgan Chase's Dimon is now pressing members of Congress to return to "the old days" of loose regulations.[67] "Banks are under assault," he complained. "We have five or six regulators coming at us on every issue."[68]

The campaign to chip away at Dodd-Frank picked up speed within Congress as Republicans wielded their new majorities and some Democrats advocated for financial interests in their districts.[69] President Obama threatened vetoes to retain the new controls over finance passed after the 2008–2009 crisis, but the lobbyists and their congressional allies are skilled at moving givebacks through the legislative process. They will put President Obama in uncomfortable situations: swallow concessions, or veto legislation he supports?

And, of course, backroom deals that undercut regulatory responsibilities or revive the backstop of government bailouts can be hidden from public view. Experienced lobbyists and their allies are skilled at burying these goodies deep within bills that are debated late at night and rushed through with quick votes that leave no time for lawmakers—let alone journalists and concerned citizens—to examine the legislation.

As old habits remain, America's history of weak financial management contorts policy debates. Well-intentioned reformers fret that financial firms are "too big," and therefore government will invariably bail them out. This fear is reasonable but backward. Canada has a far more consolidated financial system and avoided the sinkhole of TARP and Fed bailouts by aggressively intervening to prevent banks from risky speculation and subsequent bailouts. In the United States policymakers start with the assumption of regulatory incompetence and favoritism, and then work from there to the government's exposure to bailing out the high-flyers.[70] Many policymakers and regulators, a former high-ranking official lamented, "quietly subscribe to the view that bailouts are inevitable."[71]

Call it defeatism—or realism.

The Vulnerability of US Finance and the Opportunity for Reform

Historical patterns are hard to break, but not impossible. The mutually reinforcing ties among the Fed, organized financial interests, and enclaves of sympathetic lawmakers that sustained Fed power for decades is now susceptible to disruption and reform—especially as future financial crises descend on the United States. Two strains in particular are creating an opening for building more coherent and effective financial management.

A Loud and Broad Backlash

The backlash against the Fed remains loud. "Enough is enough," Senator Warren proclaimed on the floor of Congress in December 2014, as Congress moved toward weakening Dodd-Frank. By spotlighting one of the hidden deals buried by lobbyists and their allies inside a large must-pass spending bill, Warren defeated a provision to restore the prospect of government bailouts. "Congress [is] on the verge of ramming through a provision," she proclaimed, "that would do nothing for the middle class [and] do nothing for community banks...but raise the risk that taxpayers will have to bail out the biggest banks once again."[72] On another occasion, she lambasted the Fed boss of its New York office for yet another instance of lax and ineffective oversight: "You need to fix [the problem], Mr. Dudley, or we need to get someone who will."[73]

Resistance is coming not only from expected critics, but also from previously quiescent and longtime supporters. Republican senator Richard Shelby (R-AL)—top dog on the mighty Banking Committee—declares that it is time to end the Fed's free hand: "When they are putting taxpayer resources at risk, we need transparency and accountability."[74] Martin Feldstein, a conservative economist and former aide to Ronald Reagan, is ready to put the shackles on Fed rescues by enacting a double whammy: "formal Treasury concurrence backed by Congressional pre-authorization."[75]

The broad uneasiness with the Fed partly stems from uncertainty over the possible repercussions of its interventions and its $4 trillion balance sheet after Bernanke's fourfold increase. Even informed supporters of the Fed's intervention worry that it may spark the next round of crises—soaring inflation owing to the expanded money supply, or the pumping up of new asset-price bubbles for a new round of destructive boom/bust cycles.[76] Distilling the widespread apprehension about the scope and implications of central bank power, a *New York Times* columnist who followed the 2008–2009 crisis and its aftermath summarized the calls for increased "scrutiny of the Fed" as "absolutely justified, given the immense powers they enjoy."[77]

The pushback against the Fed is eroding one of the most important features of its institutional history: quiet, subterranean development. It worked in the shadow of the Treasury for much of the twentieth century and assumed greater independence through gradual steps that usually evaded notice by the untrained eye.

Sustained resistance to the Fed is altering central bank politics. It is puncturing the Fed's quiet, tight-knit alliance with congressional sponsors and lobbyists and inviting in new lawmakers and pressure groups to question earlier assumptions and policies.

Looking to the Future: Spotlights and Scrutiny

During past blowbacks, the Fed comforted itself with the expectation of future calm. "Ride out the storm," was the mindset, "and the Fed will slide back into the secure shadows where its power[s] are not challenged." Not so after 2008–2009. The pushback shows no signs of relenting, and, indeed, the future may well bring more public and elite scrutiny.

Doubt has bred scrutiny. A more aggressive Inspector General Office is now on the scene after Dodd-Frank expanded its responsibilities, Congress pressured it to closely monitor the Fed, and new leadership took over. Since the 2008–2009 crisis, the number of audit reports increased by threefold from eight in 2007 to 23 in the fall of 2014.[78] By the fall of 2015, the pipeline is chock-full of 63 ongoing investigations.[79] It is not only churning out critical reports, it is distributing them to lawmakers and journalists who are regularly reporting them.

The Inspector General (IG) is locking in as an alert watchdog of the Fed. Its mandates include producing "objective audits, evaluations, investigations, and other reviews" and keeping "Congress fully and currently informed."[80] To guard against capture, the Fed IG is subject to rigorous selection and review.[81] The motivation for professional success reinforces its legal mandate and independence: the current Fed IG has a track record in the Office of Inspector General at the Environmental Protection Agency, State Department, and the Department of Commerce. Being a slacker is a bad career move.

The invigorated IG is contributing to a new environment of public accountability and disclosure moving into the future. Republicans are on record as enthusiastically supporting legislation to audit the Fed. Although the Fed has ferociously opposed the Republican initiatives, the truth is that it is an expansion of a pattern of audits that dates from 1978—hardly a radical new invention.[82] The Fed's objection is not to audits per se, but to letting the sunshine into its decision-making.

Meanwhile, Democrats are also pushing for more transparency by taking advantage of the investigative powers of the IG and the Government Accounting Office (GAO). Senator Bernie Sanders, for instance, turned to the GAO to dig out information on the Fed's "$16 trillion in secret loans to bail out American and foreign banks and businesses." "This is a clear case," Senator Sanders insisted, of "socialism for the rich and rugged, you're-on-your-own individualism for everyone else."[83]

In the past the Fed discouraged this kind of scrutiny with warnings that politicians would use inside information to pressure central banks to make unwise decisions about the money supply and destroy the country's credibility in capital markets by slashing interest rates to win votes. But the Fed's warning has become less persuasive. The heaviest blow against deference has been dealt by the Fed itself: acting unilaterally in secret to make massive commitments during 2008–2009 demonstrated to unnerved Americans and lawmakers that too little scrutiny can risk ruin. Echoing a view gaining traction across party lines in Congress, a Republican lawmaker recently called out the "Fed's clamor for independence" as a ruse "to circumvent any sort of congressional accountability."[84] This critical view of the central bank treats the Fed's claims to secrecy as self-serving rather than as a honorable defense of the public interest.

For the attentive, the strength of the Fed's warnings also has been dimmed by the experience of other capitalist countries, which combine responsible monetary policy with prudent transparency and effective financial management. In Canada, Parliament reviews private banks every five years; other oversight activities provide a time delay and a cushion for the Bank of Canada to operate without fear that the airing of different perspectives among central bank officials will spook financial markets.

Canada's experience is not an exception. The track record of central banks in a number of capitalist countries indicates that sunshine deters (rather than invites, as the Fed has long warned) political irresponsibility. Transparency invites scrutiny not only of central banks but also of elected officials: they risk punishment if they reverse central bank decisions and increase the risk of inflation.[85]

The genie is out of the bottle. The Fed prospered in the past because it practiced the art of secrecy. As Nobel Prize–winning economist Joseph Stiglitz put it, "secrecy serves as a cloak behind which special interests can most effectively advance their interests, outside of public scrutiny."[86] The new scrutiny of the Fed invites more—not less—information in the future.

The New Politics of the Fed

Breaking out of America's pattern of Fed unilateralism and deference to finance will require a new politics of accountability. Tall order. After all, deep partisan divisions already threaten essential government functions—from passing budgets that keep the government operating to raising the ceiling on the national debt. Dysfunction is compounded by a rational political calculation to let the Fed act alone because it creates an "out" for lawmakers. For years, the Fed has taken the risk and heat for acting while the elected class kept its political ammunition dry to bask in successful crisis management and to criticize the Fed if the populist winds demanded it.[87]

Two dynamics are forming that can change the politics of the Fed and create an opening for displacing the pattern of deference to Wall Street, and for starting to build a new model that stabilizes America's financial system.

Dynamic #1: Acquiescing to the Fed is no longer an easy vote in an era with more investigations and disclosures. Lawmakers are coming to appreciate that supporting the Fed or passively looking the other way in deference to its operations can bring challenges from both the left and right in the next election. They also face criticism from newly active organized groups. Advocates for consumers, community banks, and other interests are unable to match the resources of financial lobbyists, but they are now able to capitalize on the cracks in the Fed's longtime alliance and are finding congressional and media allies willing to give voice to their criticisms. Scrutiny is reordering the political motivations of financial management and introducing incentives for Congress to share responsibility or consider it.

Dynamic #2: The next financial crisis. It does not take a crystal ball to appreciate that another financial crisis is coming and that the Fed will enter it as a beleaguered agency. The next crisis will have many sources, but the Fed may be the fall guy. For its critics and the unnerved, more financial turmoil combined with criticism from the media and politicians will confirm existing suspicions about the Fed's ineffectiveness and cozy ties to big finance. That is one of the costs of its strained legitimacy: the Fed enters the next crisis without the benefit of the doubt.

Another casualty: legislative support for extraordinary measures like TARP is likely to be smaller, and deference to the Fed will be more vulnerable to open resistance. The cumulative effect may well be enough to disrupt the Fed's alliance with organized finance and congressional enablers.

AN AGENDA FOR REFORM: INTEGRITY AND ACCOUNTABILITY

The United States is approaching a moment of choice: accept its destructive pattern of ineffective regulation and perverse incentives, or design new institutions that create organizations and incentives that steer finance away from excessive risk and crisis. It is time for America to take a new direction in managing the financial system.

The twin objectives are public accountability and effectiveness. One without the other is a recipe for disaster. The aim is to break the enduring hold of Wall Street and private banks over the Fed and to consolidate the disjointed, competing regulatory agencies to establish coherent rules and regulatory action.

A Public Responsibility

When the Fed was enacted in 1913, its backbone was a regional latticework of private banks. To this day America—and no other democratic country—cedes to private banks significant influence over the commitment of public funds and authority. Private banks dominate the nomination of regional bank presidents who serve on the Fed's key policy committee, the Federal Open Market Committee (FOMC).[88]

The privileging of private banks in the Fed may have fitted the America that existed a century ago. Banks and other financial firms were dispersed geographically, creating a practical need to stockpile money around the country to respond to runs on banks. The Fed's unusual structure also reassured skittish banks that the fledgling Fed would be responsive to them.

The twenty-first century presents, however, qualitatively different circumstances. Decentralization in a regional system makes less practical sense when financial transactions are global in scope; after all, the necessity of transporting bags of money has been replaced by lightning quick electronic transfers. Power and accountability are also out of whack. Putting the enormous power of the Fed in the hands of private bankers breaks from America's principles of democratic governance and fuels hostility across the ideological spectrum. The now incessant bubbling of discontent about the Fed originates, at its most basic level, in questions about its legitimacy—public power wielded, in part, by and for private interests.

It is time to weaken further the power of private banks over regional banks and the FOMC. Dodd-Frank chipped away at their roles on the Fed's boards, but more should be done.[89] In today's global financial environment, the sway of private banks over the nomination of regional bank presidents should be diminished by reducing their relative numbers on governing boards, including the FOMC.

An opening wedge in reorganizing the Fed's antiquated and normatively offensive structure is to shift the selection of the New York Fed's president to the president of the United States, and to strip private interests of control over this important position.[90] The head of the New York Fed directs the most power regional bank in the Fed system; he is the FOMC's vice chair and assumes a leadership role in America's financial capitol.[91] Senator Richard Shelby (R-AL) joined Senator Jack Reed (D-RI) in supporting legislation to pull this position within the normal constitutional system of presidential nomination and senate confirmation.

The make-up of the Fed's Board of Governors needs to be restructured to reduce the dominance of Wall Street insiders and to introduce a broader set of informed perspectives. Senator Joe Manchin (D-WV) joined his colleague Elizabeth Warren to push for appointing members of the Fed's Board with "meaningful background in overseeing or investigating big banks."[92] Another avenue is to widen the range of perspectives from private banks by including community banking.[93]

Regional Fed banks should also be encouraged to diversify its boards. Their current rules limit board memberships to private banks. Expanding the constituencies on regional Fed banks will tap the experience and perspectives in the business and civic communities.

The theme is to better tether the exercise of formal government authority to the public interest. In the past, the Fed's power rested on its swelling institutional might and on private banks and investment firms. Is it any surprise that the Fed routinely settled on policies that aided both while inflaming doubts about its legitimacy? The path to improving the Fed's credibility is to make its central bank more accountable to lawmakers and to the diversity of financial interests in the country.

Building Accountable Institutions

Woodrow Wilson coined the term "checks and balances" as a stinging criticism of James Madison and other writers of the Constitution. Wilson observed an America struggling with the growing pains of industrialization and social transformation in the late nineteenth and early twentieth centuries and bemoaned the lack of useable government authority and administrative capacity. The "radical defect in our federal system," Wilson said, is "that it parcels out power" according to "a 'literary theory' of checks and balances." The curse of this system, he argued, is that it hindered the development of society as "a living organism" that "must obey the laws of life, not of mechanics."[94] The

Constitution's framers frittered away useful powers that may have been marshaled to serve broad public purposes.

The principle of marshaling authority and capacity for public purposes is embodied in Canada's approach to financial management: consolidating (instead of dispersing) the authority and capacity to monitor and regulate banks, investors, and insurance. Canada demonstrates that greater accountability can coexist with some degree of prudent independence for central bank decisions. This approach flows against the pattern in the United States of attempting to check the Fed by dispersing authority across disparate agencies; the unintended effect has been to neuter effective public management and to enable lobbyists to infiltrate government offices.

Taking seriously the best practices in Canada and other Western countries will be strenuously opposed, of course, by the Fed and its allies. Part of the coming assault will equate reasonable accountability with absurd scenarios such as Congress setting interest rates. Of course, this is neither feasible nor proposed by reasonable observers.

It is time to listen to Woodrow Wilson's scholarly advice and to learn from Canada's best practices. Effective management of finance requires an accountable and administratively coherent regulatory structure with a clear mission to protect the stability of the financial system. This may be the single most important step to reconcile financial management and the public good. Fusing the numerous, often competing priorities and responsibilities of state and national government offices will require an historic effort—but one that America must start to make.

CENTRAL BANKING IN THE PUBLIC INTEREST

The second Gilded Age is upon us, as is a new generation of titans whose fortunes rival those amassed by David Rockefeller and John Pierpont Morgan. The top 1 percent of families took home 23.9 percent of all pretax income in 1928, and the "bottom" 90 percent received 50.7 percent. Jump forward to 2012, when the share at the top was 22.5 percent and much of the rest of America received *less* than half.[95] Wealth is even more unequally distributed. Wealth is 10 times more concentrated today than income; its concentration is comparable to the 1920s.[96]

The Great Recession was an economic grim reaper. It hit the top income groups hard but they bounced back. By contrast, the rest of America suffered a sharp decline in income during the crisis and largely missed out on a recovery.[97] The Great Recession also struck the main source of wealth for many Americans—their homes.

The pushback against the Fed is occurring in an environment of resentment that has been fanned by the economic travails of Middle America and the widening disparities during the Great Recession. The Tea Party and Occupy Wall Street, as well as progressive and conservative populists, target the Fed as contributing to the amassing of great wealth. The general public also appears to blame the Fed for inequality.[98] Since the 2008–2009 crisis, large majorities of up to two-thirds continue to conclude that the gap between the rich and the poor is widening and bristle at the country's pattern that "unfairly favor powerful interests" and help "just a few people at the top...to get ahead."[99] This broad public antipathy to unfairness, which has persisted years after the overall economy improved and the official rate of unemployment declined, presents a headwind for the central bank moving forward.

Fed officials are starting to wake up to the central bank's public association with growing inequality. Echoing an earlier mea culpa by Alan Greenspan, Donald Kohn (former Fed vice chair and frequent media flak for the Fed) confessed that he "deeply regrets" the impact of the crisis on consumers.[100] Janet Yellen has publicly discussed economic inequality.[101]

The sympathetic talking points have not, however, translated into practical policy to directly assist homeowners and small businesses and to break the cycles of profiteering followed by collapse that we see from central bankers in Canada and England. "We cannot [accept]," the governor of the Bank of England explained to Parliament, that there is "nothing you can do" about boom-and-bust cycles. "We cannot afford a counsel of despair given the damage that has been wreaked on the rest of the economy."[102] England's response was a series of policy initiatives to head off brazen risk-taking and to aid everyday people.[103] By contrast, the Fed's contrite press releases are part of the latest public relations strategy—publicly profess contrition while continuing business as usual.[104]

The lack of a serious policy shift reflects the Fed's institutional orientation and relations with finance. Under normal circumstances the Fed's routine operations rely on policy instruments—manipulating capital markets—that sustain and facilitate finance, and those who most benefit from this one sector of the economy.[105] In the lead-up to the crisis in 2008–2009, the Fed's abdication of its regulatory responsibilities opened the door to the Great Recession and its widening of economic disparities. When the Fed responded to the crisis, it funneled enormous sums to a select few firms and discouraged or dragged its feet in directly supporting homeowners (in contrast to what the British did). The Fed's decision to pursue quantitative easing by flooding financial markets with unprecedented sums supplied the government's most significant stimulus in the absence of fiscal policy. It helped most but the gains for the few were lopsided: it sent Wall Street to record new highs that disproportionately benefited the holders of wealth.

The reality of rising inequality since 2008 is, of course, more complicated than Fed policies alone: Congress failed to use fiscal policy to adequately respond to the 2008–2009 crisis and the sources of inequality are broader than Fed policies.[106] It is also true that unemployment and economic disparities would have been worse without the Fed.

Nonetheless, the parceling out of blame does not absolve the Fed for its part in enabling the trend toward inequality. Its responses to the 2008–2009 crisis facilitated the return of high finance to its go-go days immortalized in Hollywood's *The Wolf of Wall Street*. Profits from finance are now as large a proportion of the overall economy as they were in the early 2000s, and more than twice their average during the 70 years after the crash of 1929. Pay for those in securities is far above that of the average

American worker and on course to return to Olympian heights.[107] Meanwhile, the risk-taking mania is also making a comeback. About a one-fifth of finance service workers making over half a million a year report that they "must sometimes engage in unethical or illegal activity to be successful," and that their company's pay "incentivize employees to compromise ethics or violate the law."[108]

What are the worries? Several. By facilitating the financial sector in its current form, the Fed is sustaining a significant distortion of the overall US economy. The large financial sector drains talent, stymies the productivity that drives economic growth, and invites boom-and-bust cycles. The president of the American Finance Association popped the myth that the Wall Street boom helps America: "There is no...evidence to support the notion that all the growth of the financial sector in the last 40 years has been beneficial to society."[109]

Another worry is the Groundhog Day scenario. America's pattern of deferring to finance and risk-taking is once again in place, and the consequences are predictable.

Will America do better and build effective financial management that breaks out of the cycles of risk-taking, profiteering, and collapse? Hurdles stand in the way to redesigning the structure of monetary policy. And yet American history is littered with policies that endure for generations and then collapse during periods of crisis. The financial crises of the nineteenth and early twentieth centuries represented one of those periods, as did the Great Depression of the 1930s. As the Fed attempts to go about its business today, the foundations of its support and operational integrity are damaged. As it limps along, it risks becoming a discredited vestige of a bygone era—vulnerable to breakdown and replacement when the next financial crisis hits, as it will.

Now is the time to prepare for a new day when America will build effective financial management within the structures of democratic accountability.

Notes

1: Why Fed Power Matters

1. Edmund Andrews and Stephen Labaton, "Geithner, With Few Aides, Is Scrambling," *New York Times*, March 8, 2009, www.nytimes.com/2009/03/09/business/economy/09treasury.html.
2. Minutes of a conference call meeting of Fed governors and FOMC, February 7, 2009. The Board of Governors publishes the minutes of the Federal Open Market Committee (FOMC) meetings five years after the meetings. They can be accessed at www.federalreserve.gov/monetarypolicy/fomchistorical2008.htm. We cite from this source in this note and later notes.
3. Ronald Steel, *Temptations of a Superpower* (Cambridge, MA: Harvard University Press, 1995), 55.
4. Gregory Mankiw, *Principles of Microeconomics*, 3rd ed. (Mason, OH: Thompson/South-Western, 2004).
5. J. Lawrence Broz, "Origins of the Federal Reserve System: International Incentives and the Domestic Free-Rider Problem," *International Organization* 53 (Winter 1999): 39–44; and "The Origins of Central Banking: Solutions to the Free-Rider Problem," *International Organization* 52 (Spring 1998): 231–268.
6. Finn E. Kydland and Edward C. Prescott, "Rules Rather than Discretion: The Inconsistency of Optimal Plans," *Journal of Political Economy* 85 (June 1977): 473–492; Robert Barro, "The Control of Politicians: An Economic Model," *Public Choice* 14 (Spring 1973): 19–42.
7. James Madison, Federalist Paper #10 in *The Federalist*, ed. Jacob Cooke (Middletown, CT: Weslyan University Press, 1961), 56–65.
8. Greta R. Krippner, *Capitalizing the Crisis: The Political Origins of the Rise of Finance* (Cambridge, MA: Harvard University Press, 2011), 27–28, 34–37, 47–48; and Krippner's paper "The Financialization of the American Economy," *Socio-Economic Review* 3 (2005): 173–208.

9. Stephen G. Cecchetti and Enisse Kharroubi, "Why Does Financial Sector Growth Crowd Out Real Economic Growth," February 2015, Bank for International Settlements, www.bis.org/publ/work490.pdf.

10. Ratna Sahay, Martin Cihak, Papa N'Diaye, Adolfo Barajas, Ran Bi, Diana Ayala, Yuan Gao, Annette Kyobe, Lam Nguyen, Crhistian Saborowski, Katsiaryna Svirydzenka, and Seyed Reza Yousefi, "Rethinking Financial Deepening: Stability and Growth in Emerging Markets," International Monetary Fund, May 2015, www.imf.org/external/pubs/ft/sdn/2015/sdn1508.pdf.

11. One study finds that Fed officials as well as central banks in 19 other countries who built their careers in finance are more likely to favor monetary policies that fend off inflation (even when it is not present) than those who have worked in the public sector. Christopher Adolph, *Bankers, Bureaucrats, and Central Bank Politics: The Myth of Neutrality* (New York: Cambridge University Press, 2013).

12. Ben Bernanke, "Monetary Policy and Inequality," Brookings Institution, June 1, 2015, www.brookings.edu/blogs/ben-bernanke/posts/2015/06/01-monetary-policy-and-inequality#.VW4LoLfvPuU.twitter.

13. When the media focuses on the Fed's decisions on interest rates, it is a simplification. The Fed (specifically, its Federal Open Market Committee) does not literally determine a set point—like putting the temperature of our offices at 68 degrees. The rate that the media covers is a target, which until relatively recently was not announced publicly by FOMC. The actual work is done by the Fed's New York office and its trading desk on Wall Street, which sells and buys government securities on the open market to approach the target Federal funds rate, as it is known. In particular, it buys securities with the intent of pushing rates lower (making money cheaper by making it more plentiful), or sells them with the aim of raising rates (making money more expensive by making it less plentiful). It remains active in buying or selling securities until it reaches its target. This is the process that sets the rate charged to banks and credit unions that trade their balances held at the Fed. In addition to trading their excess reserves, banks do receive interest from the Fed on their required reserves that are held in deposit. This is the deposit rate. Banks sometimes cannot get access to sufficient reserves to meet their required balance at the Fed; this happens when other banks refuse to lend enough at the federal fund rate. As a result, the banks that are short have to borrow directly from the Fed and are charged what is known as the discount rate. Unlike the federal fund rate that is set through trades on the open market for government securities, the Fed sets the deposit and discount rates directly.

14. Mark J. Perry, "The Fed's $3.5T QE Purchases Have Generated Almost Half a Trillion Dollars for the US Treasury since 2009," AEI, January 12, 2015, www.aei.org/publication/since-2009-feds-qe-purchases-transferred-almost-half-trillion-dollars-treasury-isnt-gigantic-wealth-transfer/.

15. Edward Wolff, *The Asset Price Meltdown and the Wealth of the Middle Class* (New York: New York University Press, 2012).

16. The ability of banks to profit on low interest rates might have been constrained—outside the crisis circumstances of 2008–2009—by competition that forced them to pass on lower costs to consumers. Markus K. Brunnermeier and Yuliy Sannikov, "Redistributive Monetary Policy" (Princeton, NJ: Princeton University manuscript, August 2012), http://scholar.princeton.edu/sites/default/files/04c%20Redistributive%20Monetary%20Policy.pdf.

17. Facundo Alvaredo, Anthony B. Atkinson, Thomas Piketty, and Emmanuel Saez, "The Top 1 Percent in International and Historical Perspective," *Journal of Economic Perspectives* 27 (Summer 2013): 3–20; Robert Pear, "Median Income Rises, But Is Still 6% Below Level at Start of Recession in 2007," *New York Times*, August 22, 2013; Jesse Bricker, Arthur B. Kennickell, Kevin B. Moore, and John Sabelhaus, "Changes in U.S. Family Finances from 2007 to 2010: Evidence from the Survey of Consumer Finances," *Federal Reserve Bulletin*, June 2012, www.federalreserve.gov/Pubs/Bulletin/2012/articles/scf/scf.htm.

18. Emmanuel Saez and Thomas Piketty, updated tables and figures for "Income Inequality in the United States, 1913–1998," September 2013, http://ow.ly/GIXXX.

19. "Debt and Taxes," *New York Times*, editorial page, December 1, 2013, http://ow.ly/Ff4Bi.

20. Tanzina Vega, "Minorities Fall Further Behind Whites in Wealth During Economic Recovery," *New York Times*, December 13, 2014, http://ow.ly/FVd0v. Debbie Gruenstein Bocain, Wei Li, Carolina Reid, and Roberto G. Quercia, "Lost Ground, 2011: Disparities in Mortgage Lending and Foreclosures," Center for Responsible Lending, November 2011, www.responsiblelending.org/mortgage-lending/research-analysis/lost-ground-2011.html. Pew Research Center, "Twenty-to-One: Wealth Gaps Rise to Record Highs Between Whites, Blacks and Hispanics," Pew Research Trends, July 2011, www.pewsocialtrends.org/files/2011/07/SDT-Wealth-Report_7-26-11_FINAL.pdf.

21. Ylan Q. Mui, "Americans Saw Wealth Plummet 40 Percent from 2007 to 2010, Federal Reserve Says," *Washington Post*, June 11, 2012, www.washingtonpost.com/business/economy/fed-americans-wealth-dropped-40-percent/2012/06/11/gJQAllsCVV_story.html.

22. The failure to use fiscal policy as a tool of macroeconomic policy is ably addressed by Mark Blyth, *Austerity: The History of a Dangerous Idea* (New York: Oxford University Press, 2013). Sources of inequality are discussed here: Thomas Piketty, *Capital in the Twenty-First Century* (Cambridge, MA: Belknap Press, 2014), Part III; Thomas Piketty, "Putting Distribution Back at the Center of Economics: Reflections on *Capital in the Twenty-First Century*," *Journal of Economic Perspectives* 29 (Winter 2015): 67–88, and wide-ranging commentary in this issue of the *JEP*.

23. Bank of England, "The Distributional Effects of Asset Purchases," July 12, 2012, www.bankofengland.co.uk/publications/Documents/news/2012/nr073.pdf

24. Alan Blinder, "Is Government Too Political?" *Foreign Affairs* 76 (November/December 1997): 115–126.

25. Edmund Burke, "Speech to the Electors of Bristol," November 3, 1774, *The Works of the Right Honourable Edmund Burke* (London: Henry G. Bohn, 1854–1856). The chorus for technocracy in America includes Walter Lippmann, *The Phantom Public* (New York: Harcourt, Brace, 1925); Daniel Moynihan and Patricia Ingraham, "The Suspect Handmaiden: The Evolution of Politics and Administration in the American State," *Public Administration Review* 70 (2010): 229–237; Frank J. Goodnow, *Politics and Administration: A Study in Government* (New York: Macmillan, 1900); Leonard D. White, ed., *Introduction to the Study of Public Administration* (New York: Macmillan, 1926). The model of elite governance is rigorously scrutinized in James Druckman and Lawrence R. Jacobs, *Who Governs? Presidents, Public Opinion, and Manipulation* (Chicago: University of Chicago Press, 2015).

26. Joseph Schumpeter, *Capitalism, Socialism, and Democracy* (New York: Harper, 1950).

27. Technocrats pose a false choice between democracy and technocracy; what is required, as we argue in the conclusion, is a division of labor that carves out limited spheres of independence for central banks while creating active structures of governance. Mark Warren, "Deliberative Democracy and Authority," *American Political Science Review* 90 (March 1996): 46–60.

28. Chris Isidore, "Bernanke: Fed Will Make Profit on Bailout," CNNMoney, December 7, 2009, http://money.cnn.com/2009/12/07/news/economy/bernanke_speech/; Jacob Lew quoted in Jonathan Weisman, "U.S. Declares Bank and Auto Bailouts Over, and Profitable," *New York Times*, December 19, 2014, http://ow.ly/GlWcj.

29. Sean Fieler and Jeffrey Bell, "The Unaccountable Fed," *Wall Street Journal*, April 7, 2011.

30. Taking the institutional interest of the Fed seriously has been surprisingly neglected. The interesting paper, for instance, by Pepper Culpepper and Raphael Reinke, focuses on the power of banks not only in the domestic arena through lobbying and campaign contributions, but also in global markets to defy regulators. What is missing, however, is the Fed's national and international administrative and monetary capacity. Culpepper and Reinke, "Structural Power and Bank Bailouts in the United Kingdom and the United States," *Politics & Society* 42 (December 2014): 427–454.

31. Financial Crisis Inquiry Commission (FCIC), *Final Report of the National Commission of the Causes of the Financial and Economic Crisis in the United States* (Washington, DC: Government Printing Office, 2011), xvii, xviii, 3, 416.

32. A succinct review of the Fed monetary policy meetings is provided by Matthew O'Brien, "How the Fed Let the World Blow Up in 2008," *The Atlantic*, February 26, 2014, www.theatlantic.com/business/archive/2014/02/how-the-fed-let-the-world-blow-up-in-2008/284054/.

33. FCIC, *Final Report*, xvii–xviii.

34. Edmund Andrews, "Greenspan Concedes Error on Regulation," *New York Times*, October 23, 2008, www.nytimes.com/2008/10/24/business/economy/24panel.html?_r=0; Stephen Holmes serves up a probing review of Greenspan's 2013 book *The Map and the Territory*, taking him to task for "remain[ing] in thrall to free-market ideology" and "defending financiers against charges...that there is something basically 'unfair' about their accumulation of vast fortunes when most of their fellow citizens are struggling." "How the World Works," *London Review of Books*, May 23, 2014.

35. Quoted in Stephen Labaton, "Agency's '04 Rule Let Banks Pile Up New Debt," *New York Times*, October 2, 2008, http://ow.ly/GKa0G.

36. Financial Inquiry Commission, xviii–ixx.

37. Joe Nocera, "Sheila Bair's Bank Shot," *New York Times*, July 9, 2011, http://ow.ly/HVCKp; Sheila Bair, *Bull by the Horns: Fighting to Save Main Street from Wall Street and Wall Street from Itself* (New York: Free Press, 2012).

38. Robert A. Dahl, *Democracy and Its Critics* (New Haven, CT: Yale University Press, 1989); Deborah Stone, *Policy Paradox: The Art of Political Decision Making,* 3rd ed. (New York: Norton, 2001); Lawrence Brown and Lawrence R. Jacobs, *The Private Abuse of the Public Interest* (Chicago: University of Chicago Press, 2008).

39. 9-11 Commission, *Report of the National Commission on Terrorist Attacks Upon the United States* (Washington, DC: US Government Printing Office, 2004); Diane Vaughan, *The Challenger Launch Decision: Risky Technology, Culture, and Deviance at NASA* (Chicago: University of Chicago Press, 1997); Scott Sagan, "Review Symposium," *Administrative Science Quarterly* 42 (June 1997): 401–405.

40. Edmund Andrews, "Greenspan Concedes Error on Regulation," *New York Times*, October 23, 2008, www.nytimes.com/2008/10/24/business/economy/24panel.html?_r=0.

41. Jose Fernandez-Albertos, "The Politics of Central Bank Independence," *Annual Review of Political Science* 18 (2015): 217–237, especially 221; Christopher Crowe and Ellen Meade, "The Evolution of Central Bank Governance Around the World," *Journal of Economic Perspectives* 21 (2007): 69–90.

42. We are grateful to Erik Jones for his feedback on this dynamic.

43. The "Antifederalists" protested the Constitution's ratification including these: Federal Farmer, Letter VII, December 31, 1787; Cato, Letter VII, *The New-York Journal*, January 3, 1788. Herbert J. Storing, *What the Anti-Federalists Were For: The Political Thought of the Opponents of the Constitution* (Chicago: University of Chicago Press, 1981).

44. There are hurdles of practical accountability: congressional dysfunction is one, and others flow from the practical needs for prudent information sharing; conducting open meetings on setting monetary policy would, of course, create havoc in financial markets and prove unworkable. Delay in fulsome information releases is one of many strategies. We consider these thorny but important practical issues in coming chapters. The point here is that abdication of authority to the Fed is not a fate that America must accept; there are proven models of accountability that check unilateralism by central banks and deliver effective financial management.

45. Druckman and Jacobs, *Who Governs?*; Lawrence Jacobs, Fay Lomax Cook, and Michael Delli Carpini, *Talking Together: Public Deliberation in America and the Search for Community* (Chicago: University of Chicago Press, 2009); Warren, "Deliberative Democracy and Authority," 46–60.

46. Congress passed the Troubled Asset Relief Program (TARP) in the fall of 2008 to authorize expenditures of $700 billion to stabilize the financial sector.

47. FCIC, *Final Report,* 374–377; Office of the Special Inspector General for the Troubled Asset Relief Program (SIGTARP) Quarterly Report to Congress, January 30, 2010. www.sigtarp.gov/Quarterly%20Reports/January2010_Quarterly_Report_to_Congress.pdf.

48. FCIC, *Final Report,* 375.

49. FCIC, *Final Report,* 377.

50. Dean Baker quoted in Gretchen Morgenson, "Banks, at Least, Had a Friend in Geithner," *New York Times,* February 2, 2013.

51. Brunnermeier and Sannikov, " Redistributive Monetary Policy."

52. Mark Blyth, *Austerity: The History of a Dangerous Idea* (New York: Oxford University Press, 2013), ch. 3, 1, and ch. 2, 35.

53. Government Accounting Office, "Troubled Asset Relief Program," January 2012, US GAO-12-229.

54. Morgenson, "Banks, at Least, Had a Friend in Geithner."

55. Quoted in announcement of Bernanke's appointment, April 28, 2015. Mary Childs, "Bernanke Joins Pimco: Second Consulting Job in Two Weeks," *Bloomberg News,* April 29, 2015, www.bloomberg.com/news/articles/2015-04-29/bernanke-joins-pimco-second-consulting-job-in-two-weeks.

56. "Citadel's Ken Griffin Tops Hedge Fund Earners," *Bloomberg News,* May 5, 2015, www.bloomberg.com/news/videos/2015-05-05/citadel-s-ken-griffin-tops-hedge-fund-earners.

57. Adolph, *Bankers, Bureaucrats and Central Bank Politics,* 33.

58. Eric Lichteblau, "Ex-Regulators Get Set for Lobby on New Financial Rules," *New York Times,* July 27, 2010.

59. The implication of generations of research in sociology on "career lines" is that the job movements by Fed officials are shaped, in part, by the past experiences of individuals and their anticipation of future opportunities. Everett Hughes, "Institutional Office and the Person," *American Journal of Sociology* 43, no. 3 (1937): 404–413; Howard S. Becker and Anselm Strauss, "Careers, Personality and Adult

Socialization," *American Journal of Sociology* 62, no. 3 (1956): 253–263; Richard W. Scholl, "Career Lines and Employment Stability," *Academy of Management Journal* 26 (March 1983): 86–103.

60. Adolph, *Bankers, Bureaucrats, and Central Bank Politics.*

61. Adolph, *Bankers, Bureaucrats, and Central Bank Politics.*

62. One of the most vivid such accounts is offered by Neil Barofsky, who riled Wall Street with his stinging reports as the first inspector general of TARP. See his book *Bailout: How Washington Abandoned Main Street While Rescuing Wall Street* (New York: Free Press, 2012), xxi–xxiii.

63. In addition to Dudley, the presidents of three regional bank presidents (as of 2016) had worked at Goldman Sachs: Robert Steven Kaplan (Dallas), Neel Kashkari (Minneapolis), and Patrick Harker (Philadelphia).

64. Philip Mirowski, *Never Let a Serious Crisis Go to Waste* (London: Verso, 2013), 18. For the FRBNY statements, see www.ny.frb.org/aboutthefed/ Dudley_Financials_2008_2010.pdf and www.ny.frb.org/aboutthefed/ Dudley_Financials_2011.pdf. Also see "New York Fed Fails to Amend Conflict Rules after Dudley Waiver," *Bloomberg News*, July 22, 2011, and the US Government Accountability Office report highlighting the problem: *Securities and Exchange Commission: Existing Post-Employment Controls Could be Further Strengthened*, GA-11-654, available at www.gao.gov/new.items/d11654.pdf.

65. Marver H. Bernstein, *Regulating Business by Independent Commission* (Westport CT: Greenwood Press, 1955); Theodore Lowi, *The End of Liberalism: The Second Republic of the United States* (New York: Norton, 1979).

66. Simon Kwan. "Cracking the Glass-Steagall Barriers," Federal Reserve Bank of San Francisco Economic Letter 97-08, March 21, 1997; Binyamin Appelbaum. "Fed Held Back as Evidence Mounted on Subprime Loan Abuses," *Washington Post*, September 27, 2009; James Kwak, "Cultural Capture and the Financial Crisis," in *Preventing Regulatory Capture*, ed. Daniel Carpenter and David Moss (New York: Cambridge University Press, 2014), 71–98 (especially 72–73).

67. Appelbaum, "Fed Held Back." Strained defenses for the Fed's disastrous policies before 2008 tend to hang on the claim that they represented prevailing understandings of what was in the public interest. Among the flaws with these claims are that they violated existing law, failed to impose established rules, and ignored warnings of threats to the public good. Kwak, "Cultural Capture and the Financial Crisis," 73–75.

68. Michael Abramowitz and Steven Mufson, "Papers Detail Industry's Role in Cheney's Energy Report," *Washington Post*, July 18, 2007, www .washingtonpost.com/wp-dyn/content/article/2007/07/17/AR2007071701987 .html.

69. Kwak, "Cultural Capture and the Financial Crisis," 71–98. One of the most effective efforts to track the political influence on US financial policy to ideology, institutions, and interests is by Nolan McCarty, Keith Poole, and Howard Rosenthal, *Political Bubbles: Financial Crises and*

the Failure of American Democracy (Princeton, NJ: Princeton University Press, 2013).

70. Quoted in Joe Becker and Gretchen Morgenson, "Geithner, Member and Overseer of Finance Club," *New York Times*, April 26, 2009, www .nytimes.com/2009/04/27/business/27geithner.html?pagewanted=all.

71. Simon Johnson and James Kwak, *13 Bankers: The Wall Street Takeover and the Next Financial Meltdown* (New York: Pantheon Books, 2010).

72. Andrews, "Greenspan Concedes Error on Regulation"; FCIC, *Final Report*, xviii, 23, 28, 35; Kristin Jones, "Top Regulators Once Opposed Regulation of Derivatives," ProPublica, October 6, 2008, www .propublica.org/article/top-regulators-once-opposed-regulation-of-derivatives.

73. Alexis de Tocqueville, *Democracy in America*, trans. by George Lawrence, ed. J. P. Mayer (New York, [1835] 1988).

74. Jonathan Martin and Mike Allen, "McCain Calls Lobbyists 'Birds of Prey,'" *Politico*, August 20, 2008, www.politico.com/story/2008/08/mccain-calls-lobbyists-birds-of-prey-012678.

75. Mancur Olson, *The Logic of Collective Action: Public Goods and the Theory of Groups* (Cambridge, MA: Harvard University Press, 1971).

76. Kwak, "Cultural Capture and the Financial Crisis," 71–98, especially 92.

77. There are sobering challenges in persuasively attributing the policies of regulators to the takeover by special interests as opposed to reflecting competing definitions of the public interest, bureaucratic deadlock, and coincidence. One critique of claims of regulatory capture has been offered by Carpenter and Moss, who insist on a stringent behavioral approach to studying agency behavior based on observed and indisputable evidence of intent and action by regulators to service the requests of industry. Daniel Carpenter and David Moss, "Introduction," in *Preventing Regulatory Capture*, 1–22; Daniel Carpenter, *Reputation and Power: Organizational Image and Pharmaceutical Regulation at the FDA* (Princeton, NJ: Princeton University Press, 2010).

Carpenter and Moss's admonition deserves attention. Indeed, our own review of the career trajectories of Fed officials finds that certain authoritative decision-makers did enjoy careers in finance but their numbers were limited. Based on the information we were able to assemble, the vast majority of Fed officials never worked at a financial firm; most spent their careers at the Fed, worked for US or international firms outside of Wall Street and finance, or came from academia. Authority to make consequential decisions further dilutes the number of cases with ties to finance: some of the relatively few Fed staff with careers in finance worked in the central bank's technical offices that lacked significant decision-making authority—research and statistics office, consumer and community affairs, information technology, and operations and payment systems.

There is an important caveat, however, that underscores the limits of the stringent behavioral approach: tracing career trajectories of current

Fed officials is very difficult or impossible in many cases because the central bank does not provide this information and even laborious online searches failed. Our findings caution us from assuming "capture" and an all-encompassing revolving door process. Yet we also resist narrow empirical tests that close down needed research. Finding reliable data suitable for statistical tests of intent and action is implausible for studying agencies and regulatory actions (and inactions) where decision-making is concealed (as in the case of the Fed). The limits on social science methodologies to isolate and measure the magnitude of influence by finance does not preclude observational techniques and methods that study career lines and detect consequential processes and impacts of lobbying on senior Fed officials. Moreover, anchoring influence to "action" ignores the impact of finance on the Fed in producing inaction—as we document in subsequent chapters. Even Carpenter and Moss's edited volume includes chapters that illustrate the limits of their stringent behavioral method (e.g., Chapters 4 and 6).

A reasonable approach is to adopt multimethod approaches and recognize finance as one of a set of persistent pressures that, in concrete situations, may act alone or in conjunction with other forces. The inability to conclude that the financial sector captured the Fed and other agencies "should not end our inquiry," according to James Kwak in his chapter for the volume edited by Carpenter and Moss (74). We agree.

78. Theda Skocpol, "Bringing the State Back In," in *Bringing the State Back In*, ed. Peter B. Evans, Dietrich Rueschemeyer, and Theda Skocpol (New York: Cambridge University Press, 1985); Michael Levine and Jennnifer Forrence, "Regulator Capture, Public Interests, and the Public Agenda," *Journal of Law, Economics, and Organizations* 6 (1990): 167–198; Nicholas Bagley and Richard Revesz, "Centralized Oversight of the Regulatory State," *Columbia Law Review* 106 (October 2006): 1260–1329; Lawrence Jacobs, *The Health of Nations* (Ithaca, NY: Cornell University Press, 1993); Steven Croley, "Public Interested Regulation," *Florida State University Law Review* 28 (Fall 2000): 9–15. How agencies define their missions internally and the set of organizations that populate its environment and scrutinize its behavior influence whether the agency pursues narrow interests or broader social interests. The Fed's own interests as well as the pressure of finance exemplified the former; the latter is illustrated by Social Security, which serves a vast swathe of America in including all seniors as well as the disabled, dependents left without a parent, and others.

79. Broz, "The Origins of Central Banking" and "Origins of the Federal Reserve System."

80. The Fed also rakes in cash from financial services related to the processing of check and electronic payment and other activities.

81. The Fed's expenses in 2014 include $590 million for its board and $563 million for the new Consumer Financial Protection Bureau. In addition,

it pays a 6 percent dividend on the investment that private banks have in the Fed's 12 regional banks. A clear description of this arrangement is available here: David Dayen, "This Is the Fed's Most Brazen and Least Known Handout to Private Banks," *New Republic*, March 9, 2014, www.newrepublic.com/article/116913/federal-reserve-dividends-most-outrageous-handout-banks; Samantha Sharf, "Fed Sending $98.7 Billion of 2014 Profits to U.S. Treasury," *Forbes*, January 9, 2015, www.forbes .com/sites/samanthasharf/2015/01/09/fed-sending-98-7-billion-of-2014-profits-to-u-s-treasury/; Marvin Goodfriend, "Central Banking in the Credit Turmoil: An Assessment of Federal Reserve Practice," *Journal of Monetary Economics* 58 (January 2011): 1–12.

82. Most of this astronomical income was interest on the Fed's huge purchases of bonds (also known as "quantitative easing"), but even in 2005–2007 the Fed was transferring $21.5 billion to $34.6 billion to the Treasury.

83. Luigi Zingales, "Preventing Economists' Capture," in *Preventing Regulatory Capture*, 124–151, especially 128–129.

84. Edward Prescott, "Should Bank Supervisors Disclose Information About Their Banks?" *Economic Quarterly* 94 (Winter 2008): 1–16.

85. Ben Bernanke, "Financial Reform to Address Systemic Risk," Speech to the Council on Foreign Relations, Washington, DC, March 10, 2009, http://ow.ly/WmlA9.

86. James Kwak argues that deference to finance serves the public interest, in the view of many central bank staff. Kwak, "Cultural Capture and the Financial Crisis," 71–98. As a more general matter, the mix of institutional self-interest and public interest among government agencies is discussed in Sidney Shapiro and Ronald Wright, "The Future of the Administrative Presidency: Turning Administrative Law Inside-Out," *Miami Law Review* 65 (2011): 577–603; Levine and Forrence, "Regulatory Capture, Public Interest, and the Public Agenda"; Howard Latin, "Regulatory Failure, Administrative Incentives, and the New Clean Air Act," *Environmental Law Review* 21 (1991): 1647–1720.

87. Thomas Mayer, "Introduction," in *The Political Economy of American Monetary Policy*, ed. Thomas Mayer (New York: Cambridge University Press, 1990); William J. Bernhard, Lawrence Broz, and William Clark, "The Political Economy of Monetary Institutions," *International Organization* 56 (Autumn 2002): 693–723; Nathaniel Beck, "Congress and the Fed: Why the Dog Does Not Bark in the Night," in *The Political Economy of American Monetary Policy*; Kevin Grier, "Congressional Influence on U.S. Monetary Policy," *Journal of Monetary Economics* 28 (1991): 201–220, and "Congressional Oversight Committee Influence on U.S. Monetary Policy Revisted," *Journal of Monetary Economics* 38 (1996): 571–579.

88. Max Weber, *Essays in Sociology*, eds. Hans Gerth and C. Wright Mills (Oxford: Oxford University Press, 1946), 253–255, 262.

89. Morris Fiorina, *Congress: Keystone of the Washington Establishment*, 2nd ed. (New Haven, CT: Yale University Press, 1989); David W. Brady and Craig Volden, *Revolving Gridlock: Politics and Policy from Jimmy Carter to George W. Bush*, 2nd ed. (Boulder, CO: Westview Press, 2005).

90. Stephen Skowronek, *Building a New American State: The Expansion of National Administrative Capacities, 1877–1920* (New York: Cambridge University Press, 1982); De Tocqueville, *Democracy in America*, 394–395; J. P. Nettl, "The State as a Conceptual Variable," *World Politics* 20 (July 1968): 559–592; Werner Sombart, *Why Is There No Socialism in the United States?* trans. Patricia M. Hocking and C. T. Husbands (White Plains, NY: International Arts and Sciences Press, 1976); Louis Hartz, *The Liberal Tradition in America: An Interpretation of American Political Thought since the Revolution* (New York: Harcourt, Brace and World, 1955). More contemporary studies of America's feeble administration include Brown and Jacobs, *The Private Abuse of the Public Interest*; Thomas Mann and Norman Ornstein, *The Broken Branch: How Congress Is Failing America and How to Get It Back on Track* (New York: Oxford University Press, 2006) and *It's Even Worse Than It Looks: How the American Constitutional System Collided with the New Politics of Extremism* (New York: Basic Books, 2012); Lawrence Jacobs and Desmond King, eds., *The Unsustainable American State* (New York: Oxford University Press, 2009); Desmond King and Robert Lieberman, "Ironies of the American State," *World Politics* 61 (July 2009): 547–588; Pew Research Center, "Public Trust in Government," www.people-press.org/2013/01/31/trust-in-government-interactive/.

91. Michael Glennon, *National Security and Double Government* (New York: Oxford University Press, 2015); Arthur M. Schlesinger Jr., *The Imperial Presidency* (Boston: Houghton Mifflin, 1973); Richard Pious, *The American Presidency* (New York: Basic Books, 1979); Harold Koh, *The National Security Constitution* (New Haven, CT: Yale University Press, 1990); Louis Fisher, *Presidential War Power*, 3rd ed. (Lawrence: University Press of Kansas, 2013).

92. The discrepancy between presidential and Fed power stems in large part from the distinct constitutional, political, and informational features of domestic as opposed to foreign policy. Even presidents find that their prerogatives on the domestic front are more limited and vulnerable to challenge and reversal than they are in foreign and military power. For instance, executive orders, regulatory reviews, and other White House tools are subject to reversal by future presidents. Robert Stein and Kenneth Bickers, *Perpetuating the Pork Barrel: Policy Subsystems and American Democracy* (New York: Cambridge University Press, 1997).

93. The autonomy of government agencies is built on technical capacity and leeway from constraining institutional checks. Although the Fed's independence is unrivalled in contemporary domestic policymaking, the historic roots of government autonomy lay with the development of the departments of Treasury and Agriculture during the Progressive Era.

Daniel P. Carpenter, *The Forging of Bureaucratic Autonomy* (Princeton, NJ: Princeton University Press, 2001).

94. Woodrow Wilson, *Constitutional Government in the United States* (New York: Columbia University Press, 1908); Robert Dahl, *A Preface to Democratic Theory* (Chicago: University of Chicago Press, 1956); E. E. Schattschneider, *The Semi-Sovereign People: A Realist's View of Democracy in America* (New York: Holt, Rinehart and Winston, 1960).

95. Douglass North and Barry Weingast, "Constitutions and Commitment: The Evolution of Institutions Governing Public Choice in Seventeenth-Century England," *Journal of Economic History* 49 (1989): 803–832.

96. Quoted in John Brinsley and Anthony Massucci, "Volcker Says Fed's Bear Loan Stretches Legal Power," *Bloomberg News*, April 8, 2008.

97. Skocpol, "Bringing the State Back In"; Jacobs and King, *The Unsustainable American State*; Lawrence R. Jacobs and Joe Soss, "The Politics of Inequality in America: A Political Economy Framework," *Annual Review of American Politics* 13 (2010): 341–364.

98. For an account of the Fed's recipe of monetary responses, see "Monetary Policy since the Onset of the Crisis," remarks by Ben S. Bernanke, Federal Reserve Bank of Kansas City Economic Symposium, August 31, 2012. And for an evaluation, see discussion of "Crunch Time: Fiscal Crises and the Role of Monetary Policy," remarks by Jerome H. Powell, Board of Governors of the FRS, US Monetary Policy Forum conference, New York, February 22, 2013. For an early assessment, see Marc Labonte, *Financial Turmoil: Federal Reserve Policy Responses* (Washington, DC: Congressional Research Service, April 9, 2009).

99. Fernandez-Albertos, "The Politics of Central Bank Independence," 217–237, 231.

100. FCIC, *Final Report*, 373.

101. Alan Blinder, "Quantitative Easing: Entrance and Exit Strategies," *Federal Reserve Bank of St. Louis Review* (November/December 2010): 473, 469.

102. Blinder, "Quantitative Easing," 476; also see Martin Feldstein, "What Powers for the Federal Reserve?" *Journal of Economic Literature* 48 (March 2010): 134–145; Goodfriend, "Central Banking in the Credit Turmoil," 1–12.

103. Christopher Adolph carefully documents how central banks (including the Fed) are now making fiscal policy decisions. *Bankers, Bureaucrats, and Central Bank Politics*, 230.

104. Wilson, *Constitutional Government in the United States* and *Congressional Government: A Study in American Politics* (Boston: Houghton Mifflin, 1885); James MacGregor Burns, *Deadlock of Democracy: Four-Party Politics in America* (Englewood Cliffs, NJ: Prentice-Hall, 1963); Mann and Ornstein, *The Broken Branch*.

105. Bob Ivry, Bradley Keoun, and Phil Kuntz, "Secret Fed Loans Gave Banks $13 Billion Undisclosed to Congress," *Bloomberg News*, November 27, 2011, www.bloomberg.com/news/2011-11-28/secret-fed-loans-undisclosed-to-congress-gave-banks-13-billion-in-income.html.

106. Donald Kettl, *Leadership at the Fed* (New Haven, CT: Yale University Press, 1988), 159–160; Greta Krippner. *Capitalizing the Crisis*, 107–108.

107. Ivry, Keoun, and Kuntz, "Secret Fed Loans"; but cf. Ben Bernanke, "Letter to Congressional Leaders," December 6, 2011, www .documentcloud.org/documents/271227-emergency-lending-financial-crisis-20111206.html#document/p1.

108. Gavin Finch and Liam Vaughan, "European Banks Devour ECB Emergency Funds," *Bloomberg News*, December 21, 2011, www .bloomberg.com/news/articles/2011-12-21/european-banks-devour-ecb-emergency-funds-amid-frozen-markets.

109. Martin van Vliet quoted in Finch and Vaughan, "European Banks Devour ECB Emergency Funds."

110. The polls of Bernanke's favorability rating were conducted by, among others, Bloomberg Poll, December 3–7, 2009, www.pollingreport.com/budget8.htm.

111. The AIG questions are the following: "As you may know, the Federal Reserve will loan up to $85 billion to the giant insurance company American International Group, also known as AIG, which will put the federal government in control of the company. How closely have you been following the news about this: very closely, somewhat closely, not too closely or not at all?" "Do you favor or oppose the Federal Reserve's decision to make the loan to AIG?" USA Today/Gallup Poll, September 17, 2008, www.pollingreport.com/business3 .htm.

112. Ivry, Keoun, and Kuntz, "Secret Fed Loans." Bernanke challenged, without evidence, Bloomberg's accounting in his "Letter to Congressional Leaders." His own accounting reports only a fraction of the Fed's loans and guarantees: remarks by Ben S. Bernanke, "Monetary Policy Objectives and Tools in a Low-Inflation Environment," Conference sponsored by the Federal Reserve Bank of Boston, Boston, MA, October 15, 2010.

113. Office of the Special Inspector General for TARP. Quarterly Report to Congress, October 26, 2010, www.sigtarp.gov/Quarterly%20Reports/October2010_Quarterly_Report_to_Congress.pdf.

114. Suzanne Mettler, *The Submerged State: How Invisible Government Policies Undermine American Democracy* (Chicago: University of Chicago Press, 2011).

115. Morgenson, "Banks, at Least, Had a Friend in Geithner."

116. Feldstein, "What Powers for the Federal Reserve?"; John Taylor, "Fed Policy Is a Drag on the Economy," *Wall Street Journal*, January 28, 2013, www.wsj.com/articles/SB100014241278873233752045782679432366558414; Neil Irwin, "Quantitative Easing Is Ending. Here's What It Did, in Charts," *New York Times*, October 29, 2014, www.nytimes .com/2014/10/30/upshot/quantitative-easing-is-about-to-end-heres-what-it-did-in-seven-charts.html?_r=0&abt=0002&abg=1.

117. FCIC, *Final Report*, xvii–xviii.

118. Stephen Cecchetti, "Crisis and Responses: The Federal Reserve in the Early Stages of the Financial Crisis," *Journal of Economic Perspectives* 23 (Winter 2009): 70–71; Goodfriend, "Central Banking in the Credit Turmoil," 9–10.

119. FCIC, *Final Report*, 414.

120. "The Political Price of Backing Invaluable TARP," *Washington Post*, July 5, 2010, www.washingtonpost.com/wp-dyn/content/article/2010/07/04/AR2010070403831.html.

121. Ron Paul, *End the Fed* (New York: Grand Central Publishing, 2009), ch. 10.

122. Joshua Zumbrun, "More than Half of U.S. Wants Fed Curbed or Abolished," *Bloomberg News*, December 9, 2010, www.bloomberg.com/news/articles/2010-12-09/more-than-half-of-americans-want-fed-reined-in-or-abolished.

123. There have been penetrating studies of the origins of the financial crisis by journalists (e.g., Gillian Tett, *Fool's Gold: How Unrestrained Greed Corrupted a Dream, Shattered Global Markets, and Unleashed a Catastrophe* [Boston: Little Brown, 2009]; Gretchen Morgenson, *Reckless Endangerment: How Outsized Ambition, Greed, and Corruption Led to Economic Armageddon* [New York: Times Books, 2011]) and by a student of political economy (Krippner, *Capitalizing the Crisis*).

124. Kettl, *Leadership at the Fed*; John T. Woolley, *Monetary Politics* (New York: Cambridge University Press, 1984). More focused studies have been conducted of the financial crisis by Philip Wallach and the Fed's relations with Congress by Sarah Binder. Philip Wallach, *To the Edge: Legality, Legitimacy, and the Responses to the 2008 Financial Crisis* (Washington, DC: Brookings Institution, 2015).

125. Jacob Hacker and Paul Pierson, *Winner-Take-All Politics* (New York: Simon & Schuster, 2010); Larry Bartels, *Unequal Democracy: The Political Economy of the New Gilded Age* (Princeton, NJ: Princeton University Press, 2008); Lawrence Jacobs and Theda Skocpol, eds., *Inequality and American Democracy: What We Know and What We Need to Learn* (New York: Russell Sage Foundation, 2005).

126. Mirowski, *Never Let a Serious Crisis Go to Waste*, 194; Lawrence H. White, "The Federal Reserve System's Influence on Research in Monetary Economics," *Economics Journal Watch* 2, no. 2 (August 2005): 325–354.

127. White, "Federal Research System's Influence," 336.

128. Edward Kane quoted in White, "The Federal Reserve System's Influence," 325–354, especially 327.

129. Zingales, "Preventing Economists' Capture," 124–125.

130. Ryan Grim, "Priceless: How the Federal Reserve Bought the Economics Profession," *Huffington Post*, originally posted October 23, 2009, and revised May 13, 2013, http://ow.ly/GFxPQ.

131. Grim, "Priceless."

132. This section draws on Lawrence Jacobs and Joe Soss, "The Politics of Inequality in America: A Political Economy Framework," *Annual Review of American Politics* 13 (2010): 341–364.

133. Relying on concrete observation to document influence is one—among several—well-established approaches to research on politics and policymaking. Dahl, *A Preface to Democratic Theory*; Carpenter and Moss, "Introduction," in *Preventing Regulatory Capture*, 1–22.

134. From a transcript of a phone call on December 17, 1936, reported in Morgenthau Diaries and quoted in Kettl, *Leadership at the Fed*, 58 note 37.

135. Quoted in Kettl, *Leadership at the Fed*, 84.

136. This mode of analysis is one of the oldest and most revered in the social sciences. Max Weber, "Class, Status, Party," in *Essays in Sociology*, 108–195; Mustafa. Emirbayer, "Manifesto for a Relational Sociology," *American Journal of Sociology* 103, no. 2 (1997): 281–317; Charles Tilly, "To Explain Political Processes," *American Journal of Sociology* 100, no. 6 (1995): 1594–1610.

137. Kwak, "Cultural Capture and the Financial Crisis"; Adolph, *Bankers, Bureaucrats, and Central Bank Politics*.

138. Global financial markets generate common pressures on individual nation states, but domestic institutions and policy trajectories create meaningful variations in the responses of particular states. In our analysis, we focus on the historic development of domestic policymaking and institutions, with a keen attention to how they condition the response of the US government and the Fed to global markets and international regimes. Peter Hall and David Soskice, eds., *Varieties of Capitalism: The Institutional Foundations of Comparative Advantage* (New York: Oxford University Press, 2001); Bruce Bueno de Mesquita and Alastair Smith, "Domestic Explanations of International Relations," *Annual Review of Political Science* 15 (2012): 161–181; Michael Barnett and Martha Finnemore, "The Power of Liberal International Organizations," in Michael Barnett and Raymond Duvall, *Power in Global Governance* (New York: Cambridge University Press, 2005), 161–184; Fred Block, *Revising State Theory: Essays in Politics and Postindustrialism* (Philadelphia: Temple University Press, 1987); Charles E. Lindblom, *Politics and Markets: The World's Political Economic Systems* (New York: Basic Books, 1977).

139. Analysts have long used well-designed thought experiments based on plausible counterfactuals that examine "policy options that were available, considered, and narrowly defeated." Giovanni Capoccia and R. Daniel Kelemen, "The Study of Critical Junctures: Theory, Narrative, and Counterfactuals in Historical Institutionalism," *World Politics* 59, no. 3 (April 2007): 341–369, especially 356. Also helpful are Gary King, Robert O. Keohane, and Sidney Verba, *Designing Social Inquiry* (Princeton, NJ: Princeton University Press, 1994), 77–80;

Martin Bunzl, "Counterfactual History: A User's Guide," *American Historical Review* 109, no. 3 (2004): 845–858.

140. MacKinlay Kantor, "If the South Had Won the Civil War," *Look Magazine* 24 (November 22, 1960): 30–62; Tom Wicker, "If Lincoln Had Not Freed the Slaves," in Robert Cowley, ed., *What If?* Vol. 2 (New York: Putnam, 2001), 152–164.

141. Creative destruction has been discussed for decades before it was popularized by Joseph Schumpeter. Schumpeter, *Capitalism, Socialism, and Democracy*, 82–83; Werner Sombart, *Why Is There No Socialism in the United States?*, ed. C. T. Husbands (White Plains, NY: M. E. Sharpe, 1976).

2: THE RISE OF THE FED STATE

1. E. E. Schattschneider, *The Semi-Sovereign People: A Realist's View of Democracy in America* (New York: Rinehart and Winston, 1960), 71.

2. There are important historical studies of the political transformation of finance that we reference extensively below. Discussions of contemporary US politics neglects, however, the Fed and financial policy and its roots in American political development.

3. The importance of temporal sequencing and the significance of initially small institutional changes that open new trajectories for later development is a key insight of historical institutionalism. Theda Skocpol and Paul Pierson, "Historical Institutionalism in Contemporary Political Science," in *Political Science: State of the Discipline*, ed., I. Katznelson and H. Milner (New York: Norton, 2002), 693–721.

4. Edwin Walter Kemmerer, *The ABC of the Federal Reserve System* (Princeton, NJ: Princeton University Press, 1936), 5.

5. PBS, "Jesse James' Bank Robberies," www.pbs.org/wgbh/americanexperience/features/general-article/james-robberies.

6. Quora, "How Much Physical Money Is Inside the Average Retail Bank?" November 27, 2011, www.quora.com/How-much-physical-money-is-inside-the-average-retail-bank.

7. Ben Bernanke, "Clearinghouses, Financial Stability, and Financial Reform," Remarks to the 2011 Financial Markets Conference, Atlanta, April 4, 2011, 3.

8. Louis Hartz, *Economic Policy and Democratic Thought* (Cambridge, MA: Harvard University Press, 1948), and Marc Stears, *Progressives, Pluralists, and the Problem of the State* (New York: Oxford University Press, 2000), ch. 4.

9. President Andrew Jackson, "Veto Message Regarding the Bank of the United States," July 10, 1832, http://avalon.law.yale.edu/19th_century/ajveto01.asp.

10. J. Lawrence Broz, "Origins of the Federal Reserve System: International Incentives and the Domestic Free-Rider Problem," *International Organization* 53 (Winter): 48–51. In comparison to European economies, US banks were ill-equipped to serve as needed intermediaries to facilitate (at relatively low rates) the payment of exporters and the collection from importers. They had a limited number of financial instruments (such as bankers' acceptances, commercial paper, and Treasury bills) to sell and purchase and small secondary markets, which put them at a disadvantage against their competitors in Germany, Britain, and other leading trade countries.

11. Democratic Party Platform of 1896, July 7, 1896, www.presidency.ucsb.edu/ws/?pid=29586.

12. One proposal known as the Subtreasury Plan would permit farmers to store harvests in federal warehouses when prices were low in exchange for government loans up to 80 percent of the market value of the crops. Sidney Rothstein, "Macune's Monopoly: Economic Law and the Legacy of Populism," *Studies in American Political Development* 28 (April 2014): 80–106.

13. A number of studies have examined the losing battles of populist against monopolies and monetary policies that favored banks and wealthy interests. Lawrence Goodwyn, *Democratic Promise: The Populist Movement in America* (New York: Oxford University Press, 1976); James Livingston, *Origins of the Federal Reserve System: Money, Class, and Corporate Capitalism, 1890–1913* (Ithaca, NY: Cornell University Press, 1986); Charles Postel, *The Populist Vision* (New York: Oxford University Press, 2007).

14. Quoted in Elizabeth Sanders, *Roots of Reform* (Chicago: University of Chicago Press, 1999), 139.

15. Democratic Party Platform of 1896, July 7, 1896, www.presidency.ucsb.edu/ws/?pid=29586.

16. Walter Dean Burnham, "The Changing Shape of the American Political Universe," *American Political Science Review* 59 (1965): 23, and *Critical Elections and the Mainsprings of American Politics* (New York: Norton, 1970), 71–90; Schattschneider, *The Semi-Sovereign People*, 78–85; cf. V. O. Key, "A Theory of Critical Elections," *Journal of Politics* 17 (1955): 3–18; see for review Richard McCormick, "Walter Dean Burnham and 'The System of 1896,'" *Social Science History* 10 (Autumn 1986): 245–262. The "System of 1896" thesis generated a number of critical evaluations of its analysis of the realignment of political parties and electoral participation. Less attention has been focused on a second vital element of their argument, the transformation of US governance; this is our focus. For extensive review, see David Mayhew, "Electoral Realignments," *Annual Review of Political Science* 3 (2000): 449–474.

17. McCormick, "Walter Dean Burnham," 253; Michael Kazin, *A Godly Hero: The Life of William Jennings Bryan* (New York: Knopf, 2006).

18. Democratic Party Platform of 1912, June 25, 1912, www.presidency.ucsb
    .edu/ws/?pid=29590.
19. Livingston, *Origins of the Federal Reserve System*, 26.
20. Scott C. James, *Presidents, Parties, and the State: A Party System
    Perspective on Democratic Regulatory Choice, 1884–1936* (Cambridge:
    Cambridge University Press, 2006); Goodwyn, *Democratic Promise*, 519;
    Postel, *The Populist Vision*, 280.
21. For a readable account of the Jekyll Island tete-a-tete, see Liaquat
    Ahamed, *Lords of Finance* (New York: Penguin and London: Windmill
    Books, 2009), 54–59. Senator Nelson Aldrich was not only chair of the
    Finance Committee, but also at this point more central to the political
    process than President William Taft or the House Speaker. See Eric
    Schickler, *Disjointed Pluralism* (Princeton, NJ: Princeton University
    Press, 2001), 72–83; and Jeffrey A. Jenkins "The Evolution of Party
    Leadership," in *The Oxford Handbook of the American Congress*, ed.
    Eric Schickler and Frances E. Lee (Oxford: Oxford University Press,
    2011), 696–697.
22. Broz, "Origins of the Federal Reserve," 57–59.
23. One of the key forums for Aldrich's efforts to rally attention to the need
    for financial reform and to his proposal for a new central bank was the
    National Monetary Commission that was created by the 1908 Aldrich-
    Vreeland Act.
24. Broz, "Origins of the Federal Reserve," 56–57 includes the details.
25. Broz, "Origins of the Federal Reserve," which quotes and cites in detail
    numerous Warburg memoranda, writings, and speeches collected in Paul
    M. Warburg, *The Federal Reserve System: Its Origin and Growth*, 2 vols.
    (New York: Macmillan, 1930).
26. Lawrence Broz argues that banks were indifferent about investing their
    time and resources. Their participation in establishing a generic central
    bank represented a "good" that would be widely shared, including with
    free riders who did not work for its passage. The resolution of this
    "collective action problem" was to create selective rewards to incentivize
    banks to work to pass the law. In effect, Broz reverses the usual critique
    of banks as slavishly rigging the Fed to their benefit. Instead, the reward
    of a strong currency supplied the incentives necessary to persuade banks
    to build a public good that served the country as a whole. Broz, "Origins
    of the Federal Reserve System," 39–70. For an account that does locate
    the Fed's origin in capitalism, see Livingston, *Origins of the Federal
    Reserve System*, who argues that "the origins of the Federal Reserve
    System lies in the awakening and articulation of capitalist class
    consciousness" (18).
27. Although the Fed's founding was premised in part on regulating the
    supply of money to stabilize banks and the economy, its original
    approach to monetary policy was quite different from today's strategy.
    The contemporary Fed's monetary policy is countercyclical—restrict the
    amount of money in circulation during economic expansion to tamp down

the risk of inflation and expand it during contractions to stimulate growth. When the Fed was created, however, the prevailing strategy was to issue additional money during expansion to encourage further growth and restrict it to during downturns.

28. A tug-of-war over implementing the agreed-upon structure broke out over where to locate the 12 regional Fed branches. Regional Banks were located in the largest financial centers in the country; they were also established in underserved areas in the South to create new hubs to challenge the dominance of Northeast banks and to reward regions dominated by Democrats, who controlled the White House and Congress in 1913. Sarah Binder and Mark Spindel, "Monetary Politics: Origins of the Federal Reserve," *Studies in American Political Development* 27 (April 2013): 1–13.

29. John T. Woolley, *Monetary Politics* (New York: Cambridge University Press, 1984), 35–37.

30. Ahamed, *Lords of Finance*, 173.

31. Allan H. Meltzer, *A History of the Federal Reserve: Volume I: 1913–1951* (Chicago: University of Chicago Press, 2003), 1.

32. Donald Kettl, *Leadership at the Fed* (New Haven, CT: Yale University Press, 1988), 4.

33. Albert Hart, ed., *Selected Addresses and Public Papers of Woodrow Wilson* (New York: Boni and Liverbright Publishers, 1918), 158–159.

34. Meltzer, *A History of the Federal Reserve: Volume I*, 1; Kettl *Leadership at the Fed*, 1; Stephen Skowronek, *Building a New American State: The Expansion of National Administrative Capacities, 1877–1920* (New York: Cambridge University Press, 1982); J. K. Galbraith, *The Great Crash 1929* (Harmondsworth: Penguin, 1961), 32.

35. Galbraith, *The Great Crash*, 32.

36. See Marriner S. Eccles, "Statement Before the Senate Finance Committee on Investigation of Economic Problems," February 25, 1933, for his five-point action plan, cited in Thorvald Grung Moe, "Marriner S. Eccles and the 1951 Treasury-Federal Reserve Accord: Lessons for Central Bank Independence," Levy Economics Institute Working Paper No. 747, January 2013, www.levyinstitute.org/pubs/wp_747.pdf, 11.

37. Robert L. Hetzel and Ralph F. Leach, "The Treasury-Fed Acccord: A New Narrative Account," Federal Reserve Bank of Richmond, *Economic Quarterly* 87, no. 1 (2001): 33–55.

38. Kettl, *Leadership at the Fed*, 13–16; Thorvald Grung Moe, "Marriner S. Eccles and the 1951 Treasury-Federal Reserve Accord: Lessons for Central Bank Independence, Levy Economics Institute of Bard College, Working Paper, January 2013.

39. From a transcript of a phone call on December 17, 1936, reported in Morgenthau Diaries and quoted in Kettl, *Leadership at the Fed*, 58 note 37.

40. For an account of this period and the trajectory leading to the Fed-Treasury Accord, see Hetzel and Leach, "The Treasury-Fed Acccord," 33–55.

41. Kettl, *Leadership at the Fed*, 28, 43.

42. Truman promised to make Eccles vice chairman, but after three months without an announcement of this appointment Eccles declined to be a candidate, remaining as an ordinary board member believing Truman too hostile to honor his promise. Cited from Eccles Papers in Kettl, *Leadership at the Fed*, 63.

43. The Treasury was left with nonmarketable bonds, but the Fed withdrew its prior guarantee of the Treasury's short-term market. Mitchel Y. Abolafia, "Central Banking and the Triumph of Technical Rationality," in *The Oxford Handbook of the Sociology of Finance*, ed., Karin Knorr Cetina and Alex Preda (New York: Oxford University Press, 2012), 97–98.

44. Meltzer, *A History of the Federal Reserve: Volume I*, 708–712; but cf. Woolley, *Monetary Politics*, 46.

45. A combination of restrictions in the 1932 legislation and caution by the Board of Governors delayed the Fed's use of 13(3). The Fed eventually capitalized on its new power as its institutional standing grew and new legislation (especially the 1991 FDIC Improvement Act) authorized it to lend directly to individuals and businesses during emergencies. Alexander Mehra, "Legal Authority in Unusual and Exigent Circumstances: The Federal Reserve and the Financial Crisis," *University of Pennsylvania Journal of Business Law* 13 (Fall 2010): 221–273; David Fettig, "The History of a Powerful Paragraph," June 1, 2008, www .minneapolisfed.org/publications_papers/pub_display.cfm?id=3485; Tim Sablik, "Fed Credit Policy During the Great Depression," Federal Reserve Bank of Richmond, March 2013, EB13–03, www.richmondfed.org/ publications/research/economic_brief/2013/pdf/eb_13-03.pdf.

46. Howard Hockley, *Lending Functions of the Federal Reserve Banks: A History* (Washington, DC: Board of Governors of the Federal Reserve System, 1973).

47. Moe, "Marriner S. Eccles and the 1951 Treasury-Federal Reserve Accord"; Kettl, *Leadership at the Fed*, 47–48.

48. Fred Block, *The Origins of International Economic Disorder* (Berkeley: University of California Press, 1977); Forrest Capie, Charles Goodhart, and Norbert Schnach, "The Development of Central Banking," in *The Future of Central Banking*, ed. Forrest Capie, Charles Goodhart, Stanley Fischer, and Norbert Schnadt (Cambridge: Cambridge University Press, 1994).

49. Lawrence H. White, "The Federal Reserve System's Influence on Research in Monetary Economics," *Economics Journal Watch* 2, no. 2 (August 2005): 325–354.

50. Moe, "Marriner S. Eccles and the 1951 Treasury-Federal Reserve Accord," 54–55.

51. Kettl, *Leadership at the Fed*, 116.

52. Kettl, *Leadership at the Fed*, 122–131.

53. The last Fed chair pushed out was in 1987, when the Reagan White House punished Paul Volcker for not being sufficiently aggressive in pursuing deregulation.

54. Terry Moe, "The Presidency and the Bureaucracy: The Presidential Advantage," in *The Presidency and the Political System*, 7th edition, ed. Michael Nelson (Washington, DC: Congressional Quarterly Press, 2003), 425–457; Matthew Dickinson, "The Executive Office of the President: The Paradox of Politicization," in Joel Aberbach and Mark Peterson, *Institutions of American Democracy* (New York: Oxford University Press, 2006), 135–173; Report of the Brownlow Committee [for President Franklin D. Roosevelt] (1937). Reprinted in *Basic Documents of Public Administration*, ed. F. C. Mosher (New York: Holmes & Meier Publishers, 1976); Richard Pious, *The American Presidency* (New York: Basic Books, 1979).

55. Bureaucratic autonomy built on technical capacity and a resulting reputation is not unique to the Fed, but was cultivated in such departments as Treasury and Agriculture in an era of Progressive expansion: Daniel P. Carpenter, *The Forging of Bureaucratic Autonomy* (Princeton, NJ: Princeton University Press, 2001).

56. One indicator of the Fed's integration into advanced social science research is the number of its staff and visitors who publish in exclusively academic journals. Thirty percent or more of the articles published over a five-year period in two well-respected economics journals (the *Journal of Monetary Economics* and the *Journal of Money, Credit and Banking*) had a coauthor who worked at the Fed, and more than double that proportion had had a Fed affiliation at some point. White, "The Federal Reserve System's Influence," 325–354, especially 326. This close connection between the economics profession and Fed policy economists is much weaker in other central banks such as the Bank of England or the ECB, as measured by who is appointed as governors and staff profiles.

57. Quoted in Kettl, *Leadership at the Fed*, 84.

58. Kettl, *Leadership at the Fed*, ch. 6, especially 159–163.

59. While central bank decisions over interest rates requires some time delay to avoid unnecessarily unsettling financial markets, the Fed has taken on (as we discuss in coming chapters) a range of fiscal policies that are normally debated in public.

60. The new oversight was triggered by a congressional resolution in 1975, the Federal Reserve Reform Act 1977, and the Humphrey-Hawkins Act 1978.

61. Quoted in Tim Todd, "The Balance of Power: The Political Battle for an Independent Central Bank, 1790–Present," Federal Reserve Bank of Kansas City, 2012, www.kansascityfed.org/publicat/balanceofpower/balanceofpower.pdf, 33.

62. Karl Blessing (president of Deutsche Bundesbank, 1958–1969) quoted in Tim Todd, "The Balance of Power."

63. The foundation for Keynesianism was John Maynard Keynes's 1936 masterpiece *The General Theory of Employment, Interest, and Money*. Paul Samuelson popularized the core insights of Keynes in his textbook

Economics (first published in 1948), helping to establish its hold on economic policy after World War II. John Maynard Keynes, *The General Theory of Employment, Interest, and Money* (London: Macmillan, 1936); Paul A Samuelson, *Economics* (New York: McGraw Hill, 1948).

64. Although the policy acceptance of monetarism did not occur until the 1970s, it had been developed decades earlier in the 1940s and 1950s. Academic research by Clark Warburton and Milton Friedman linked changes in the money supply to economic output in the short run and the price level over the long term. One of its central findings was that overexpansion of the money supply produces inflation.

65. Monetarists led by Milton Friedman assaulted the foundation of Keynesianism—using government spending to modulate consumer demand—and a lively battle ensued in the arenas of scholarly publications and policymaking. Keynesians forcefully responded to the challenge by pointing to the limits of monetarism and the effectiveness of government intervention since the 1970s. Even central banks (in the United States and elsewhere) hold back from following the strict guidelines of targeting money supply (instead of interest rates). Alan Blinder and Robert Solow, "Does Fiscal Policy Matter?" *Journal of Public Economics* 2 (1973): 319–337; J. Bradford DeLong, "The Triumph of Monetarism?" *Journal of Economic Perspectives* 14 (2000): 83–94.

66. Stuart Eisenstat quoted in William Greider, *Secrets of the Temple* (New York: Simon & Schuster, 1987), 47.

67. Neil Barofsky, *Bailout: How Washington Abandoned Main Street While Rescuing Wall Street* (New York: Free Press, 2012), xxi–xxiii.

68. The Report was conducted by the SEC's Office of Inspector General after the collapse of Bear Stearns. US SEC Office of Inspector General, Office of Audits, "SEC's Oversight of Bear Stearns and Related Entities: The Consolidated Supervised Entity Program," September 25, 2008, Report No. 446-A, www.sec.gov/about/oig/audit/2008/446-a.pdf; Statement by Chairman Cox on September 26, 2008: www.sec.gov/news/press/2008/2008-231.htm.

69. Neoliberalism should not be confused with the partisan ideology in America that favors government intervention to provide universal health insurance and other forms of activism. By contrast, neoliberalism is rooted in a philosophical tradition of minimal government and deference to private markets.

70. Legal and administrative actions against the largest mortgage businesses revealed that they deliberately discriminated against customers of color. Hispanic and African American borrowers paid higher-cost subprime loans while white borrowers of similar or weaker financial circumstances were offered lower-cost prime loans. In addition, as the financial crisis hit in 2009, the incidence of high-interest subprime mortgages being held by black households making more than $68,000 a year was more than five times greater than among whites of

similar or lower incomes. A study of Baltimore found that African American borrowers forked out 5 to 11 percent more in monthly mortgage repayments than whites; homeownership equity totaling $2 million evaporated in these areas as a result of the subprime collapse.

Investigations by the US Department of Justice that revealed racial disparities produced extraordinary settlements—loans by Countrywide led to a $335 million settlement (America's largest fair lending settlement) and disparities at Wells Fargo resulted in a $175 million settlement. Other national and local banks and mortgage companies across the country faced tough scrutiny for racial disparities in their lending practices that singled out black and Hispanic lenders for higher costs and greater vulnerability for foreclosure. Michael Powell, "Bank Accused of Pushing Mortgage Deals on Blacks," June 6, 2009, http://ow.ly/HKvZb; Christie Thompson, "Disparate Impact and Fair Housing: Seven Cases You Should Know," *ProPublica*, February 12, 2013, http://ow.ly/HKwaj; Jacob S. Rugh, Len Albright, and Douglas S. Massey, "Race, Space and Cumulative Disadvantage: A Case Study of the Subprime Lending Collapse," *Social Problems* 62 (2015): 186–218.

71. Gillian Tett, *Fool's Gold: How Unrestrained Greed Corrupted a Dream, Shattered Global Markets and Unleashed a Catastrophe* (Boston: Little Brown, 2009); Philip Augar, *Chasing Alpha* (London: Bodley Head, 2009); Hans-Werner Sinn, *Casino Capitalism* (Oxford: Oxford University Press, 2010); Lawrence J. Kotlikoff, *Jimmy Stewart Is Dead* (Hoboken, NJ: Wiley, 2010); and Raghuram F. Rajan, *Fault Lines* (Princeton, NJ: Princeton University Press, 2010).

72. "Evaluating Progress in Regulatory Reforms to Promote Financial Stability," remarks by Daniel K. Tarullo, Member Board of Governors FRS, at the Peterson Institute for International Economics, Washington, DC, May 3, 2013, especially 2–4.

73. Greta R. Krippner, *Capitalizing the Crisis: The Political Origins of the Rise of Finance* (Cambridge, MA: Harvard University Press, 2011), 27–28, 34–37, 47–48; and Krippner, "The Financialization of the American Economy," *Socio-Economic Review* 3 (2005): 173–208.

74. Greider, *Secrets of the Temple*, 45–47.

75. Kettl reviews these changes in *Leadership at the Fed*, 175–179, first set out in staff papers, then agreed at a special Saturday meeting of the FOMC (October 6, 1979) and elaborated on in a speech by Volcker (October 9, 1979) to the American Bankers' Association.

76. Kettl, *Leadership at the Fed*, 176.

77. For a discussion of Greenspan, see Stephen Holmes, "How the World Works," *London Review of Books* 36, no. 10 (May 22, 2014). For the way in which Greenspan became mired in a controversy about whether he under responded to some governors' concerns about the growth of subprime mortgages, see Sewell Chan, "Greenspan Criticized for Characterization of Colleague," *New York Times*, April 9, 2010. Governor Edward

M. Gramlich welcomed the spread of homeownership under subprime mortgages in a speech in 2000 but warned of "increasing reports of abusive lending practices, targeted particularly at female, elderly, and minority borrowers.... Predatory lending destroys people and communities and is a clear blight in this otherwise attractive picture." Remarks by Governor Gramlich at the Federal Reserve Bank of Philadelphia, Conference on Predatory Lending, Philadelphia, December 6, 2000, www.federalreserve.gov/boarddocs/speeches/2000/20001206.htm; and see his speech in 2004, www.federalreserve.gov/boarddocs/speeches/2004/20040521/default.htm.

78. On the change in pensions, see Edward A. Zelinsky, *The Origins of the Ownership Society* (New York: Oxford University Press, 2007), chs. 3, 4.

3: CONCEALED ADVANTAGE

1. Henry Paulson, *On the Brink: Inside the Race to Stop the Collapse of the Global Financial System* (New York: Business Plus, 2010), 259.
2. Testimony to Financial Crisis Inquiry, 339, http://ow.ly/BqW01.
3. Manu Raju, "Cheney: It's 'Herbert Hoover' Time," *Politico*, December 12, 2008, www.politico.com/story/2008/12/cheney-its-herbert-hoover-time-016515.
4. Senator Mel Martinez, Testimony to Financial Crisis Inquiry, 3, http://ow.ly/BqW01.
5. Erik Holm, "Buffett Buys Goldman Stake in 'Economic Pearl Harbor,'" *Bloomberg News*, September 24, 2008, www.bloomberg.com/apps/news?pid=newsarchive&sid=aRhG15OZUpzE&refer=home.
6. Chris Giles, Alan Beattie, and Ben Hall, "Scramble to Avoid Collapse," *Financial Times*, October 13, 2008, www.ft.com/cms/s/2/7c577604-97ef-11dd-b720-000077b07658.html#axzz3qWDNKmHq.
7. Email from Susan McCabe (Goldman Sachs executive) to New York Federal Reserve Board officials William Dudley, Gustavo Suarez, and Chris Burke, September 11, 2008, http://financialcrisisinquiryreport.com/html/2008-09-11_federal_reserve_ban.html.
8. FOMC Minutes, January 9, 2008.
9. Commercial paper is a promissory note issued by a corporation or bank to finance its short-term credit need. It is primarily issued by corporations with high credit ratings, and therefore commercial paper has a low risk.
10. Janet L. Yellen, "Interconnectedness and Systemic Risk: Lessons from the Financial Crisis and Policy Implementation," Remarks at the AEA/American Finance Association Joint Luncheon, San Diego, CA, January 4, 2013, 2–3.

11. Fed governors Lacker and Bullard, respectively, FOMC Minutes, June 24–25, 2008, 56, 60.

12. Bernanke at the FOMC, June 24–25, 2008, 96 (and see Plosser at FOMC meeting, March 18, 2008, 50). In contrast to Bernanke and most of the FOMC, Mishkin and Yellen were nearly alone in consistently warning that "we're in the worst financial crisis that we've experienced in the post–WWII era." Quote from Mishkin, FOMC, March 18, 2008, 69.

13. Quote by Bernanke, Mishkin, and Dudley, respectively in FOMC minutes for meetings on June 24–25, 2008 (94), July 24, 2008 (42), and October 7, 2009 (3–4).

14. High-quality collateral includes Treasury Bills, AAA-rated mortgages, and commercial paper from strong businesses.

15. The London Interbank Offered Rate or LIBOR, which is a conventional measure of the interest rates that banks charge each other, hit the highest levels in two decades. The difference between LIBOR and the rates of the US Treasury bills and the Eurodollar shot up by threefold and then ninefold from fall 2007 to fall 2008. Niel Willardson and LuAnne Pederson, "Federal Reserve Liquidity Programs: An Update," *The Region*, Minneapolis Federal Reserve Bank, June 2010, 15. A basis point is one-hundredth of a percentage point. We have learned subsequently through criminal charges and regulatory investigations that LIBOR itself was frequently manipulated by those charges with setting it along with traders to boost profit.

16. Bob Ivry, Bradley Keoun, and Phil Kuntz, "Secret Fed Loans Gave Banks $13 Billion Undisclosed to Congress," *Bloomberg News*, November 27, 2011, www.bloomberg.com/news/print/2011-11-28/ secret-fed-loans-undisclosed-to-congress-gave-banks-13-billion-in- income.html; Vaughn Ververs, "President Obama to Reappoint Federal Reserve Chair Ben Bernanke," *Politico*, August 24, 2009, http://dyn.politico.com/printstory.cfm?uuid=4F5D014A-18FE-70B2- A8A02EBC1E29A0C0; Jon Hilsenrath, "Bernanke Fights for Second Term," *Wall Street Journal*, December 4, 2009, http://online.wsj.com/ articles/SB125985187175274589.

17. Financial Crisis Inquiry Commission (FCIC), *Final Report of the National Commission of the Causes of the Financial and Economic Crisis in the United States* (Washington, DC: Government Printing Office, 2011), xvii.

18. Sheila Bair, *Bull By the Horns: Fighting to Save Main Street from Wall Street and Wall Street from Itself* (New York: Free Press, 2012), 187.

19. Ivry, Keoun, and Kuntz, "Secret Fed Loans."

20. Hilsenrath, "Bernanke Fights for Second Term."

21. Ivry, Keoun, and Kuntz, "Secret Fed Loans."

22. Atif Mian and Amir Sufi, *House of Debt: How They (and You) Caused the Great Recession, and How We Can Prevent It from Happening Again* (Chicago: University of Chicago Press, 2014).

23. Stephen G. Cecchetti, "Crisis and Responses: The Federal Reserve in the Early Stages of the Financial Crisis," *Journal of Economic Perspectives* 23 (Winter 2009): 51–75, especially 70.

24. The precise nature of the Fed's support is nuanced. The Fed loaned funds to the programs it established—especially the three limited liability companies that it set up under the name "Maiden Lane," which in turn extended guarantees. We follow the shorthand of referring to the Fed's loans and guarantees.

25. Bair, *Bull by the Horns*, 187.

26. Ivry, Keoun, and Kuntz, "Secret Fed Loans."

27. Awareness of TARP is evident in the 86 percent to 91 percent who were able to respond to questions about the government's rescue efforts rather than answering "don't know." Here is the wording of these items. "As you may recall, last October, Congress passed and President Bush signed into law a $700 billion Troubled Asset Relief Program, referred to as TARP, to aid the financial sector by purchasing failing bank assets. The first half of that money, $350 billion, was authorized and distributed late last year. Last week, the Senate approved the second half of that money, which will soon be distributed. In your opinion, was the approval of $350 billion to aid the financial sector a bad idea or a good idea?" 56 percent "bad idea," 32 percent "good idea," and 13 percent "unsure." Diageo/Hotline Poll, January 21–24, 2009. N=800 registered voters nationwide. Margin of error ± 3.5; "Do you think the Troubled Asset Relief Program, known as TARP, was necessary to prevent the financial industry from failing and drastically hurting the US economy, or was it an unneeded bailout?" 28 percent "necessary," 58 percent "unnecessary," and 14 percent "unsure." Bloomberg Poll conducted by Selzer & Co., July 9–12, 2010. N=1,004 adults nationwide. Margin of error ± 3.1; "Suppose another major bank or insurance company is on the verge of bankruptcy. If the Obama administration determines that the new problem is similar to the situation that led to the Federal government's intervention to assist troubled banks and insurance companies in recent months, would you favor or oppose the Federal government intervening in a similar fashion to stabilize that major bank or insurance company on the verge of bankruptcy?" 28 percent "favor," 62 percent "oppose," and 9 percent "unsure." Cook Political Report/RT Strategies Poll, April 8–11, 2009. N=833 registered voters nationwide. Margin of error ± 3.5.

28. Gillian Tett, *Fool's Gold: How Unrestrained Greed Corrupted a Dream, Shattered Global Markets and Unleashed a Catastrophe* (Boston: Little Brown, 2009); Gretchen Morgenson, *Reckless Endangerment: How Outsized Ambition, Greed, and Corruption Led to Economic Armageddon* (New York: Times Books, 2011); Paulson, *On the Brink*; Greta R. Krippner, *Capitalizing the Crisis: The Political Origins of the Rise of Finance*

(Cambridge, MA: Harvard University Press, 2011); FCIC, *Final Report*; Bair, *Bull by the Horns*; Simon Johnson and James Kwak, *13 Bankers: The Wall Street Takeover and the Next Financial Meltdown* (New York: Pantheon 2010); Michael Lewis, *The Big Short* (New York: Penguin, 2011); Philip Augar, *Chasing Alpha* (London: Bodley Head, 2009); Hans-Werner Sinn, *Casino Capitalism* (New York: Oxford University Press, 2010); Laurence J. Kotlikoff, *Jimmy Stewart Is Dead* (Hoboken, NJ: Wiley, 2010), For an exception, see Mark Blyth, *Austerity: The History of a Dangerous Idea* (New York: Oxford University Press, 2013), chs. 2, 7.

29. There is a long list of culprits for citizen disengagement: outright efforts by elites to manipulate public opinion and discourage public engagement, the selection of issues by the media and politicians that bore many Americans, the difficulty many individuals experience in processing information about candidates and policy choices, and cumbersome administrative barriers such as registration, which is automatic upon birth in European countries. E. E. Schattschneider, *The Semi-Sovereign People: A Realist View of Democracy in America* (New York: Holt, Rinehart and Winston 1960; Frances Fox Piven and Richard Cloward, *Regulating the Poor: The Functions of Public Welfare*, updated ed. (New York: Vintage Books 1993); Lawrence Jacobs and Robert Shapiro, *Politicians Don't Pander: Political Manipulation and the Loss of Democratic Responsiveness* (Chicago: University of Chicago Press, 2000); James Druckman and Lawrence Jacobs, *Who Governs? Presidents, Public Opinion, and Manipulation* (Chicago: University of Chicago Press, 2015).

30. A familiar observation about politics focuses on how interest groups, public opinion, and voters drive policy. There is, of course, truth to that. But there are also numerous studies demonstrating that "policies make politics"—the visibility and tangible payoff of government programs can alter perceptions of interests and selectively recruit participation into the political process. This section applies this body of research to the Fed. Suzanne Mettler, *The Submerged State: How Invisible Government Policies Undermine American Democracy* (Chicago: University of Chicago Press, 2011); Paul Pierson, "Increasing Returns, Path Dependence, and the Study of Politics," *American Political Science Review* 94 (June 2000): 251–267 and "When Effect Becomes Cause: Policy Feedback and Political Change," *World Politics* 45 (July 1993): 595–628; Suzanne Mettler and Joe Soss, "The Consequences of Public Policy for Democratic Citizenship: Bridging Policy Studies and Mass Politics," *Perspectives on Politics* 2 (March 2004): 55–73.

31. Quoted in Larry DeWitt, "Research Notes & Special Studies by the Historian's Office," Research Note #23, July 21, 2005, www.ssa.gov/history/Gulick.html.

32. Andrea Louise Campbell, *How Policies Make Citizens: Senior Political Activism and the American Welfare State* (Princeton, NJ: Princeton University Press, 2003).

33. The political effects of policy design have been identified in a wide range of policies from higher education to public assistance. See Mettler and Soss, "The Consequences of Public Policy."

34. Mettler, *The Submerged State*.

35. Mettler, *The Submerged State*; Kimberley Morgan, "Constricting the Welfare State: Tax Policy and the Political Movement Against Government," in *Remaking America: Democracy and Public Policy in an Age of Inequality*, ed. Joe Soss, Jacob Hacker, and Susan Mettler (New York: Russell Sage Foundation, 2007), 27–50.

36. J. Lawrence Broz, "Origins of the Federal Reserve System: International Incentives and the Domestic Free-Rider Problem," *International Organization* 53 (Winter 1999): 39–70 and "The Origins of Central Banking: Solutions to the Free-Rider Problem," *International Organization* 52 (Spring 1998): 231–268.

37. Email from Ralph Santasiero to New York Bank Supervisor, September 18, 2008, http://fcic.law.stanford.edu/documents/view/2121; email from Patrick Parkinson to Lucinda Brickler, September 12, 2008, http://fcic .law.stanford.edu/documents/view/624; email to Ben Bernanke from Kevin Warsh, Scott Alvarez, and Brian Madigan, July 20, 2008, http:// fcic.law.stanford.edu/documents/view/433; Til Schuermann to Arthur Angulo, September 17, 2008, http://fcic.law.stanford.edu/documents/ view/2120. These emails and others cited below were collected by the Financial Crisis Inquiry Commission.

38. Memo to Board of Directors from Michael Glasseman, Sandra Thompson, Arthur Murton, and John Thomas, January 15, 2009, http:// fcic.law.stanford.edu/documents/view/1078.

39. Memo from Federal Reserve Board and Office of the Comptroller of the Currency staff to Rick Cox (FDIC), January 10, 2009, http://fcic.law .stanford.edu/documents/view/1066.

40. Email from Til Schuermann to William Brodows, Arthur Angulo, Lorie Logan, and Joshua Frost, September 19, 2008, http://fcic.law.stanford .edu/documents/view/2123.

41. Memo from Michael Glassman, Sandra Thompson, James Wigand, and Herbert Held to Board of Directors, November 23, 2008, http://fcic.law .stanford.edu/documents/view/1019; email from William Dudley to Kevin Warsh, Lucinda Brickler, Meg McConnell, Terrence Checki, Timothy Geithner, and Patrick Parkinson, July 15, 2008, http://fcic.law.stanford .edu/documents/view/523; memo to Board of Governors from Staff, August 14, 2007, http://fcic.law.stanford.edu/documents/view/906.

42. Email from Til Schuermann to Chris McCurdy, July 11, 2008, http:// fcic.law.stanford.edu/documents/view/491; email from Lucinda Brickler, William Brodows, Chris McCurdy, and Til Schuermann to Tim Geithner, July 11, 2008, http://fcic.law.stanford.edu/documents/view/491.

43. Memo from Lucinda Brickler, William Brodows, Chris McCurdy, and Til Schuermann to Tim Geithner, July 11, 2008, http://fcic.law.stanford.edu/ documents/view/491.

44. Email Tim Clark to Robard Williams and Kevin Coffey, June 20, 2008, http://fcic.law.stanford.edu/documents/view/559.

45. From Patrick Parkinson to Joseph Sommer, July 13, 2008, http://fcic.law.stanford.edu/documents/view/278.

46. Memo from Lucinda Brickler, William Brodows, Chris McCurdy, and Til Schuermann to Tim Geithner, July 11, 2008, http://fcic.law.stanford.edu/documents/view/491.

47. Email Joseph Sommer to Patrick Parkinson, July 13, 2008, http://fcic.law.stanford.edu/documents/view/683; email from Patrick Parkinson to Joseph Sommer, July 13, 2008, http://fcic.law.stanford.edu/documents/view/683.

48. Memo from Lucinda Brickler, William Brodows, Chris McCurdy, and Til Schuermann to Tim Geithner, July 11, 2008, http://fcic.law.stanford.edu/documents/view/491.

49. Email from Patricia Mosser to Debby Perelmuter, Richard DzinaI, Susan McLaughlin, Michael Holscher, Chris Burke, Michael Schetzel, Joshua Frost, Susan Stiehm, a/KY/FRS; Alejandro LaTorre cc: William Dudley, September 10, 2008, http://fcic.law.stanford.edu/documents/view/855.

50. Email from Patrick Parkinson to Deborah Bailey, September 11, 2008, http://fcic.law.stanford.edu/documents/view/434.

51. Bernanke, FOMC, October 7, 2008, 12.

52. William Dudley, FOMC, October 28–29, 2008, 4.

53. The Lehman Brothers' episode illustrates the clash of organizational principles—the Fed's amped-up powers collided with the systems of accountability that on occasion kick into gear. In this case, the political check on the Fed's inclination boomeranged in a way that reinforced the deference to the Fed.

54. Neil Barofsky, special inspector general for TARP, recounts how the Treasury took the lead in pressuring him to delay criticisms of a new Fed facility. *Bailout* (New York: Free Press, 2012), 117–118.

55. Sherrill Shaffer quoted in Ivry, Keoun, and Kuntz, "Secret Fed Loans"; Robert G. Kaiser, *Act of Congress* (New York: Knopf, 2013), 6–13, 259.

56. FCIC, *Final Report*, 27.

57. The response by the large firms was complicated: the often secret and massive intervention paved a path toward recovery and profits, but its acceptance signaled internally the errors of senior management. Paulson, *On the Brink*, 362–368.

58. Ivry, Keoun, and Kuntz, "Secret Fed Loans."

59. Ivry, Keoun, and Kuntz, "Secret Fed Loans."

60. Max Weber, *Essays in Sociology*, ed. H. H. Gerth and C. Wright Mills (Oxford: Oxford University Press, 1946), 233; Matthew McCubbins, Roger Noll, and Barry Weingast, "Administrative Procedures as Instruments of Political Control," *Journal of Law, Economics and Organization* 3, no. 2 (1987): 243–277; David Stasavage, "Transparency, Democratic Accountability, and the Economic Consequences of Monetary

Institutions," *American Journal of Political Science* 47 (July 2003): 389–402.

61. Ivry, Keoun, and Kuntz, "Secret Fed Loans." Bernanke challenged, without evidence, Bloomberg's accounting in his "Letter to Congressional Leaders," December 6, 2011, www.documentcloud.org/documents/271227-emergency-lending-financial-crisis-20111206.html#document/p1. His own accounting reports only a fraction of the Fed's loans and guarantees. Remarks by Ben S. Bernanke, "Monetary Policy Objectives and Tools in a Low-Inflation Environment," Conference sponsored by the Federal Reserve Bank of Boston, Boston, MA, October 15, 2010.

62. Although the facilities started in 2007, we generally mark the peak of the crisis in other chapters as 2008 and 2009—this is when the financial system experienced its sharpest disruptions and the Fed took its most audacious new steps.

63. The Federal Reserve Bank of New York implemented TSLF, PDCF, CPFF, and TALF, while the Federal Reserve Bank of Boston implemented AMLF.

64. The Fed's intervention produced a good deal for JP Morgan Chase (it took over Bear Stearns at 7 percent of its market value), and it granted FDIC protections to Morgan Stanley and Goldman Sachs by allowing them to become bank holding companies.

65. William C. Dudley, "Why Financial Stability Is a Necessary Prerequisite for an Effective Monetary Policy," Andrew Crockett Memorial Lecture, BIS Annual General Meeting, June 23, 2013, 1.

66. "A Century of U.S. Central Banking: Goals, Frameworks, Accountability," Remarks by Ben Bernanke to NBER conferences, Cambridge, MA, July 10, 2013, 14.

67. Martin Feldstein, "What Powers for the Federal Reserve?" *Journal of Economic Literature* 48 (March 2010): 134–145.

68. Debate on the Fed's assertion of new powers breaks out on the FOMC in March 10, 2008, 9–10.

69. Bernanke, August 5, 2008, 3. A close review of the decision to use 13(3) by Bernanke and the Fed is provided by Philip Wallach, *To the Edge: Legality, Legitimacy, and the Responses to the 2008 Financial Crisis* (Washington, DC: Brookings Institution, 2015).

70. Timothy Geithner, *Stress Test: Reflections on Financial Crises* (New York: Crown Publishers, 2014).

71. FOMC Meetings March 10 and August 5, 2008.

72. Ben Bernanke, February 18 2011. "Global Imbalances: Links to Economic and Financial Stability," remarks by Ben S. Bernanke at the Banque de France Financial Stability Review Launch Event, Paris, France, www.federalreserve.gov/newsevents/speech/bernanke20110218a.htm.

73. Michael Glennon, *National Security and Double Government* (New York: Oxford University Press, 2015); Arthur M. Schlesinger Jr., *The Imperial Presidency* (Boston: Houghton Mifflin, 1973); Richard Pious, *The*

American Presidency (New York: Basic Books, 1979); Harold Koh, *The National Security Constitution* (New Haven, CT: Yale University Press, 1990); Louis Fisher, *Presidential War Power*, 3rd ed. (Lawrence: University Press of Kansas, 2013).

74. Schattschneider, *The Semi-Sovereign People*; Lawrence Jacobs and Theda Skocpol, eds., *Inequality and American Democracy: What We Know and What We Need to Learn* (New York: Russell Sage Foundation, 2005) and "Studying Inequality and American Democracy: Findings and Challenges," in *Inequality and American Democracy*; Richard Hall and Frank Wayman, "Buying Time: Moneyed Interests and the Mobilization of Bias in Congressional Committees," *American Political Science Review* 84 (September 1990): 797–820; Lawrence R. Jacobs and Benjamin I. Page, "Who Influences U.S. Foreign Policy?" *American Political Science Review* 99 (February 2005): 107–124; Martin Gilens, *Affluence and Influence* (Princeton, NJ: Princeton University Press, 2012); Martin Gilens and Benjamin Page, "Testing Theories of American Politics: Elites, Interest Groups, and Average Citizens," *Perspectives on Politics* 12 (September 2014): 564–581.

75. The Fed's facilities reflected and added onto its overtime development of authority and administrative capacity. The individual facilities fit into a pattern of broader institutional development, but they do not alone encapsulate the Fed as an institution. Individual facilities may fade over time while the Fed's structure remained. Pierson, "Increasing Returns," 251–267.

76. One of the most important backroom operations in global finance involves repurchase agreements or "repos"—the selling of securities on the agreement that the seller will buy them back in the future (often one day to a week later). The Fed uses repos like a monetary yo-yo—buying securities from primary dealers to pump money into the banking system, and then the primary dealers sell it back in order to pull money out of the system. This is one of the Fed's key tools for managing interest rates.

77. Alan Blinder, "Quantitative Easing: Entrance and Exit Strategies," *Federal Reserve Bank of St. Louis Review* (November/December 2010): 265–279; Marvin Goodfriend, "Central Banking in the Credit Turmoil: An Assessment of Federal Reserve Practice," *Journal of Monetary Economics* 58 (January 2011): 1–12.

78. One of the main fears is that AIG's collapse would prevent businesses from raising short-term credit by issuing commercial paper to meet payroll and fund other operations. Federal Reserve Maiden Lane II Background, www.federalreserve.gov/newsevents/reform_aig.htm.

79. Maiden Lane III purchased collateralized debt obligations to reduce the demands on AIG to make good on its credit default swaps—the insurance it sold to backstop the risk that subprime mortgages and other loans would default.

80. TALF focused on encouraging companies that owned high-caliber collateral to purchase asset-backed securities for consumer loans.

81. FOMC Conference Call, March 10, 2008.

82. FOMC Conference Call, March 10, 2008.

83. Donald Kohn, FOMC, March 10, 2008, 24–25.

84. We used ordinal measures because our analysis can reasonably rank into categories whether Fed deference and generosity are lowest or highest.

85. We created three ranked categories of collateral based on the quality and risk of the assets pledged to secure loans. The most secure collateral included safe, high-quality investment-grade securities and tri-party eligible collateral.

86. The middle category of collateral security included First Tier Asset Backed Commercial Paper, Municipal Securities, Commercial Loans, Unsecured Commercial Paper, and Fed Agency Debt, as well as Asset-Backed Securities (ABS), Newly Issued ABS, and Asset Portfolios.

87. The lowest category of collateral included securities backed by student and auto loans, loans backed by insurance premiums as well as still more risky collateral—hedges, residential mortgage loans, securities backed by credit card loans, and mortgages for residential and commercial properties.

88. AMLF was a partial exception to this arc of growing Fed intervention outside its traditional confines of depository institutions and primary dealers.

89. Blinder, "Quantitative Easing"; Feldstein, "What Powers for the Federal Reserve?"

90. FOMC Meeting, January 29–30, 2008.

91. Frank Morris, "Bernanke: 'I Had to Hold My Nose' to Bail Out Banks," July 27, 2009, www.npr.org/templates/story/story.php?storyId=111046705

92. Dudley quoted in FCIC, *Final Report*, 274; James Bullard, "The Fed's Emergency Liquidity Facilities: Why They Were Necessary," *The Regional Economist* (January 2011): 3, www.stlouisfed.org/publications/pub_assets/pdf/re/2011/a/presidents%20message.pdf; O. Armantier, E. Ghysels, A. Sarkar, and J. Shrader, "Stigma in Financial Markets: Evidence from Liquidity Auctions and Discount Window Borrowing During the Crisis," *Federal Reserve Bank of New York Staff Reports*, no. 483, 2011, www.newyorkfed.org/research/staff_reports/sr483.pdf.

93. John Beebe to Jennifer Burns, September 27, 2008, re: Wachovia Bank; PP to Deborah Bailey (DB), September 11, 2008, re: revised liquidation consortium gameplan and quests, Highly Confidential.

94. Carsten Brzeski quoted in Jack Ewing and David Jolly, "Demand Is High for Euro Loans from Central Bank," *New York Times*, December 21, 2011; Gavin Finch and Liam Vaughan, "European Banks Devour ECB Emergency Funds," *Bloomberg News*, December 21, 2011.

95. The British building society provides mortgages and savings accounts and is owned by its members. Its roots reach back to the eighteenth century, and it has some similarities with credit unions in the United States.

96. House of Commons Treasury Committee, Banking Crisis: Dealing with *the Failure of the UK Banks*, Seventh report of Session 2008-09, HC 416 (London: House of Commons Stationary Office, 2009), 60.

97. The Fed's doling out of targeted benefits was interspersed, on occasion, with the meting out of pain. While investors in Goldman, Morgan Stanley, Citigroup, Bank of America, and others that faced ruin were paid by the Fed 100 cents on the dollar, the Fed imposed harsh terms on the investors in AIG—eliciting intense protests and legal action by the former head of AIG, Maurice Greenberg. Why were banks that bought the speculative subprime loans protected but AIG punished for insuring them? Former Treasury secretary Henry Paulson testified that "politics" accounted for the disparate treatment: AIG was "a scapegoat for Wall Street and all of the bad practices people were angry about" in order to "minimize political opposition to what we were doing." Quoted in Zachary Warmbrodt and M. J. Lee, "AIG Trial Focuses on 'Harsh' Bailout," *Politico*, October 7, 2014, www.politico.com/story/2014/10/aig-trial-bailout-111679_Page2.html; Andrew Ross Sorkin, "A.I.G. Bailout, Revisionists' Version," *New York Times*, October 6, 2014, http://ow.ly/DPI7v.

98. Andrew M. Cuomo, "No Rhyme or Reason: The Heads I Win, Tails You Lose Bank Bonus Culture," Attorney General State of New York, July 30, 2009. Published by the NY State Attorney General Office, www.scribd.com/doc/17850928/Andrew-Cuomo-Bonus-Report.

99. Ivry, Keoun, and Kuntz, "Secret Fed Loans."

100. Ivry, Keoun, and Kuntz, "Secret Fed Loans."

101. Cornelia Woll, *The Power of Inaction: Bank Bailouts in Comparison* (Ithaca, NY: Cornell University Press, 2014).

102. Mian and Sufi, *House of Debt*.

103. Dawn Kopecki, "Mortgage 'Cram-Down' Bankruptcy Bill May Aid 1 Million in U.S.," *Bloomberg News*, March 6, 2009, www.bloomberg.com/apps/news?pid=newsarchive&sid=aoyMWtlsj27A.

104. The foreclosure filings were assembled by RealtyTrac. Erin Carlyle, "2014 Foreclosure Filings Hit Lowest Level Since 2006," *Forbes*, January 15, 2015, www.forbes.com/sites/erincarlyle/2015/01/15/foreclosure-filings-drop-by-18-in-2014-hit-lowest-level-since-2006-realtytrac-says/.

105. Amir Efrati and Jennifer S. Forsyth, "Power to Modify Mortgages Sits Well With Judges," *Wall Street Journal*, January 12, 2009, www.wsj.com/articles/SB123170970691971885.

106. Glenn Hubbard quoted in M. J. Lee, "Mitt Romney Adviser: Tim Geithner's Lying," *Politico*, May 11, 2014, www.politico.com/story/2014/05/mitt-romney-adviser-tim-geithner-lie-106563, and www.huffingtonpost.com/2014/05/12/mitt-romney-tim-geithner_n_5309356.html.

107. Mian and Sufi, *House of Debt*.

108. Research by the Cleveland Federal Reserve on the use of cram-downs to save family farms demonstrated their effectiveness because of meaningful negotiations by banks eager to avoid bankruptcy judges. Thomas J. Fitzpatrick IV and James B. Thomson, "Stripdowns and Bankruptcy: Lessons from Agricultural Bankruptcy Reform," *Economic Commentary No. 2010-9*, August 3, 2010, Federal Reserve Bank of Cleveland, www.clevelandfed.org/en/newsroom-and-events/publications/economic-commentary/economic-commentary-archives/2010-economic-commentaries/ec-201009-stripdowns-and-bankruptcy-lessons-from-agricultural-bankruptcy-reform.aspx.

109. Eric Etherudge, "Rick Santelli: Tea Party Time," *New York Times*, February 20, 2009, http://opinionator.blogs.nytimes.com/2009/02/20/rick-santelli-tea-party-time/.

110. Lawrence R. Jacobs and Theda Skocpol, *Health Care Reform and American Politics*, 3rd ed. (New York: Oxford University Press, 2016).

111. FCIC, *Final Report*.

112. Efrati and Forsyth, "Power to Modify Mortgages Sits Well With Judges"; Fitzpatrick and Thomson, "Stripdowns and Bankruptcy."

113. Mian and Sufi, *House of Debt*.

114. While the Fed and Treasury dragged its feet in helping homeowners, the British government tried several approaches including the successful Funding for Lending. For workers who lost jobs or had their hours cut, the British Homeowners Mortgage Support Scheme helped borrowers to defer 30 percent of interest payments on their mortgage for up to two years. The program directly assisted about 5,000 households to avoid foreclosure and appears to have encouraged lenders to renegotiate payment agreements with 135,000 households by the end of 2009, 74 percent higher than at the end of 2008.

115. Tanya Powley and Claire Jones, "Funding for Lending Scheme Viewed as a Mixed Success," *Financial Times*, August 12, 2013, www.ft.com/cms/s/0/050a2998-036a-11e3-b871-00144feab7de.html#ixzz3h6rSHJt1; Phillip Inman, "Market PMI Records Surge in Housebuilding Activity," *The Guardian*, April 2, 2014, www.theguardian.com/business/2014/apr/02/housebuilding-boosts-construction-sector-best-levels-2007. While the impact on the mortgage and housing construction industries was significant, Funding for Lending was less successful either in prodding banks to lend to small-and medium-sized businesses or in enticing them to take on new debt.

116. Hilary Osborne, "Funding for Lending Has Seen Approvals on New Loans Rise by a Third," *The Guardian*, July 31, 2013, www.theguardian.com/business/2013/jul/31/george-osborne-funding-for-lending-mortgages.

117. Schlesinger, *The Imperial Presidency*; Koh, *The National Security Constitution*; Fisher, *Presidential War Power*.

118. The prospects for presidential prerogatives on the domestic front are far more limited than they are in foreign and military power, and more

vulnerable to reversal on domestic policy. Executive orders, the use of regulatory review, and other executive tools are subject to reversal by subsequent presidents and, in salient areas, are overturned.

119. Marver Bernstein, *Regulating Business by Independent Commission* (Westport CT: Greenwood Press, 1955); George Stigler, "The Theory of Economic Regulation," *Bell Journal of Economics* 2 (1971): 3–21.

120. The new superrich, who have propelled rising economic inequality and flowed from the outsized profitability of finance, accounts (not surprisingly) for much of the growth in campaign contributions—their share rocketed up by fourfold since 1980. Adam Bonica, Nolan McCarty, Keith T. Poole, and Howard Rosenthal, "Why Hasn't Democracy Slowed Rising Inequality?" *Journal of Economic Perspectives* 27 (Summer 2013): 103–124; Nolan McCarty, "The Politics of the Pop: The US Response to the Financial Crisis and the Great Recession," in *Coping with Crisis,* ed. Nancy Bermeo and Jonas Pontusson (New York: Russell Sage Foundation, 2012).

121. Ronald C. Moe, "Exploring the Limits of Privatization," Public *Administration Review* 47 (1987): 453–460. But cf. Terry Moe, "The New Economics of Organization," *American Journal of Political Science* 28 (November 1984): 739–777; Peter Evans, Dietrich Rueschemeyer, and Theda Skocpol, eds., *Bringing the State Back In* (New York: Cambridge University Press, 1985); Stephen Skowronek, *Building a New American State: The Expansion of National Administrative Capacities, 1877–1920* (New York: Cambridge University Press, 1982).

4: THE FED'S LEGITIMACY PROBLEM

1. Quote from Brad Miller (D-NC). Bob Ivry, Bradley Keoun, and Phil Kuntz, "Secret Fed Loans Gave Banks $13 Billion Undisclosed to Congress," *Bloomberg News*, November 27, 2011, http://ow.ly/GFKtb.

2. Quote by David Jones, former economist at Federal Reserve Bank of New York. Ivry, Keoun, and Kuntz, "Secret Fed Loans."

3. Ivry, Keoun, and Kuntz, "Secret Fed Loans."

4. For instance, the Maiden Lane facilities were limited liability companies that were created by loans from the Fed amounting to about $70 billion. These loans were repaid in 2012 with interest.

5. Quote by Roberto Perli (former Fed economist and managing director at International Strategy & Investment Group in Washington) and Jim Russell (investment advisor at the large money managers Bahl & Gaynor). Joshua Zumbrun, "More than Half of U.S. Wants Fed Curbed or Abolished," *Bloomberg News*, December 9, 2010, http://ow.ly/FeBdz; Kate Gibson, "Republicans Looking to Turn Up Heat on Fed in 2015," CNBC, November 18, 2014, http://ow.ly/FVsz4.

6. The Fed's predicament is a problem of legitimacy rather than a fleeting controversy or a bout of bad press that will soon pass and allow it to resume its unilateral control over monetary and, increasingly, fiscal policy. We draw on long-standing analysis of legitimacy as arising from legal systems, authority, and competent performance. We situate the threat to the Fed's legitimacy in its contradictory relationship with private markets: it both makes claims to serve as the steward of the national interest and operates as the protector of finance. The crisis of 2008–2009 required Fed interventions to sustain private finance and, in turn, tarnished its public persona as separate and apart from it. Max Weber, *Economy and Society*, trans. G. Roth (Berkeley: University of California Press, 1978); Claus Offe, *Contradictions of the Welfare State*, ed. John Keane (Cambridge, MA: MIT Press, 1984); Jurgen Habermas, "What Does a Crisis Mean Today? Legitimation Problems in Late Capitalism," *Social Research* 40 (Winter 1973): 643–667.

7. Norbert Michel, "Is the Federal Reserve Running on Empty?" *Forbes*, September 2, 2014, http://ow.ly/FZu2q.

8. Nicholas Lemann, "The Hand on the Lever: How Janet Yellen Is Redefining the Federal Reserve," *New Yorker*, July 21, 2014, http://ow.ly/G4LU3.

9. Peter J. Henning, "Fed's New 'Cop on the Beat' Role Puts It in a Bind," *New York Times*, November 24, 2014, http://dealbook.nytimes.com/2014/11/24/the-fed-in-a-bind/.

10. We draw on polls conducted by reputable survey organizations that publicly share information about their methods, survey parameters, and question wording. For the most part, we relied on the Ipoll Databank that is curated by the Roper Center for Public Opinion Research. Polls that were not archived by the Roper Center or did not provide standard survey information to assess its methods and quality were not used.

11. The question wording is: "Do you approve or disapprove of the way [Paul Volcker/Alan Greenspan/Ben Bernanke/Janet Yellen] is handling [his/her] job as chairman of the Federal Reserve?"

12. The scoring of when economic recessions and expansion start and end is conducted by the National Bureau of Economic Research and its "Business Cycle Dating Committee," www.nber.org/cycles/recessions.html.

13. This discussion is based on Pavlina R. Tcherneva, "Reorienting Fiscal Policy: A Bottom-up Approach," *Journal of Post-Keynesian Economics* 37, no. 1 (Fall 2014): 43–66.

14. We were unable to locate polls that examine detailed questions about the Fed's rescue maneuvers and its connection to rising economic inequality.

15. Greenberg Quinlan Rosner Research, March 22–29, 2006. Based on 1,044 interviews with national adults.

16. For clarity of presentation, dates after 1988 on x-axis are not evenly spaced. The following question wording was generally used by the

surveys: Do you approve or disapprove of the way [Paul Volcker/Alan Greenspan/Ben Bernanke/Janet Yellen] is handling [his/her] job as chairman of the Federal Reserve?

17. The question wording is: "As I read some names and groups, please tell me how much confidence you have in each to do or to recommend the right thing for the economy—a great deal, a fair amount, only a little, or almost none. How about... Federal Reserve Chairman [Paul Volcker/ Alan Greenspan/Ben Bernanke/Janet Yellen]?"

18. Our discussion reflects a distinction that survey researchers make between the public's evaluation of the performance by individual political authorities (like presidents or Fed chairs) and its assessment of major government institutions. Fay Lomax Cook, Lawrence Jacobs, and Dukhong Kim, "Trusting What You Know: Information, Knowledge, and Confidence in Social Security," *Journal of Politics* 72 (April 2010): 1–16; Arthur Miller, "Political Issues and Trust in Government, 1964–70," *American Political Science Review* 68 (September 1974): 951–972 and "Rejoinder to Comment by Jack Citrin: Political Discontent or Ritualism," *American Political Science Review* 68 (1974): 989–1001; Jack Citrin, "Comment: The Political Relevance of Trust in Government," *American Political Science Review* 68 (1974): 973–988.

19. The question wording is: "How would you rate the job being done by... the Federal Reserve Board? Would you say it is doing an excellent, good, only fair, or poor job?"

20. The following question wording was generally used by the surveys: As I read some names and groups, please tell me how much confidence you have in each to do or to recommend the right thing for the economy—a great deal, a fair amount, only a little, or almost none. How about Federal Reserve Chairman [Paul Volcker/Alan Greenspan/Ben Bernanke/Janet Yellen]?

21. The Gallup question was: "How would you rate the job being done by [agency/department]? Would you say it is doing an excellent, good, only fair, or poor job?" The survey was conducted July 10–12, 2009, and interviewed 1,018 national adults. See www.gallup.com/poll/121886/cdc-tops-agency-ratings-federal-reserve-board-lowest.aspx?version=print.

22. The following question wording was generally used by the surveys: How would you rate the job being done by the Federal Reserve Board? Would you say it is doing an excellent, good, only fair, or poor job?

23. Michael X. Delli Carpini and Scott Keeter, *What Americans Know about Politics and Why It Matters* (New Haven, CT: Yale University Press 1996), ch. 3.

24. A significant body of research has tracked the public's substantial knowledge of public policy and reasonable formation of core preferences. Benjamin I. Page and Robert Y. Shapiro, *The Rational Public: Fifty Years of Trends in American's Policy Preferences* (Chicago: University of Chicago Press, 1992); Delli Carpini and Keeter, *What Americans Know;*

Fay Lomax Cook and Lawrence R. Jacobs, "Assessing Assumptions about Attitudes toward Social Security: Popular Claims Meet Hard Data," in *The Future of Social Insurance: Incremental Action or Fundamental Reform,* ed. Peter Edelman, Dallas Salisbury, and Pamela Larson (Washington, DC: Brookings Institution, 2002), 82–118.

25. The wording is: "How would you rate the job being done by [agency/department]? Would you say it is doing an excellent, good, only fair, or poor job?" Source: Gallup Polling: http://www.gallup.com/poll/121886/CDC-Tops-Agency-Ratings-Federal-Reserve-Board-Lowest.aspx?g_source=2009%20Job%20agencies&g_medium=search&g_campaign=tiles

26. Who is the Chair of the Federal Reserve Board?

27. The question wording is: "I am going to read a series of statements. For each please tell me if you believe or do not believe the statement.... The Federal Reserve is out of control." Winston Group, April 13–14, 2010, 1,000 interviews with nationally registered voters.

28. The question reads: "Some people say the Federal Reserve has too much power and is not accountable to the Congress. Others say it is best to have an independent body that can make unpopular decisions. Do you think the Federal Reserve should be more accountable to Congress or left as an independent body, or should it be abolished entirely?" Bloomberg Poll, December 4–7, 2010, interviews with 1,000 national adults.

29. The question wording: "Would you favor or oppose a law that would allow Congress to conduct an annual internal review of the Federal Reserve?" Princeton Survey Research Associates International, September 13–17, 2012, 1,006 interviews with a sample of national adults. A second survey was conducted by Rasmussen Reports based on interviews with 1,000 national adults, November 6–7, 2013.

30. Lyle Gramley quoted in Zumbrun, "More Than Half of U.S. Wants Fed Curbed or Abolished."

31. Testimony by Paul A. Volcker, Committee on Banking, Finance and Urban Affairs, House of Representatives, February 10, 1982, https://fraser.stlouisfed.org/scribd/?item_id=22397&filepath=/docs/historical/house/cmp/1980s/CMP_97HR_02101982.pdf#scribd-open

32. There is a large body of research that pursues a Congress-oriented approach to Fed rates. The most trenchant version of this account is Sarah Binder and Mark Spindel, "Congress and the Federal Reserve," in *Congress and Policy Making in the 21st Century*, ed. Jeffrey Jenkins and Eric Patashnik (New York: Cambridge University Press, 2016), 187–207. Additional research includes Kevin Grier, "Congressional Influence on US Monetary Policy," *Journal of Monetary Economics* 28 (1991): 201–220, and "Congressional Oversight Commmittee Influence on US Monetary Policy Revisted," *Journal of Monetary Economics* 38 (1996): 571–579; Thomas Mayer, "Introduction," in *The Political Economy of American Monetary Policy*, ed. Thomas Mayer (New York: Cambridge University Press, 1990).

33. Binyamin Appelbaum, "New Limits on the Fed Pose Risks, Yellen Says," *New York Times*, July 15, 2015, www.nytimes.com/2015/07/16/business/yellen-federal-reserve-house-testimony-oversight.html?_r=0.

34. Quoted in Zumbrun, "More Than Half of U.S. Wants Fed Curbed or Abolished."

35. Dan Balz, "Perry Warns of Fed Treason, Challenges Obama," *Washington Post*, August 16, 2011, http://ow.ly/FeJ0G.

36. Yellen won confirmation in January 2014 by a 56–24 margin, with many members prevented from voting by the weather. Bernanke's approval was 70 to 30, which was the narrowest winning margin up to 2010. In his first Senate vote to win confirmation in 2006 and before the crisis, the decision was unanimous.

37. Edmund Andrews, "Bernanke, a Hero to His Own, Can't Shake Critics," *New York Times*, August 19, 2009, http://ow.ly/GFycK; Joshua Zumbrun and Jeff Kearns, "Yellen's Record-Low Senate Support Reflects Fed's Politicization," *Bloomberg News*, January 7, 2014, http://ow.ly/FeU78.

38. Gretchen Morgenson, "The Week That Shook the Fed," *New York Times*, November 23, 2014, http://ow.ly/FS78C; Senate Permanent Subcommittee on Investigations, "Wall Street Bank Involvement with Physical Commodities," November 20, 2014, http://ow.ly/G0U2M.

39. As the crisis blossomed, the Fed's leaders mentioned inflation 597 times during the June and September 2008 FOMC meetings even though inflation remained tepid then and for years afterward. Meanwhile, the disaster enveloping American and global financial markets received scant attention; the FOMC meetings referred to systemic risk or crisis 39 times. Compiled by Matthew O'Brien, "How the Fed Let the World Blow Up in 2008," *The Atlantic*, February 26, 2014; Mark Felsenthal and Pedro da Costa, "Bernanke Says Recovery on Track but Jobs to Lag," Reuters, June 9, 2010.

40. Rich Miller, "The Republican Plan to Rein in Janet Yellen's Federal Reserve," *Business Week*, March 6, 2014, http://ow.ly/FWKuo.

41. The press and congressional reformers framed the Fed and its dealings with finance as bordering on improper or over the line into outright favoritism. As we suggested in earlier chapters, our analysis points to a more complicated set of relationships.

42. Morgenson, "The Week That Shook the Fed"; Andrews, "Bernanke, a Hero to His Own."

43. Henning, "Fed's New 'Cop on the Beat.'"

44. Jessica Silver-Greenberg, Ben Protess, and Peter Eavis, "New Scrutiny of Goldman's Ties to the New York Fed after a Leak," *New York Times*, November 19, 2014, http://ow.ly/G4F5M.

45. Jake Bernstein, "Lawsuit Claims N.Y. Fed Fired Regulator Who Raised Questions about Goldman Sachs," *Washington Post*, October 10, 2013, http://ow.ly/Fgddh.

46. Pedro Nicolaci da Costa, "Sen. Warren Wants Hearings Over New York Fed's Relationship with Banks," *Wall Street Journal*, September 26, 2014, http://ow.ly/FWJ8R.
47. Zumbrun and Kearns, "Yellen's Record-Low Senate Support."
48. Jeff Kearns, "Fed $4 Trillion Assets Draw Lawmaker Ire Amid Bubble Concern," *Bloomberg News*, December 17, 2013, http://ow.ly/FgbPZ.
49. Morgenson, "The Week That Shook the Fed"; "Wall Street Bank Involvement with Physical Commodities," November 20, 2014, http://ow.ly/G0U2M; www.hsgac.senate.gov/subcommittees/investigations/hearings/wall-street-bank-involvement-with-physical-commodities-day-one.
50. Marc Labonte, "Federal Reserve: Oversight and Disclosure Issues," Washington, DC, Congressional Research Service, September 19, 2014, http://ow.ly/S6RcC.
51. Miller, "The Republican Plan to Rein in Janet Yellen's Federal Reserve"; Zumbrun, "More Than Half of U.S. Wants Fed Curbed Abolished"; "50 Shades of Fed," Washington Post Wonkblog, June 1, 2014, http://ow.ly/FZH9A. The GOP proposal to tie the Fed's interest rates to a formula resuscitates a debate over "rules versus discretion." Milton Friedman advocated for the former in order to limit the discretion of central banks over monetary supply. Pragmatists, including Republican appointees like Alan Greenspan, accepted that unforeseen contingencies require discretion to respond. Milton Friedman, "The Role of Monetary Policy," *American Economics Review* 58 (1968): 1–17; Jose Fernandez-Albertos, "The Politics of Central Bank Independence," *Annual Review of Political Science* 18 (2015): 217–237.
52. Quoted in Zumbrun, "More Than Half of U.S. Wants Fed Curbed or Abolished."
53. Victoria McGrane and Ryan Tracy, "Sen. Shelby Presses Democrats on Bill Aiding Smaller Banks," *Wall Street Journal*, April 29, 2015, www.wsj.com/articles/sen-shelby-seeking-doable-banking-legislation-1430313591; Greg Robb, "Shelby Takes It Easy on Fed in New Banking Bill," *MarketWatch*, May 12, 2015, www.marketwatch.com/story/shelby-takes-it-easy-on-fed-in-new-banking-bill-2015-05-12.
54. Barney Jopson and Sam Fleming, "Wall Street Wary of 'Audit the Fed' Campaign," *Financial Times*, April 7, 2015, www.ft.com/cms/s/0/d57644fe-dcbc-11e4-b70d-00144feab7de.html#axzz3iAdHxiNW.
55. Jopson and Fleming, "Wall Street Wary of 'Audit the Fed' Campaign."
56. Ylan Q. Mui, "Top Senate Panel Looks to Tighten Oversight of Federal Reserve," *Washington Post*, May 12, 2015, www.washingtonpost.com/news/wonkblog/wp/2015/05/12/top-senate-panel-looks-to-tighten-oversight-of-federal-reserve/; Robb, "Shelby Takes It Easy on Fed."
57. Partisan divisions over the scope of Dodd-Frank's regulatory intervention produced near party-line votes on its passage, though there were a few brave souls who broke ranks. With Congress under the control of Democratic majorities, three Republicans and two

independents voted in favor of passage in the Senate, and three Republicans joined 234 Democrats in the House.

58. Letter from Senators Warren and Merkley to President Obama, May 29, 2014, http://online.wsj.com/public/resources/documents/Merkley-Warren LetteronFinancialReformFedNoms.pdf.

59. David Harrison, "Senate Duo Takes Aim at Fed's Lending Powers," *Wall Street Journal Blog*, May 13, 2015, http://blogs.wsj.com/ economics/2015/05/13/senate-duo-takes-aim-at-feds-lending-powers/.

60. Jopson and Fleming, "Wall Street Wary of 'Audit the Fed' Campaign."

61. Isaac Boltansky (senior vice president at Compass Point Research) quoted in Mui, "Top Senate Panel Looks to Tighten Oversight of Federal Reserve."

62. Andrews, "Bernanke, a Hero to His Own."

63. Zumbrun and Kearns, "Yellen's Record-Low Senate Support."

64. FOMC, October 28–29, 2008, 149.

65. Gibson, "Republicans Looking to Turn Up Heat"; Miller, "The Republican Plan to Rein in Janet Yellen's Federal Reserve."

66. National Association of Federal Credit Unions, "Yellen Reiterates Need for Fed Independence," July 17, 2014, http://ow.ly/FZPZ2.

67. Quoted in Binyamin Appelbaum, "Janet Yellen Warns Congress Against Adding to Fed's Oversight," *New York Times*, July 15, 2015, www .nytimes.com/2015/07/16/business/yellen-federal-reserve-house-testimony-oversight.html?_r=0.

68. Board of Governors of the Federal Reserve System, "News Release," November 20, 2014, http://ow.ly/G2S97.

69. Morgenson, "The Week That Shook the Fed."

70. Quote from Ted Kaufman (D-DE) and Byron Dorgan (D-ND). Ivry, Keoun, and Kuntz, "Secret Fed Loans."

71. Quoted in Ivry, Keoun, and Kuntz, "Secret Fed Loans."

72. Quote from Neil Barofsky. Ivry, Keoun, and Kuntz, "Secret Fed Loans."

73. Ivry, Keoun, and Kuntz, "Secret Fed Loans."

74. The Congress-centered account offers a rich and detailed insight into the legislative process. It does neglect, though, the Fed's commitment to pursuing its own institutional interests and "core values" and willingness to revert to strategic maneuvering to achieve them—in addition to the epoch-defining decline in the Fed's legitimacy. Terry Moe, "The New Economics of Organization," *American Journal of Political Science* 28 (November 1984): 739–777; Peter Evans, Dietrich Rueschemeyer, and Theda Skocpol, eds., *Bringing the State Back In* (New York: Cambridge University Press, 1985); Stephen Skowronek, *Building a New American State: The Expansion of National Administrative Capacities, 1877–1920* (New York: Cambridge University Press, 1982).

75. "Monitoring the Financial System," Speech by Bernanke at the 49th Annual Conference on Bank Structures and Competition, Federal Reserve Board of Chicago, May 10, 2013, 1.

76. This section's examination of Dodd-Frank drew on this reliable guide to its core provisions: www.law.cornell.edu/wex/dodd-frank_title_I.

77. The rapid revolution in finance that now makes it possible for a relatively few firms to crash the financial and economic systems on a global scale is illustrated by the origins of the term "macroprudential." It was coined only four decades ago and became widely used as a framework in the past decade. Piet Clement, "The Term 'Macroprudential': Origins and Evolution," *Bankers for International Settlements Quarterly Review*, March 2010, http://ow.ly/Gn6tK.

78. For a review of the Fed's implementation of Dodd-Frank, see statement by Daniel K. Tarullo, Member Board of Governors of FRS before the US Senate Committee on Banking, Housing and Urban Affairs, July 11, 2013, www.federalreserve.gov/newsevents/testimony/tarullo20130711a .htm.

79. In practice, the Fed's job will require close attention to international negotiations known as the Basel Accords, which were started in 1988 and substantially revised in 2004 and again after the 2008 crisis. These international standards are necessary because capital is traded on global markets.

80. Dodd-Frank's Volcker Rule shares Glass-Steagall's goal of focusing commercial banks on taking deposits and handling checking accounts instead of engaging in risky speculation. But there are several differences. Glass-Steagall prohibited certain types of institutions that both took consumer deposits and acted as investors by making trades; the Volcker Rule prohibited the activities of trading but allowed banks to multitask. After Dodd-Frank, a bank backed up by the Federal Deposit Insurance Corporation could take deposits *and* invest as long as it avoided excessive risks and kept its distance from private equity funds. The slippery slope is that banks cannot make risky trades, but they are permitted to hedge their investments using strategies practiced by speculators. Setting up and policing the Volcker Rule is inherently problematic.

81. Rebecca Thiess, "Paying Off for Consumers: How the Consumer Financial Protection Bureau Is Getting the Job Done," *US News and World Report*, July 24, 2014, www.usnews.com/opinion/economic-intelligence/2014/07/24/four-years-after-dodd-frank-the-cfpb-is-paying-off.

82. Andrews, "Bernanke, a Hero to His Own."

83. Statement by Ben S. Bernanke before the US Senate Committee on Banking, Housing and Urban Affairs, February 17, 2011.

84. The Council represents 15 regulatory agencies and is showing early signs of exercising its power to direct some of the same nonbank firms (AIG, Prudential, and GE Capital) that the Fed claims responsibility to oversee. This kind of sharing of responsibilities is intended to put an end to the Fed's free reign: it now faces multiple and competing agencies. In addition to checking unilateral Fed activities, the Council may prove

over time more effective than the Fed in regulating derivatives and protecting the financial system from risk. J. Nicholas Ziegler and John T Woolley, "After Dodd-Frank: The Post-Enactment Politics of Financial Reform in the United States," IRLE University of California, Berkeley Working Paper 110-14, September 2014.

85. Rich Miller, "Dodd-Frank Law May Hinder Crisis Response by US Policy Makers," *Bloomberg News*, November 22, 2011, http://ow.ly/G7bbC; www .bloomberg.com/news/articles/2011-11-22/dodd-frank-may-hamper-policy-makers-shielding-banking-system-in-a-crisis.

86. The Commodity Futures Trading Commission was assigned responsibility for derivatives and swaps—the exchange of securities or currency or similar types of investments. SEC was handed security-based swaps.

87. Dodd-Frank's design follows one of the most consistent themes in American political development: the turn to institutional fragmentation to prevent coherent and effective administration. Dodd-Frank may give rise to well-rehearsed agency tactics: end-runs to the White House or Congress, press leaks, deceptive reports, and more to outflank rivals. Skowronek, *Building a New American State*; Theodore Lowi, *The End of Liberalism: The Second Republic of the United States*, 2nd ed. (New York: Norton, 1979).

88. Congress does have the option to withhold the names of firms that receive assistance. It is unclear if elected officials would risk the political blowback of hiding the assistance to the biggies in finance and risking the political blowback when it eventually became public.

89. David Jones (Fed economist) quoted in Ivry, Keoun, and Kuntz, "Secret Fed Loans."

90. Dodd-Frank adds to the list of audits that are conducted of the Fed. Nonetheless, auditors are explicitly prohibited by law from examining the Fed's operations related to foreign central banks and its deliberations and decisions relating to monetary policymaking and the Federal Open Market Committee. The Republican "Audit the Fed" proposal would lift these restrictions.

91. Donald Kohn quoted in Miller, "Dodd-Frank Law May Hinder Crisis Response."

92. Dodd-Frank Act 2010, Title XI Section 1101; Tim Sablik, "Fed Credit Policy During the Great Depression," Federal Reserve Bank of Richmond, March 2013, EB13-03, http://ow.ly/GpnVp.

93. Testimony by Jeffrey Lacker, House Committee on Financial Services, June 26, 2013, http://ow.ly/GprIB.

94. Quotes from John Williams (president, San Francisco Fed Bank) and Robert J. Samuelson, "Dodd-Frank's Achilles' Heel," *Washington Post*, July 27, 2014, http://ow.ly/G77DJ. Williams quoted in Miller, "Dodd-Frank Law May Hinder Crisis Response."

95. John Williams quoted in Miller, "Dodd-Frank Law May Hinder Crisis Response."

96. Glenn Hutchins, "'Audit' the Fed and You Blunt Our Last Working Economic Tool," *Financial Times*, July 17, 2015.

97. Stanley Fischer, July 17, 2015, speaking at a question and answer session at the US Chamber of Commerce, reported in www.ft.com/cms/s/0/fe83a13a-2c93-11e5-8613-e7aedbb7bdb7.html#axzz3qWDNKmHq. Fischer's speech is part of a rolling campaign by Board of Governors' members to stave off congressional or other efforts to impose tighter oversight: Governors Jerome Powell and Charles Plasser (who ended his term in June 2015) made speeches, as did Fischer, in the opening months of 2015 opposing a bill that would require oversight of the FOMC's interest rate setting decisions on the grounds that this would politicize the decision-making process and compel FOMC members to temper their discussions.

5: PREPARING FOR THE NEXT FINANCIAL CRISIS

1. Kate Gibson, "Republicans Looking to Turn Up Heat on Fed in 2015," CNBC, November 18, 2014, http://ow.ly/FVsz4.

2. Art Rollnick, "Defend the Fed," *Star Tribune*, August 11, 2012, www.startribune.com/defend-the-fed/165781736/; Daniel Indiviglio, "Why We Need the Fed," *Atlantic Monthly*, January 14, 2011, http://ow.ly/FhReF.

3. Timothy A. Canova, "The Federal Reserve We Need," *American Prospect*, October 7, 2010.

4. Philip Keefer, "Elections, Special Interests, and Financial Crisis," *International Organization* 61 (2007): 607–641; Guillermo Rosas, *Curbing Bailouts: Bank Crises and Democratic Accountability in Comparative Perspective* (Ann Arbor: University of Michigan Press, 2009); Frances Rosenbluth and Ross Schaap, "The Domestic Politics of Banking Regulation," *International Organization* 57 (2003): 307–336; Jose Fernandez-Albertos, "The Politics of Central Bank Independence," *Annual Review of Political Science* 18 (2015): 217–237.

5. While the Madisonian insistence on public accountability is necessary to reintegrate America's central bank into the country's norms of governance, coherent regulation is necessary to achieve regulatory effectiveness. The application of Madisonianism by Dodd-Frank is problematic because it is a recipe for ineffectiveness. But it is possible— as Canada demonstrates—to create legislative and institutional accountability and regulatory coherence.

6. Max Boot and Jeane J. Kirkpatrick, "America's Destiny Is to Police the World," *Financial Times*, February 19, 2003; Frederick Jackson Turner, "The Significance of the Frontier in American History" (1893), republished in John Mack Faragher, ed., *Rereading Frederick Jackson Turner* (New York: Henry Holt, 1994), 31–60; Louis Hartz, *The Liberal Tradition in America: An Interpretation of American Political Thought*

since the Revolution (New York: Harcourt, Brace and World, 1955). The self-serving silences and inventions that undergird American exceptionalism are laid bare in Rogers M. Smith, "Beyond Tocqueville, Myrdal and Hartz: The Multiple Traditions in America," *American Political Science Review* 87 (1993): 549–566.

7. Cornelia Woll, *The Power of Inaction: Bank Bailouts in Comparison* (Ithaca, NY: Cornell University Press, 2014).

8. Woll, *The Power of Inaction.*

9. England's return to regulation followed the collapse of Northern Rock in 2007—the first run on a British bank in 140 years—and the subsequent parliamentary investigation that faulted the responsible government overseer (Financial Services Authority [FSA]) for having "failed dreadfully in its supervision of the banking sector." House of Commons Treasury Committee, *Banking Crisis: Regulation and Supervision,* Fourteenth Report of Session 2008–09. HC 767 (London: House of Commons, the Stationary Office, 2009), 3. Also see House of Commons Treasury Committee, Fifth Report of the Session 2007–08, vol. 1, *The Run on the Rock,* HC 56–1 (London: The Stationary Office, January 24, 2008). The British Government responded by helping borrowers and reining in bankers. Responding to the recommendation of the Independent Commission on Banking chaired by Sir John Vickers, Parliament greatly increased the capital that banks had to have on hand to cushion their investments, established new protections to create a ring fence around retail banking to distance it from proprietary trading activities, and took a roster of other steps.

10. This distinction between accepting and reordering private markets and social relations is familiar in the field of comparative policy. Gosta Esping-Andersen, *The Three Worlds of Welfare Capitalism* (Princeton, NJ: Princeton University Press, 1990).

11. John C. Courtney and Pietro S. Nivola, *Know They Neighbor: What Canada Can Tell Us about Financial Regulation,* Brookings Briefing Paper, April 23, 2009, 1–2, www.brookings.edu/research/papers/2009/04/23-canada-nivola.

12. Seymour Martin Lipset's *Continental Divide: The Values and Institutions of the United States and Canada* (New York: Routledge, 1990) stresses Canadian distinctiveness—the collectivist holdover from Britain, a credible socialist party, and cultural traditions that embraced hierarchy.

13. NBC News and the *Wall Street Journal* poll July 30–August 3, 2014, asked: "Right now, do you think the United States is in an economic recession, or not?" Forty-nine percent indicated that the country is in a recession; 46 percent believed it was not. The sample was 1,000 adults nationwide; the margin of error is 3.1 points. Although the rate of unemployment has declined, the official measure of unemployment excludes the long-term and permanently unemployed who have either given up searching or search with little prospect of finding a job. By June 2015, there were still close to two million (1.9) workers classified as

marginally unemployed but not included in the official unemployment count and 6.5 million workers held part-time positions after failing to find full-time employment or having their hours reduced. Matthew O'Brien, "The Fed Absolutely Shouldn't Give Up on the Long-Term Unemployed," *The Atlantic*, January 21, 2015.

14. Tony Porter, "Canadian Banks in the Financial and Economic Crisis," paper for the Policy Responses to Unfettered Finance Workshop, North-South Institute, Ottawa, June 8–9, 2010. Tony Porter, "Canada, the FSB and the International Institutional Response to the Current Crisis," and David Longworth, "The Global Financial Crisis and Financial Regulation: Canada and the World," both in Robinton Medhora and Dane Rowlands, eds., *Crisis and Reform: Canada and the International Financial System* (Waterloo, ON: Centre for International Governance Innovation and Carleton University, 2014), 71–86, 87–102.

15. Jack Mintz (University of Calgary) speaking to the Senate's Standing Committee on Banking, Trade and Commerce hearing on regulation and the global crisis, November 5, 2009, www.parl.gc.ca/Content/SEN/Committee/402/bank/13evb-e.htm?Language=E&Parl=40&Ses=2&comm_id=3.

16. Canada stood apart from the United States and Europe by adopting capital adequacy rules that helped lead the way for the international Basel Accord and its regular revisions. For a good historical account, see Donald Brean, Lawrence Kryzanowski, and Gordon S. Roberts, "Canada and the United States: Different Roots, Different Routes to Financial Sector Regulation," *Business History* 53 (2011): 249–269.

17. Canada's asset-to-capital rules of 20 to 1 were both higher and more stringent than the lax rules in the United States (ranging from 25 to 1 to over 33) and Europe (often well over 30). Capital requirements for Canadian banks exceed international minimum standards set by Basel II. Porter, "Canadian Banks in the Financial and Economic Crisis," 4; Kevin Lynch, "Avoiding the Financial Crisis: Lessons from Canada," *Options Politiques*, May 2010, 12–15, 13.

18. Silla Brush and Erik Wasson, "Senate Republicans Try New Tactic in Reining in Dodd-Frank," *Bloomberg News*, July 21, 2015, www.bloomberg.com/news/articles/2015-07-21/senate-republicans-said-to-mull-new-tactic-for-easing-dodd-frank.

19. Louis W. Pauly and Michael Gavin, "Continental Divide? Canada's Experience during the Financial Crisis of 2008," Paper to the Nuffield College, Oxford University conference on "Governing the Fed," October 2012, 3; Porter, "Canadian Banks in the Financial and Economic Crisis," 3–4; Quillin cited in World Bank, "Crisis-Proofing Financial Integration: Canada," http://siteresources.worldbank.org/ECAEXT/Resources/258598-1284061150155/7383639-1323888814015/8319788-1324485944855/03_canada.pdf.

20. Mark Carney speaking to the Standing Senate Committee on Banking, Trade and Commerce, October 28, 2009, www.parl.gc.ca/Content/SEN/

Committee/402/bank/12eva-e.htm?Language=E&Parl=40&Ses=2&c omm_id=3. Carney was poached by the UK's Chancellor of the Exchequer a few years later to become governor of the Bank of England.

21. The liveliest account of the rise of securitization is Gillian Tett, *Fool's Gold* (Boston: Little, Brown, 2009), chs. 6–9.

22. Pauly and Gavin, "Continental Divide?," 4.

23. This account was provided to the New York State's Attorney General Andrew M. Cuomo when his office conducted a review of compensation by the financial system after TARP. Andrew M. Cuomo, *No Rhyme or Reason: The "Heads I Win, Tails You Lose" Bank Bonus Culture*, July 30, 2009. Published by the NY State Attorney General Office, www.scribd .com/doc/17850928/Andrew-Cuomo-Bonus-Report.

24. Moody's Banking Sector Outlook and the World Economic Forum both ranked the Canadian banking sector's soundness at the top. Remarks by Jean Boivin (Bank of Canada's deputy governor), March 28, 2011, 4. Boivin's response can be found at www.fin.gc.ca/n14/14-114-eng.asp.

25. Pauly and Gavin, "Continental Divide?," 4; World Bank, "Crisis-Proofing Financial Integration: Canada," http://siteresources.worldbank.org/ ECAEXT/Resources/258598-1284061150155/7383639-1323888814015/ 8319788-1324485944855/03_canada.pdf.

26. Brean, Kryzanowski, and Roberts, "Canada and the United States," 265–266.

27. Porter, "Canadian Banks in the Financial and Economic Crisis," 6; Brean, Kryzanowski, and Roberts, "Canada and the United States," 260; Canadian Bankers Association, "Global Banking Regulations and Banks in Canada," September 18, 2014, www.cba.ca/en/media-room/50- backgrounders-on-banking-issues/667-global-banking-regulations-and- banks-in-canada; International Monetary Fund, *Canada: Financial System Stability Assessment—Update*, February 2008, IMF Country Report No. 08/59 (Washington, DC: IMF), 6; IMF Public Information Notice No 00/11, February 18, 2000, "IMF Concludes Article IV Consultation with Canada," www.imf.org/external/np/sec/pn/2000/pn0011. htm; Financial Stability Board, *Peer Review of Canada: Review Report*, January 30, 2012, www.financialstabilityboard.org/2012/01/r_120130/, 12.

28. Financial Stability Board, *Peer Review of Canada*, 8.

29. Canada's economy (including exports and investments) did temporarily shrink in late 2008 and early 2009, but it recovered quickly and avoided a financial implosion. Michael D. Bordo, Angela Redish, and Hugh Rockoff, "Why Didn't Canada Have a Banking Crisis in 2008 (Or In 1930, Or 1907, Or...)?" NBER Working Paper Series, Working Paper 17312 (Cambridge, MA: NBER August 2011), 17; Remarks by Jean Boivin, Deputy Governor Bank of Canada, Montreal CFA Society, "The 'Great' Recession in Canada: Perception versus Reality," March 28, 2011; Philip Cross, "The Post-Recession Recovery of Canadian Exports, 2009–2011," *Statistics Canada*, December 2012, www.statcan.gc.ca/ pub/11-010-x/2011009/part-partie3-eng.htm.

30. Although the extraordinary interventions pursued in the United States were not necessary, Canadian banks benefited from liquidity supplied by their government as well as some US government support after 2008. David Macdonald, *The Big Banks' Big Secret: Estimating Government Support for Canadian Banks During the Fiscal Crisis* (Ottawa: Canadian Centre for Policy Alternatives, April 2012), 46; Pauly and Gavin, "Continental Divide?"

31. Boivin, "The 'Great' Recession in Canada," 2.

32. Our examination of regulatory intervention differs, in certain respects, from the familiar formalist approach for comparatively classifying central banks. This approach typically defines transparency with regard to requirements for central banks to publish or report key information and equates accountability with mandates for central bank officials to appear before lawmakers or face the prospect of policy reversals. David Stasavage, "Transparency, Democratic Accountability, and the Economic Consequences of Monetary Institutions," *American Journal of Political Science* (July 2003): 389–402; Philip Keefer and David Stasavage, "The Limits of Delegation: Veto Players, Central Bank Independence, and the Credibility of Monetary Policy," *American Political Science Review* 97 (August 2003): 407–423.

33. Ipsos Reid, December 6–9, 2010, http://ow.ly/GzHmg; Canadian Bankers' Association, "Global Banking Regulations and Banks in Canada," March 13, 2015, www.cba.ca/en/media-room/50-backgrounders-on-banking-issues/667-global-banking-regulations-and-banks-in-canada; Canadian Bankers Association, "Global Banking Regulations and Banks in Canada," September 18, 2014.

34. Hugh Heclo developed the concept of "social learning" to explain the tendency of decision-makers to factor in the experiences and consequences of past policies as they formulated subsequent action. Hugh Heclo, *Modern Social Politics in Britain and Sweden* (New Haven, CT: Yale University Press, 1974).

35. Pauly and Gavin, "Continental Divide?"; Lawrence Kryzanowski and Gordon S. Roberts, "Canadian Banking Insolvency, 1922–1940," *Journal of Money, Credit and Banking* 25 (1993): 361–376.

36. A number of studies have investigated social learning and the government's initiation of independent analyses and policy innovation in varying historical periods, countries, and policy areas—from social welfare to economic policy. Heclo, *Modern Social Politics in Britain and Sweden*, 305–306; Theda Skocpol, "Bringing the State Back In: Strategies of Analysis in Current Research," in *Bringing the State Back In*, ed. P. Evans, D. Rueschemeyer, and T. Skocpol (New York: Cambridge University Press, 1985), 12; Peter Hall, "Policy Paradigms, Social Learning, and the State: The Case of Economic Policy Making in Britain," *Comparative Politics* 25 (April 1993): 275–296.

37. Woll, *The Power of Inaction*.

38. The big five are Royal Bank of Canada, TD (Toronto Dominion) Canada Trust, Bank of Novia Scotia, Bank of Montreal, and Canadian Imperial Bank of Commerce. The National Bank of Canada, the next largest, is

also folded into the group. Together these banks make up over 70 percent of total banking assets in Canada.

39. Where the US banking system remained fragmented within states until the 1980s, Canada has a history of creating national banks, which stretched across the entire country, and centralized regulation. Historically, the Canadian federal government controlled the power to charter and regulate banks. By contrast, states controlled the chartering of banks during the nineteenth century and rivaled the national banking system as it developed. The Federal Reserve system continues to reflect this federalist legacy with the power granted to regional banks. Charles W. Calomiris and Stephen H. Haber, *Fragile by Design: The Political Origins of Banking Crises and Scarce Credit* (Princeton, NJ: Princeton University Press, 2014).

40. For detailed analyses, see David Xiao Chen, H. Evren Damar, Hani Soubra, and Yaz Terajima, "Canadian Bank Balance-Sheet Management: Breakdown by Types of Canadian Financial Institutions," Bank of Canada Discussion Paper 2012–17, September 2012.

41. There is a large and long-standing body of social science research on the ills of concentrated economic and political power including the following seminal studies: Adam Smith, *Wealth of Nations* (New York: Knopf, 1991 [1776]); Robert Michels, *Political Parties: A Sociological Study of the Oligarchical Tendencies of Modern Democracy* (Glencoe, IL: Free Press, 1958 [1911]). Here is a review of economic research on oligopoly: William Samuelson and Stephen Marks, *Managerial Economics*, 7th ed. (New York: Wiley, 2011).

42. Robert Dahl, *A Preface to Democratic Theory* (Chicago: University of Chicago Press, 1956) and *Who Governs? Democracy and Power in an American City* (New Haven, CT: Yale University Press, 1963); Lawrence R. Jacobs, "Political Parties and Economic Inequality," *CQ Guide to Political Parties*, ed. Marjorie Hershey (Washington, DC: Congressional Quarterly Press, 2014). Contemporary studies of the ill effects of concentrated economic and political resources include Martin Gilens and Benjamin I. Page, "Testing Theories of American Politics: Elites, Interest Groups, and Average Citizens," *Perspectives on Politics* 12 (September 2014): 564–581, and Martin Gilens, *Affluence and Influence* (Princeton, NJ: Princeton University Press, 2014).

43. A large body of research stresses the durable and reinforcing dynamics of institutional trajectories as well as the path dependence of financial management. Paul Pierson, "Increasing Returns, Path Dependence and the Study of Politics," *American Political Science Review* 94 (2000): 251–267; Calomiris and Haber, *Fragile by Design*; Bordo, Rockoff, and Redish, "Why Didn't Canada Have a Banking Crisis?"

44. Brean, Kryzanowski, and Roberts, "Canada and the United States," 249–269.

45. The process of reviewing private banks for charters occurs every five years.

46. Porter, "Canadian Banks in the Financial and Economic Crisis"; Calomiris and Haber, *Fragile by Design*, 316–317; and D. J. Mason,

"Commercial Banking in the U.S. versus Canada," *Graziadio Business Review* 10, no. 4 (2007), http://gbr.pepperdine.edu/2010/08/commercial-banking-in-the-u-s-versus-canada/.

47. Mark Copelovitch and David Singer, "Financial Regulation, Monetary Policy, and Inflation in the Industrialized World," *Journal of Politics* 70 (2008): 663–680; Charles Goodhart and Dirk Schoenmaker, "Should the Functions of Monetary Policy and Banking Supervision Be Separated?" *Oxford Economic Papers* 47 (1995): 539–560; Carmine DiNoia and Giorgio DiGiorgio, "Should Banking Supervision and Monetary Policy Tasks Be Given to Different Agencies?" *International Finance* 2 (1999): 361–378.

48. In its peer review of Canada in 2012, the Financial Stability Board praises the country's coordination of regulatory agencies: "In spite of Canada's relatively complex regulatory structure, cooperation between relevant agencies during the crisis appears to have been swift and effective." America's regulators and the Fed failed to understand the systemic implications of the faltering mortgage business for the financial industry during the 2008–2009 crisis, but their Canadian counterparts connected the dots: "Risks in the household sector and their implications for the financial sector as determined by the Department of Finance, Bank of Canada and OSFI, led to a series of changes to the mortgage insurance framework decided by the Department of Finance"; "Peer Review of Canada: Review Report," January 30, 2012, 16, www .financialstabilityboard.org/wp-content/uploads/r_120130.pdf.

49. OSFI can direct a trust and loan company or bank to enlarge its capital base and capital-to-loan ratios through the imposition of institution-specific capital charges. Lynch, "Avoiding the Financial Crisis," 12.

50. Porter, "Canadian Banks in the Financial and Economic crisis," 3.

51. Canada imposes tighter limits than the United States on the favor-trading that results from the revolving door, according to the OECD standards for preventing conflicts of interest. OECD, Public Governance and Territorial Development, "Revolving Doors, Accountability and Transparency—Emerging Regulatory Concerns and Policy Solutions in the Financial Crisis," Expert Group on Conflict of Interest, May 5, 2009, GOV/PGC/ETH (2009), 4, 2, 36, 60–61, www.oecd.org/officialdocuments/publicdisplaydocumentpdf/?doclanguage=en&cote=GOV/PGC/ETH(2009)4.

52. Office of the Superintendent of Financial Institutions, "Structure and Operations," http://ow.ly/GL9JR; SOFI, conducted four surveys of the mass public in 2013–2014 to gauge its confidence and trust. "Consultations and Surveys," http://ow.ly/GLawx.

53. The international reviews—known as the Financial Services Assessment Program (FSAP)—was a joint initiative of the IMF and World Bank and was created in 1999 to help test national financial systems in the light of the Asian financial crisis. Canada participated in these assessments in 1999, 2008, and 2004. The United States participated in two FSAPs in 2010 and 2014; see www.imf.org/external/pubs/ft/scr/2008/cr0859.pdf

and www.imf.org/external/pubs/ft/scr/2014/cr1429.pdf; IMF Canada:
Financial System Stability Assessment—Update, 2, www.imf.org/
external/pubs/ft/scr/2014/cr1429.pdf.

54. Financial Stability Board, "Peer Review of Canada: Review Report,"
January 30, 2012, 16, www.financialstabilityboard.org/wp-content/
uploads/r_120130.pdf.

55. Financial Stability Board, Peer Review of the United States: Review
Report, August 27, 2013, 6, 7, www.financialstabilityboard.org/2013/08/
pr_130827 and www.financialstabilityboard.org/2013/08/pr_130827.

56. Lou Pauly, "Canadian Autonomy and Systemic Financial Risk after the
Crisis of 2008," in *Crisis and Reform: Canada and the International
Financial System; Canada Among Nations*, ed. Rohinton Medhora and
Dane Rowlands (Waterloo, ON: Canadian Institute for Governance
Innovation, 2014), 161–180, especially 166.

57. J. D. Wagster, "Canadian Bank Capital During the Great Depression of
the 1930s: A Comparison to the Basel III Requirements," *Journal of
Banking Regulation* 13 (2012): 89–98.

58. Office of Inspector General for the Federal Reserve and the Consumer
Financial Protection Bureau, "The Board Should Enhance Its Supervisory
Processes as a Result of Lessons Learned from the Federal Reserve's
Supervision of JP Morgan Chase & Company's Chief Investment Office,"
Board Report #2014-SR-B-017, October 17, 2014, http://ow.ly/I0Jc7.

59. Dodd-Frank did create a new office within the Treasury Department—
the Federal Insurance Office—but the authority to supervise insurance
providers remains with states. Outside the finance industry, there are
pockets of insurance provisions—health insurance, for instance—that do
come under federal regulatory supervision.

60. Dodd-Frank largely gave brokers and exchanges a pass. In a classic "kick
the can down the road" tactic, it called for a study by the SEC to develop
uniform standards for brokers and investment advisers who work with
retail customers.

61. Suzi Ring, "London Whale Escapes $1.5 Million Fine as FCA Drops
Case," *Bloomberg News*, July 9, 2015, www.bloomberg.com/news/
articles/2015-07-09/london-whale-escapes-1-5-million-fine-as-u-k-fca-
drops-case.

62. Office of Inspector General for the Federal Reserve and the Consumer
Financial Protection Bureau, "The Board Should Enhance Its Supervisory
Processes as a Result of Lessons Learned from the Federal Reserve's
Supervision of JP Morgan Chase & Company's Chief Investment Office,"
Board Report #2014-SR-B-017, October 17, 2014, http://ow.ly/I0Jc7. JP
Morgan Chase was fined $1 billion by UK and US regulators for inadequate
management of the London office, though it escaped prosecution.

63. Office of Inspector General for the Federal Reserve and the Consumer
Financial Protection Bureau, "Audit Reports," http://ow.ly/I0Kau. At the
same time as the Inspector General was scorching the Fed for its
ineffectual oversight of JP Morgan Chase, a newspaper report found that

the New York Fed's confidential documents were leaked by an official to Goldman Sachs to help one of its clients. Jessica Silver-Greenberg, Ben Protess, and Peter Eavis, "New Scrutiny of Goldman's Ties at the New York Fed After a Leak," *New York Times*, November 19, 2014.

64. Conflicts among agencies, pressure from lobbyists, and complicated policy issues stalled the rollout of Dodd-Frank. Appreciating the vulnerability created by this deadlock, Obama decided in August 2013 to call together and galvanize the key regulators from the Treasury, Comptroller of the Currency, Security and Exchange Commission, Commodity Futures Trading Commission, Consumer Financial Protection Bureau, and the Fed. But even four and a half years after Dodd-Frank's passage, 37 percent of its deadlines to finalize new rules were missed and 24 percent were not even designed. Davis Polk, "Dodd-Frank Progress Report," December 2014, www.davispolk.com/sites/default/files/December2014_Dodd.Frank_.Progress.Report.pdf; "Bedeviled by Dodd-Frank Details," Editorial, *Washington Post*, August 22, 2013.

65. Frank Partnoy, "The Fed's Magic Tricks Will Not Make Risk Disappear," *Financial Times*, March 5, 2015, www.ft.com/cms/s/0/8fc85ac4-b5d3-11e4-a577-00144feab7de.html#axzz3qWDNKmHq. And see Frank Partnoy, "Financial Systems, Crises and Regulation," in *The Oxford Handbook of Financial Regulation*, ed. N. Moloney, E. Ferran, and J. Payne (Oxford: Oxford University Press, 2015), 68–95.

66. Jesse Eisinger, "Tough Talk on Dodd-Frank Rules Misses Relevant Points," *New York Times*, October 8, 2014, http://ow.ly/FidUF.

67. Dimon quoted in Tony Braithwaite, "Dimon Says Banks 'Under Assault,'" *Financial Times*, January 15, 2014.

68. Tanya Agrawal and David Henry, "JP Morgan Hit by Legal Costs, Dimon Says Banks 'Under Assault,'" *Reuters*, January 14, 2015, www.reuters.com/article/2015/01/14/us-jpmorgan-results-idUSKBN0KN19C20150114.

69. Before Republicans formally took control of both chambers of Congress in January 2015, Democrats rushed to strike a budget deal in December. The bargain started the process of chipping away at Dodd-Frank by allowing banks to use federally insured savings in derivative trading. Once Republicans did take control, the pace of reversal picked up with proposals quickly introduced to block steps to bring derivative trading out of the shadow into the light of public inspection, to delay (for two years) new rules to prohibit large banks from holding risky securities, and to remove the Security and Exchange Commission as a regulator of private equity firms engaging in securities trading. Gretchen Morgenson, "Kicking Dodd-Frank in the Teeth," *New York Times*, January 10, 2015.

70. Calomiris and Haber, *Fragile by Design*.

71. Sheila Bair, "'No More Bank Bailouts' Cannot Be an Empty Slogan," *Financial Times*, August 8, 2014.

72. "'Enough Is Enough': Elizabeth Warren Launches Fiery Attack after Congress Weakens Wall Street Regs," *Wonkblog*, December 12, 2014,

www.washingtonpost.com/news/wonkblog/wp/2014/12/12/enough-is-enough-elizabeth-warrens-fiery-attack-comes-after-congress-weakens-wall-street-regulations/.

73. Quoted in Peter Eavis, "New York Fed Is Criticized on Oversight," *New York Times*, November 21, 2014. The president of the New York Fed is William C. Dudley.

74. Bob Ivry, Bradley Keoun, and Phil Kuntz, "Secret Fed Loans Gave Banks $13 Billion Undisclosed to Congress," *Bloomberg News*, November 27, 2011, http://ow.ly/GFKtb.

75. Martin Feldstein, "What Powers for the Federal Reserve?" *Journal of Economic Literature* 48 (March 2010): 134–145.

76. Jeff Kearns, "Fed $4 Trillion Assets Draw Lawmaker Ire Amid Bubble Concern," *Bloomberg News*, December 17, 2013, http://ow.ly/FgbPZ.

77. Gretchen Morgenson, "The Week That Shook the Fed," *New York Times*, November 23, 2014, http://ow.ly/FS78C.

78. Damian Paletta, "Fed's Little-Known Inspector General Moves Front and Center," *Wall Street Journal*, November 20, 2014, http://blogs.wsj.com/economics/2014/11/20/feds-little-known-ig-moves-front-and-center/.

79. Office of Inspector General Board of Governors of the Federal Reserve System and Consumer Financial Protection Bureau, "Semiannual Report to Congress: October 1, 2014–March 31, 2015," http://oig.federalreserve.gov/reports/oig-semiannual-report-mar2015.pdf.

80. The Office of Inspector General was established in 1978 and subsequently revised to create an IG for the Fed and then expand and refine its responsibilities. Of particular importance, Dodd-Frank expanded the Fed IG's scope of responsibility to include additional reviews, reporting requirements, and oversight of the Bureau of Consumer Financial Protection. For a history of the IGs, see Wendy Ginsberg and Michael Greene, "Federal Inspectors General: History, Characteristics, and Recent Congressional Actions," Congressional Research Service, December 8, 2014, http://ow.ly/SvXJi.

81. The Inspector General of the Fed is selected out of a pool of IGs by the Fed chair and is subject to peer reviews by other IGs. The Council of Inspectors General on Financial Oversight (CIGFO), which was created by Dodd-Frank, is an independent council devoted to effectiveness and rooting out wrongdoing. The Council is also charged with pulling together the disparate IGs responsible for financial regulators to consider the broader financial sector. Office of Inspector General Board of Governors of the Federal Reserve System and Consumer Financial Protection Bureau, "Semiannual Report to Congress: October 1, 2014–March 31, 2015," http://oig.federalreserve.gov/reports/oig-semiannual-report-mar2015.pdf; Ginsberg and Greene, "Federal Inspectors General."

82. Marc Labonte, "Federal Reserve: Oversight and Disclosure Issues," Washington, DC: Congressional Research Service, September 19, 2014, http://ow.ly/S6RcC. See Chapter 4 for detailed discussion of the widening use of audits to improve transparency.

83. Office of US Senator Bernie Sanders, "The Fed Audit," Thursday, July 21, 2011, www.sanders.senate.gov/newsroom/press-releases/the-fed-audit.

84. Representative Sean Duffy (R-WI) quoted in Binyamin Appelbaum, "New Limits on the Fed Pose Risks, Yellen Says," *New York Times*, July 15, 2015, www.nytimes.com/2015/07/16/business/yellen-federal-reserve-house-testimony-oversight.html?_r=0.

85. Stasavage, "Transparency, Democratic Accountability, and the Economic Consequences."

86. Joseph Stiglitz, "The Private Uses of Public Interests: Incentives and Institutions," *Journal of Economic Perspectives* 12 (Spring 1998): 15–16.

87. This kind of blame avoidance is standard fare in politics. Christopher Hood, *The Blame Game* (Princeton, NJ: Princeton University Press, 2013). David Stockman made a similar point about why politicians defer to the Fed. See Christopher Whalen, "Washington & Wall Street: Is the Federal Reserve Responsible for Fiscal Gridlock?" October 21, 2013, www.breitbart.com/big-government/2013/10/21/washington-wall-street-is-the-federal-reserve-responsible-for-fiscal-gridlock/.

88. The FOMC, which sets monetary and other crucial policy, includes the presidents of all 12 regional Fed banks; five vote at any one time along with the seven members of the Board of Governors. Although the approval of the Fed's Board of Governors is required, the private banks dominate the nomination of the regional presidents: they select six of the nine members of the board of directors that make the recommendation. For a careful analysis of the FOMC at work before the crisis, see Cheryl Schonhardt-Bailey, *Deliberating American Monetary Policy* (Cambridge, MA: MIT Press, 2013).

89. Dodd-Frank moved the nomination of regional bank presidents out of the direct hands of banks, but they still wield significant indirect influence through their election of board members, who are supposed to represent the public as well as industry interests. See www.newyorkfed.org/aboutthefed/org_nydirectors.html.

90. Simon Johnson and Ronald Kurtz, "Testimony Submitted to the House Financial Services Committee, Hearing on Legislation to Reform the Federal Reserve on Its 100-Year Anniversary," July 10, 2014, http://ow.ly/G0Xhp.

91. The New York president takes the lead in implementing monetary policy by trading US Securities and other activities and has been instrumental in assessing and negotiating financial rescues during crises in 2008–2009 and earlier.

92. "The Fed Needs Governors Who Aren't Wall Street Insiders," *Wall Street Journal*, November 17, 2014, www.warren.senate.gov/?p=blog&id=656.

93. Sheila Bair, "Obama's Treasury Pick Is Another Bank Watchdog Straight from Wall Street," *Fortune*, December 5, 2014, http://fortune.com/2014/12/05/sheila-bair-antonio-weiss-lazard-treasury/.

94. Woodrow Wilson, *Congressional Government: A Study in American Politics* (Boston: Houghton Mifflin, 1885) and "What Is Progress?"

in *The New Freedom* (New York: Doubleday, Page & Company, 1913).

95. Emmanuel Saez, "Striking It Richer: The Evolution of Top Incomes in the United States," Department of Economics, University of California, Berkeley, September 3, 2013, http://eml.berkeley.edu/~saez/saez-UStopincomes-2012.pdf.

96. Emmanuel Saez and Gabriel Zucman, "Wealth Inequality in the United States Since 1913: Evidence from Capitalized Income Tax Data," National Bureau of Economic Research Paper, October 2014.

97. Emmanuel Saez and Thomas Piketty, Updated Tables and Figures for "Income Inequality in the United States, 1913–1998," September 2013, http://ow.ly/GIXXX.

98. Chapter 4 examines public opinion toward the Fed.

99. A large pool of polls are available here: www.pollingreport.com/budget .htm. The two cited are the following: "The economic system in this country unfairly favors powerful interests. The economic system in this country is generally fair to most Americans." Pew Research Center, February 18–22, 2015. N=1,504 adults nationwide. Margin of error ± 2.9; "Which comes closer to your view? In today's economy, everyone has a fair chance to get ahead in the long run. OR, In today's economy, it's mainly just a few people at the top who have a chance to get ahead." CBS News/New York Times Poll, May 28–31, 2015. N=1,022 adults nationwide. Margin of error ± 3; Pew Research Center, "Five Years after Market Crash, US Economy Seen as 'No More Secure.'" September 12, 2013, http://ow.ly/GIPRq.

100. Rich Miller, "Dodd-Frank Law May Hinder Crisis Response by US Policy Makers," *Bloomberg News*, November 22, 2011, http://ow.ly/G7bbC.

101. Janet Yellen, "Perspectives on Inequality and Opportunity from the Survey of Consumer Finances," Remarks at the Conference on Economic Opportunity and Inequality, Federal Reserve Bank of Boston, October 17, 2014.

102. Mervyn King, "House of Commons Treasury Committee, Banking Crisis: Regulation and Supervision," 14th report of the Session, 2008–2009 (London: The Stationary Office, July 21, 2009), www.publications .parliament.uk/pa/cm200809/cmselect/cmtreasy/767/767.pdf.

103. The British responses are discussed in Chapter 4.

104. Binyamin Applebaum, "Yellen Issues a Warning on the Risks of Rising Inequality," *New York Times*, October 18, 2014, http://ow.ly/FiiNx.

105. We discuss the Fed's implication with rising inequality in greater detail in Chapter 1.

106. For discussion of the breakdown of fiscal policy to manage economic downturns, see Mark Blyth, *Austerity: The History of a Dangerous Idea* (New York: Oxford University Press, 2013). The broader sources of inequality are discussed here: Thomas Piketty, "Putting Distribution Back at the Center of Economics: Reflections on *Capital in the Twenty-First Century*," *Journal of Economic Perspectives* 29 (Winter 2015): 67–88, and commentary in this issue of the *JEP*.

107. Average pay per full-time worker in the finance industry was 2.2 times more (on average) than that of the average American worker from 1929–1999; it had reached 3.6 times in 2013 and has likely widened still more (the peak was 4.2 in 2007). Neil Irwin, "Wall Street Puts Crisis Behind, and Prospers," *New York Times*, May 18, 2015, www .nytimes.com/2015/05/19/upshot/wall-street-is-back-almost-as-big-as-ever.html?_r=0. Also see Thomas Philippon and Ariell Reshef, "Wages and Human Capital in the U.S. Finance Industry: 1909–2006," *Quarterly Journal of Economics* (2012): 1551–1609.

108. Ann Tenbrunsel and Jordan Thomas, "The Street, the Bull, and the Crisis: A Survey of the US and UK Financial Services Industry," May 2015, www.secwhistlebloweradvocate.com/LiteratureRetrieve .aspx?ID=224757.

109. Luigi Zingales, "Does Finance Benefit Society?" January 2015, Prepared for the 2015 AFA Presidential Address, 3, http://faculty .chicagobooth.edu/luigi.zingales/papers/research/Finance.pdf; Ratna Sahay, Martin Cihak, Papa N'Diaye, Adolfo Barajas, Ran Bi, Diana Ayala, Yuan Gao, Annette Kyobe, Lam Nguyen, Christian Saborowski, Katsiaryna Svirydzenka, and Seyed Reza Yousefi, "Rethinking Financial Deepening: Stability and Growth in Emerging Markets," International Monetary Fund, May 2015, www.imf.org/external/pubs/ ft/sdn/2015/sdn1508.pdf; Stephen G. Cecchetti and Enisse Kharroubi, "Why Does Financial Sector Growth Crowd Out Real Economic Growth," February 2015, Bank for International Settlements Working Paper No 490, www.bis.org/publ/work490.pdf.

Index